Coding Android Apps

As Android apps continue to grow in popularity and an associated job market emerges, the ability to develop software and applications for Android smartphones will only grow more relevant in the foreseeable future. Compiled from materials used in over a decade of teaching undergraduate and graduate students majoring in computer science and information technology, this book is a hands-on, step-by-step guide to coding Android apps that have been rigorously tested.

KEY FEATURES

- Each chapter begins with a list of student learning outcomes that can be used for assessment purposes and syllabus construction.
- The mechanics of Android app creation is presented in a very detailed, step-by-step progression, with accompanying screenshots and code explanations.
- New topics are introduced chapter-by-chapter in a very logical and gradational instructional manner.
- Very detailed exercises are provided at the end of each chapter and can be used for class activities and as homework assignments. Each chapter includes multiple exercises of varying difficulty.
- Video lessons are available as supplementary resources for each chapter to quickly illustrate in a demonstrative and visual manner the Java and XML code and Android Studio development actions covered in the chapter.

This book is particularly appealing for students of mobile apps development courses offered in computer science and information technology departments, as well as information systems disciplines within business schools, at both the undergraduate and graduate levels.

Margaret Kozak Polk, PhD, is an Associate Professor at Carroll University in Waukesha, Wisconsin, since August 2020. Prior to that she was a Professor of Computer Science at Dominican University in River Forest, Illinois. She has over 25 years of experience teaching computer science and information technology courses. She earned a PhD in computer science, with an emphasis in artificial intelligence, at the Illinois Institute of Technology.

Coding Android Apps

Margaret Kozak Polk

CRC Press
Taylor & Francis Group
Boca Raton London New York

CRC Press is an imprint of the
Taylor & Francis Group, an **informa** business
A CHAPMAN & HALL BOOK

First edition published 2025
by CRC Press
2385 NW Executive Center Drive, Suite 320, Boca Raton FL 33431

and by CRC Press
4 Park Square, Milton Park, Abingdon, Oxon, OX14 4RN

CRC Press is an imprint of Taylor & Francis Group, LLC

ISBN: 978-1-032-26059-4 (hbk)
ISBN: 978-1-032-25888-1 (pbk)
ISBN: 978-1-003-28632-5 (ebk)

DOI: 10.1201/9781003286325

Typeset in Palatino
by KnowledgeWorks Global Ltd.

Access the Instructor and Student Resources: https://www.routledge.com/9781032260594

I love you, my Von!

Contents

1

Introduction

While the intent of this book is to teach the reader how to code Android mobile apps, it is also provided to encourage a captivating future our industry can enjoy. Readers are supplied with the tools required for the coding of traditional applications, but additional exercises are meant to stimulate the imagination. However, like an architect preparing a set of building plans, your final product will evolve only as you use the components you learn to code, layer by layer and step by step.

Before we launch into our step-by-step approach on how to code using today's Android Studio technology, it's useful to pause to briefly review some of the major mobile phone breakthroughs that got us here; how quickly innovations are progressing; and where industry researchers, dreamers, and pioneers predict the future to be.

If you think the mobile phone is a recent dream someone had in their garage, basement, or even the result of a well-funded think tank, then think again. Alexander Graham Bell launched the dream over 140 years ago circa 1876 when he not only invented the telephone but in addition, two years later, foresaw that someday "The day will come when the man at the telephone will be able to see the distant person to whom he is speaking" (Bell, 1906).

Later, in 1926, renowned scientist and inventor Nikola Tesla dreamed of a device, almost 100 years ago, that would transform the lives of its users. In an interview, he once stated, "We shall be able to communicate with one another instantly, irrespective of distance. … and the instruments through which we shall be able to do this will be amazingly simple compared with our present telephone. A man will be able to carry one in his vest pocket" (Chong, 2015).

Interestingly, in 1922, around the same time as Tesla's vision, a silent film newsreel recently discovered by British Pathe called "Eve's Wireless" was circulating as a demonstration of a wireless mobile telephone. It took two people to operate, had to be attached to a fireplug, had to have an antenna wired to an umbrella and was then broadcast over radio waves, and only two people could connect and talk (Clark, 2011).

Today, the popular futuristic dreams continue on separate but similar roadmaps. On a universal basis, the objective of these dreams or destination is to create a sentient machine, robotically based or biologically based. The robotic path involves creating the entity through computing parts. For a few

DOI: 10.1201/9781003286325-1

years now Android technology has been used to control robots; in fact, practically anyone can use their Android smartphone today to build a robot for under $75 (The Physics arXiv Blog, 2020).

The destination in the second path is the same, a sentient machine, and involves creating the entity through component parts but begins with the biological source. Presently in development or already on the market are automated implementations of human parts, thereby integrating computing components into a human being. And Android plays a significant role. For example, a current contribution of the Massachusetts Institute of Technology to the Android effort is a prosthetic hand as an Android-based controller to direct five different hand gestures (Hamdan et al., 2020). The *BrainGate* Consortium reported that paralyzed individuals were able to operate Android tablets using brain implants (Scudellari, 2018), supporting a premise that implants can facilitate the functioning of a droid.

Many prognosticators foresee dire consequences in purposely handing our freedoms and decision-making over to machines. This group, however, admits that super intelligent malevolent machines as portrayed in "I-robot" or as Hal in "2001 a Space Odyssey" or as the "Terminator" are not real possibilities at this time. The reality is that all of the above are far beyond the science of today. Simply put, machines portraying consciousness, self-awareness, and free will still remain in the bailiwick of science fiction.

This is not to diminish the importance of stressing the moral imperative underscoring the ethical, responsible use of technology. For those more socially oriented, the impact of existing Android technology as well as that on the drawing board is not only about the macro dream of the large corporations and well-funded research institutions but is also significantly impacting small- and medium-sized businesses, educational institutions, and not-for-profits, as well as each of us in our everyday lives.

Why Study Android App Coding?

In practicality today, mobile communication is so integrated into our lives that many people feel lost without a cell phone. There was a time when mobile phones were predominantly used for calendaring, making calls, and sending texts. Now, made possible through the development of mobile applications, the smartphone is a multifunctional device that not only communicates but allows a person to create their own palette of apps according to their specific needs, and there are thousands from which to choose. In fact, many people are using sophisticated phone cameras to record life in real time.

This book was written primarily as a textbook for undergraduates. Most of whom are now looking at careers that will span two to three decades which make the knowledge of existing technologies and devices imperative, nevertheless, and of equal importance are the imminent and future innovations. The defining feature of success for smartphones will be not only in their ability to run well and look good but also to give connection to the extended capabilities via third-party apps transition technology.

Simply put, new devices in the communication technology market will substantially expand. The World Economic Forum reports that there are more mobile phones than people in the world (Richter, 2023). According to Statista, in 2023, the number of smartphone users in the world was around 6.93 billion, and in the United States alone, the number of smartphone users is predicted to continuously increase from 2024 to 2028 (Statista, 2024). And, *StatCounter* reports that the Android mobile operating system holds the largest market share globally, as of December 2023, at 70.48% (Statcounter, 2024).

In addition, there were over 3.5 million apps available for download on the Google Play Store as of January of 2024 (42matters, 2024). According to *TechReport*, mobile apps are where 70% of all US digital media time is spent, and an average smartphone user engages with 30 apps per month (Laborde, 2023).

Individuals concerned with return on educational investment will find it encouraging to hear that *Payscale*, in a salary analysis of Android software developers, identified an annual average base salary of $97,293 with bonuses of up to $17,000 (Laborde, 2023). *Zippia* reports the job outlook for Android developers in the United States to grow 21% from 2018 to 2028. And, in January of 2024, *Indeed* reported a listing of 1,790 Android developer jobs (Indeed, 2024).

So, it follows that career opportunity based on new phones, new products, and the communication technology field will substantially expand in terms of size (dollar volume), innovation, and need for Android savvy developers. But the innovation will not take centuries and will not be measured by new products here or there but rather in the enormous number of products all introduced in less than a decade.

About This Book

So, let's get started and here is your roadmap. The only requisite knowledge is experience with the Java programming language, as it is the foundational computer language upon which Android coding in this book is based. The material is organized and covered in depth in a tested learnable time frame, organized in chapters. Learning objectives are identified on a chapter-by-chapter basis. The first eight chapters should be covered on a sequential basis as each chapter builds upon the previous. Each chapter, after Chapter 2, includes substantial exercises instructors may wish to utilize for homework assignments. Many of the exercises throughout the book build upon an exercise found in a previous chapter. Thus, the reader is able to build Android coding skills incrementally; some of the first screens will be limited graphically but will be enhanced in subsequent chapters. Royalty-free graphic images pertinent to an exercise, and thus to most apps coded in this book, are provided for download, but readers are free to use any appropriate royalty-free images they find on their own as well.

Video lessons are also available as supplementary material to this book. The content of this book and its supplementary materials were developed on a Windows system, but students utilizing Android Studio on Mac computers have also successfully used this content.

Students of this text should have some acquaintance with programming in the Java computer language. This book is the collective result of over a decade of experience of teaching Android apps development. The material in this book has been used successfully in a course where students had only a one-semester course in Java as a prerequisite. As experience with coding has taught us, coding requires focus, sometimes long hours, and a level of frustration when something is just not working. But the author can personally share a story about a conversation with one of the true pioneers, one of the first people to ever make a cell phone call. It is my sincere hope that the hard work you do and the knowledge you gain will give you the same excitement in your voice someday that this early pioneer communicated even all these years later.

Overview of the Chapter Topics

Chapters 2 through 8 detail the coding and implementation of Android apps in a very methodical stepwise manner. Chapter 2 introduces the Android Studio development environment supported by Google. The reader will learn how to create an app project and Android Virtual Devices (AVDs), also known as emulators, on which to install and execute apps. Chapter 3 introduces the mechanics of a screen layout and the use of background images, as well as how to add image resources to a layout and Android resource naming requirements. Launcher icons are also presented in Chapter 3. Chapter 4 discusses the important Android principle of resource externalization, including those for strings, colors, and dimensions. Chapter 5 begins the exploration of app interaction with a user, which is expanded upon in Chapter 7. Chapter 6 recognizes the difficulty in rendering app screen layouts on different mobile phone and tablet devices and examines strategies for dealing with these challenges. Chapter 8 adds multiple screen layouts and features to apps, detailing the mechanics for creating multiple activities and moving a user between and among activities in the use of an app.

Chapters 9 and 10 address persistent storage strategies, namely the implementation of shared preferences and SQLite databases. Chapters 11 and 12 explore the employment of navigation views including that of slide-in menus and tabbed apps.

Finally, Chapters 13 and 14 examine the incorporation of external information and communication within an app. Chapter 13 details the process of implementing web content within an app, including Google Maps. Chapter 14 focuses on the inclusion of media and communication features within an app, specifically the incorporation of audio and video content, the transmission of text messages, and the initiation of phone calls.

So, let's get started!

References

42matters. (2024). Google Play statistics and trends 2024. Retrieved January 14, 2024, from https://42matters.com/google-play-statistics-and-trends

Bell, A. G. (1906). The day will come when the man at the telephone will be able to see the distant person to whom he is speaking. https://agbmuseumstore.com/blogs/the-association/alexander-graham-bell-teacher-scientist-inventor-and-visionary

Chong, C. (2015, July 6). The inventor that inspired Elon Musk and Larry Page predicted smartphones nearly 100 years ago. *Business Insider.* https://www.businessinsider.com/tesla-predicted-smartphones-in-1926-2015-7

Clark, J. (2011, November 27). Eve's wireless. *Big Medium.* https://bigmedium.com/ideas/eves-portable-wireless-phone.html

Hamdan, M. H., Basir, M. A. A., Bahar, M. Q. S., Ramle, S. F., Albitar, D., & Jailani, R. (2020). Android based control system for prosthetic hand. *16th IEEE International Colloquium on Signal Processing & Its Applications.* (CSPA), 197–202. https://doi.org/10.1109/CSPA48992.2020.9068670

Indeed. (2024, January). Android Developer Jobs [Advertisement]. Retrieved January 14, 2024, from https://www.indeed.com/q-android-developer-jobs.html

Laborde, S. (2023, July 27). Mobile app statistics everyone should know in 2023. *TechReport.* https://techreport.com/statistics/app-statistics/

Richter, F. (2023, April 11). Charted: There are more mobile phones than people in the world. World Economic Forum with the collaboration of Statista. https://www.weforum.org/agenda/2023/04/charted-there-are-more-phones-than-people-in-the-world/

Scudellari, M. (2018, November 21). Paralyzed individuals operate tablet with brain implant. *IEEE Spectrum.* https://spectrum.ieee.org/paralyzed-individuals-operate-tablet-with-brain-implant

Statcounter. (2024). *Mobile operating system market share worldwide.* Retrieved January 14, 2024, from https://gs.statcounter.com/os-market-share/mobile/worldwide/

Statista. (2024). *Number of smartphone users in the United States from 2013 to 2028.* Retrieved January 14, 2024, from https://www.statista.com/forecasts/1145056/smartphone-users-in-the-united-states

The Physics arXiv Blog. (2020, September 8). How to turn your smartphone into a robot. *Discover.* https://www.discovermagazine.com/technology/how-to-turn-your-smartphone-into-a-robot

2

Lift Off with Android Native Apps

Learning Outcomes:

✓ *Successful installation of the Android Studio Development Environment.*
✓ *Successful creation of an Android Studio app project.*
✓ *Understanding of Application Program Interfaces (APIs) and Software Development Kits (SDKs).*
✓ *Successful setting up of Android Virtual Device (AVD) emulator devices.*
✓ *Optional deployment of apps onto physical Android devices.*
✓ *Successful identification and selection of editing preview devices.*
✓ *Familiarity with the Android Studio runtime environment.*

Before you can code your own dazzling Android apps, you will need to set up a development environment. The most popular Android development environment currently is by far Android Studio. It has replaced Eclipse ADT as the primary IDE for native Android app development. Android Studio is now the official IDE for the coding of Android device applications. It provides tools for building apps for every Android device including smartphones, tablets, wearables, and future breathtaking applications such as human medical implants

DOI: 10.1201/9781003286325-2

currently in the creation, testing, and marketing phases. Android Studio is based on the JetBrains IntelliJ IDEA software and is available free of charge for download on Windows, Mac OS X, and Linux development systems.

Student outcomes for this chapter focus on the installation of the IDE for coding Android device applications and the successful testing of the installation with a simple "Hello World" project. Following are step-by-step outlines to accomplish the desired outcomes.

Setting Up the Launch Pad for Android Studio Development

Android Studio can be installed on a Windows, Mac OS, or Linux-based computer. At the time of this writing, instructions and appropriate downloads for all of these platforms can be found at https://developer.android.com/studio#downloads.

Upon navigating to this URL, you will see select instructions for the operating system under which you will be installing Android Studio. At some point, you will be asked to read the terms and conditions for the *Android Software Development Kit License Agreement*. After agreeing to these terms, you will be prompted to continue to download Android Studio.

After downloading, run the executable file that was downloaded. You will be prompted through the Android Studio Setup wizard. Be sure to install all of the Android Studio features and components as indicated in Figure 2.1.

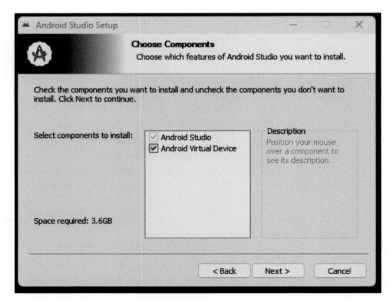

FIGURE 2.1
Android Studio Setup wizard.

Android Studio setup will then prompt you for the installation location, which on a Windows computer will most likely be C:\Program Files\ Android\Android Studio.

Creating Your First Android Studio Project

To create your Android project in Android Studio, launch the Android Studio development environment application. There is some initial setup the first time you do so, which can take some time. There are several components that need to be downloaded on a fresh install of Android Studio, including the target SDK for the project, so plan on reserving time for the completion of this download.

Once you have launched Android Studio and the required SDK components have been downloaded, Android Studio will display the welcome window as illustrated in Figure 2.2.

FIGURE 2.2
Android Studio welcome window.

Follow these steps to create a new Java Android Project:

1. Select the first option which reads "New project". Note that once you have created a project, you can select the second option to open it. If the project is created in a different version of Android Studio than the version in which you are re-opening it, you will find that you need to select the "More Actions" option to import it.

2. The "New Project" is the next window displayed as shown below. Notice all of the different platforms for which projects can be created. Most of our projects, especially initially, will be "Phone and Tablet" projects.

3. Select "Empty Views Activity" as shown in Figure 2.3 and click Next.

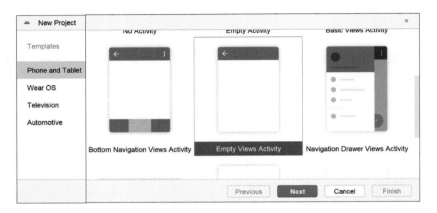

FIGURE 2.3
Empty Views Activity project type.

Let the "Package name" specification default, unless you specifically know that it should be different. You can change the name of the application to reflect the purpose of your app. In this first example, let's name the application "HelloWorld" as shown in Figure 2.4. For our purposes, make certain that the "Language" is **Java** as shown in Figure 2.4.

Browse to the appropriate location where your project is to be stored. You may do so by clicking on the folder indicated for the "Save location" in the illustration above.

A "Minimum SDK" recommendation specifies which minimum version of the Android Operating System, and therefore API, should be used. APIs are important because they provide the building blocks for common app components. Table 2.1 lists the generations of Android Operating Systems and associated APIs. The earlier the API number, the greater the number of devices on which your app will be able to run. But you can also run into problems if the API is too early, so it is wise to go with the default minimum unless you have specific reasons for not doing so.

4. Click Finish and Gradle builds the project information. Android Studio uses the open source Gradle build system. When complete, the project is created. Note this may take some time! There are many

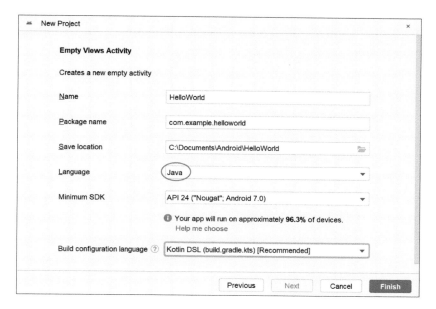

FIGURE 2.4
Android project attributes.

files created for the project. The message "Gradle project sync in progress" indicates that the project is still in creation mode.

5. Once complete, the entire folder structure of project files is displayed in the "Project" panel on the left side of the screen as shown in Figure 2.5.

Take a few minutes to acquaint yourself with the features of the development environment. There are several facets of which to be aware, as noted below.

A brief description of the purpose of each of the highlighted features noted in the Android Studio Windows IDE is displayed in Figure 2.6. The Android Studio IDE for the Mac is quite similar. Further descriptions for these items can be found on the website for Android Developers.

Main Menu – The Main Menu is a collection of all menu options available for performing various tasks within Android Studio.

Project – The Project tool is a toggle that provides a listing of all folders and files within the project.

Resource Manager – The Resource Manager provides a direct link to the color, images, and other resources of the app

More tool windows – The More tool windows icon provides a menu of the various tools provided in the IDE.

TABLE 2.1

Android Mobile Operating System Versions

Android 1.0	Acquired by Google in 2005	**API**
		1
		2
Android 1.5	**Cupcake**	3
	Released in May of 2009	
	First commercially available version	
Android 1.6	**Donut**	4
	Released in September of 2009	
	Included text-to-speech technology	
Android 2.0-2.1	Éclair	5
	Released in October of 2009	6
	Included a revamped UI and the introduction of Live Wallpapers (animated wallpapers at the home screen).	7
	Additional features include a virtual keyboard, Bluetooth 2.1 support for faster file transfers, account sync synchronization of email and contacts, and support for HTML5 and an improved navigational experience with Google Maps.	
Android 2.2	**Froyo** (Frozen yogurt)	8
	Released in May 2010	
	Introduced external storage	
	Introduced the Android Cloud to Device Messaging (C2DM) which has since been deprecated for Google Cloud Messaging.	
	Also seriously increased OS speed thanks to the Java V8 engine and JIT compiler which launched apps faster than ever.	
Android 2.3	**Gingerbread**	9
	Released later in 2010	10
	Added a redesigned keyboard, improved navigation capabilities, increased power efficiency, and more.	
	Also added improved features for communications within apps, multimedia, and sensors processing. Also added near-field communications (NFC)	
Android 3.0-3.2	**Honeycomb** → tablets	11
	User-interface improvements for tablets	12
	Added fragments, a persistent Action Bar, optimization for different screen sizes, Holo, improved graphics, multimedia, Bluetooth support, multicore processor architectures, and animation frameworks	13
Android 4.0	**Ice Cream Sandwich** = merged 2.3 and 3.0	14
	Released in 2011	15
	Incorporated into smartphone apps Honeycomb features that were available only for tablets so that developers could more easily scale apps to work on different devices	
	Added accessibility for users with disabilities	
Android 4.1-4.3	**Jelly Bean**	16
	Released in 2012	17
	Includes support for external displays, improved security, appearance, and performance enhancements	18

(Continued)

TABLE 2.1 (*Continued*)

Android Mobile Operating System Versions

Android 4.4	**KitKat**	19
	Released in October of 2013	20
	Includes several performance improvements meant to bridge older and newer Android devices	
Android 5.0	**Lollipop**	21
	Released November of 2014	22
	Redesigned UI, improvements to notifications, and improved battery performance	
	ART officially replaced Davlik	
Android 6.0	**Marshmallow**	23
	Released in October of 2015	
	Includes a new permissions architecture, new APIs for contextual assistants, improved power management system, ability to use a microSD card as primary storage, and native support for fingerprint recognition	
Android 7.0	**Nougat** –	24
	Released in September of 2016	25
	Users can now run two apps with split-screen multi-window support	
	Notification enhancements, JIT compilation, doze enhancements, optimization of background processing, data saver mode, Vulkan 3D rendering API for appropriate hardware devices, and improved call screening	
Android 8.0	**Oreo** –	26
	Released in August of 2017	
Android 8.1	**Oreo Go** –	27
	Released in December of 2017	
Android 9.0	**Pie** –	28
	Released in August of 2018	
Android 10.0	**10** – (Android Q)	29
	Released in August of 2019	
Android 11.0	**11** – (Android R for Red Velvet Cake)	30
	Released in September of 2020	
Android 12.0	**12** – Snow Cone	31
	12L – Snow Cone v2	32
Android 13.0	**13** – Tiramisu	33
Android 14.0	**14** – Upside Down Cake	34

Build – The Build tool compiles the app and its resources and produces an *apk* (Android Package Kit) that can then be installed on a physical device or an AVD for the execution and testing of an app.

Logcat – The Logcat provides a list of system messages generated by a running device.

Problems – The Problems tool lists all syntax and build errors encountered with the development of an app project.

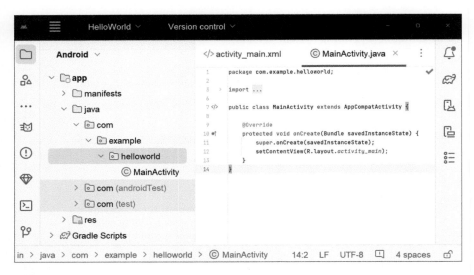

FIGURE 2.5
Android Studio project view.

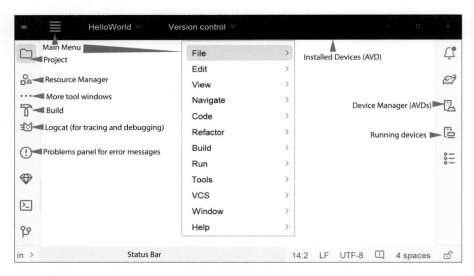

FIGURE 2.6
Android Studio IDE newer UI.

Installed Devices – The Installed Devices tool provides a drop-down list of devices available for running an app. Initially, there are no AVDs installed.

Device Manager – The Device Manager tool provides a wizard for creating an AVD that can be used to emulate a variety of Android physical devices.

Running Devices – The Running Devices panel displays the AVDs that are currently running. These are generally associated with the launch of a current app.

Status Bar – The Status Bar displays the status of the project and indicates the last Gradle build result.

This is a note for those who have worked with Android Studio in the past prior to the release of the newer user interface (UI): To revert the IDE back to the older UI, navigate through the Main Menu to *File, Settings,* and then the *"New UI"* option. The same set of actions can be taken to enable the new UI.

There is also the Android tool that when clicked displays a drop-down list of alternative views of the project files as shown in Figure 2.7. The preferred option for most activities in app development is the Android view.

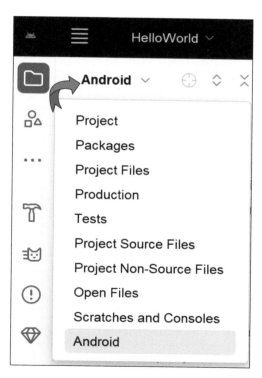

FIGURE 2.7
Variety of project views.

The primary subfolders contained within an Android project are the *manifests, java,* and *res* subfolders. Expand these subfolders and you will see their subfolders and files as shown in Figure 2.8.

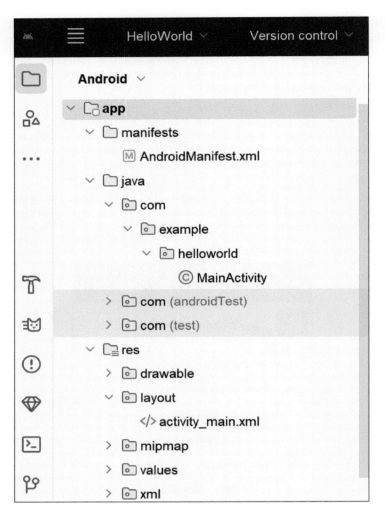

FIGURE 2.8
Project subfolder organization.

The contents of these subfolders will become more apparent as you progress through this text and develop increasingly more sophisticated applications. In the meantime, however, a brief description of the purpose of each folder and its file contents is provided below.

a. The *manifests* folder contains the *AndroidManifest.xml* file. This manifest file describes the fundamental properties of the app, including its launcher icon to be featured on the Android device's menu. Other characteristics described in this file include the name of the app, the theme style of the app design, and any special permissions that the app may require.

b. The *java* folder organizes the java code and code settings for the app. Java code is required to react to user activity within an app.

c. The *res* folder contains the resources for the app.

Resources are organized according to type and categorized within the following subfolders.

1. The *drawable* subfolder contains the image files used in the app.

2. The *layout* subfolder contains the screen (activity) layouts defined for the app. Most of the time, each different screen in the app will be defined by a specific layout file. The layout file consists of eXtensible Markup Language (XML) statements defining UI components and their attributes. The *activity_main.xml* file is created when the empty activity is created.

3. The *mipmap* subfolder shown in expanded mode above contains the launcher icons to be associated with the app. Several versions of a launcher icon are required to accommodate the myriad of Android devices and screen densities available.

4. The *values* subfolder contains the fundamental resource values for the app. These values are string constants, color specifications, size designations, or defined Cascading Style Sheets (CSS) styles and are stored according to their type within XML files correspondingly named *strings.xml, colors.xml, dimens.xml,* and *styles.xml*.

The easiest and most logical starting place in the coding of a native Android app takes place in the *activity_main.xml* (main activity) layout file that defines a screen. There is technically a difference between a screen and an activity, but for our purposes to simplify things a bit, for now you may consider an activity and a screen to be the same.

As an an app developer, you work in Android Studio with the contents of the layout file in a Graphical User Interface (GUI)-based *Design* mode or in an XML statement *Code* mode. To continue, double-click on the single file named *activity_main.xml* to open it. It may take a little time to initialize the rendering library. Thereafter, you should see your present activity layout displayed in Design mode as shown below.

An activity layout defines the visual structure for a UI, most notably a display screen. The layout is coded in XML. Note the tabs labeled *Design* and *Code* in the area underneath the Navigation Bar as shown in Figure 2.9. The present layout view is the *Design* view. While it is possible to code your entire screen layout and components in XML, you will find it much easier to use the GUI-based Design mode to generate the XML statements. Later chapters, however, will discuss the XML code further.

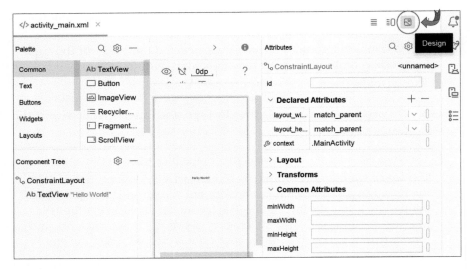

FIGURE 2.9
Layout design view.

If you click the *Code* tab, the display switches to the equivalent XML code for the current composition of the layout, as illustrated in Figure 2.10.

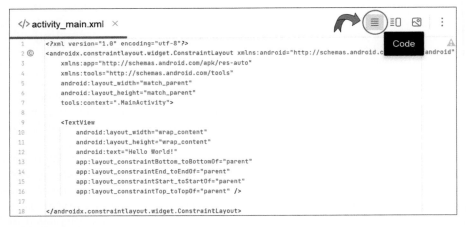

FIGURE 2.10
Layout code view.

As an app developer, you will find it helpful to be able to navigate between the *Design* view and the *Code* view but will most likely be more comfortable, at least initially, in the *Design* view.

Returning to the Design view, take a careful note of the *Component Tree* display, as shown in Figure 2.11.

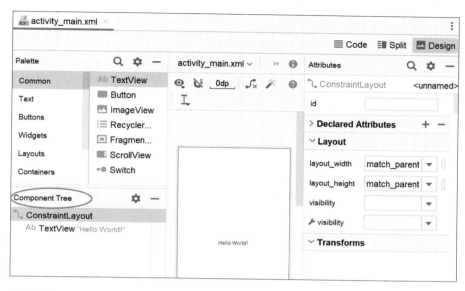

FIGURE 2.11
Layout component tree.

The Component Tree panel is named as such because it displays the components of your device's screen in a hierarchical manner. In this example, the *TextView* is contained within the *activity_main (ConstraintLayout)*. Much more will be said later on what it means to be a *ConstraintLayout*.

For now, click on the *TextView* element shown in this panel and observe that the *TextView* component is now highlighted. In addition, an "Attributes" panel of information is also displayed on the right side of the window as shown in Figure 2.12. You will most likely need to scroll to view these properties. You may also click on the ">All Attributes" item to expand the full list of properties that can be valued, a small subset of which can be seen in Figure 2.12.

The *TextView* component has many properties, of which only a few of those considered currently most relevant are displayed under the "Common Attributes" heading.

Scroll through this *TextView*'s attributes in the appropriate panel and keep scrolling until you get to the *text* property. Within this panel, attributes are listed in the left column, while their respective values are listed in the adjacent right column. It is not necessary to assign all properties a value. The current *text* property value is "Hello World!" as shown in Figure 2.13. While it is tempting to change the value by simply typing over the current value, a more detailed set of actions are required to properly change its value, as you will learn a bit later. For now, we will leave the values as they are and run our app.

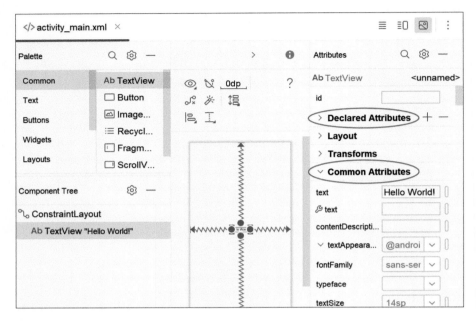

FIGURE 2.12
Selected component attributes.

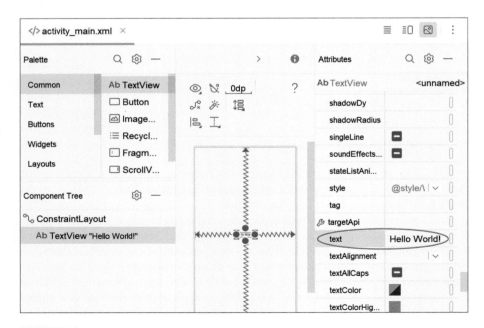

FIGURE 2.13
Focusing on a single attribute.

Running the Android App

In order to run our app, as is noted in the Android Studio User Guide (https://developer.android.com/studio/intro/index.html), Android Studio builds the app with Gradle, requests the selection of a deployment target in the form of an emulator or physically connected device, and then deploys the app to it. While you need not be concerned with Gradle for a while, a decision of run-time platform from basically two choices is required. One alternative is to set up an emulator, referred to as an AVD and deploy our app to the emulator. The other choice is to deploy our app to a physical Android device.

Using the AVD to Set Up an Emulator

An Android emulator, or AVD, was initially installed when we installed our Android Studio IDE and created our first project. It enables you to prototype, develop, and test Android apps without using a hardware device. The emulator supports Android phone, tablet, Android Wear, and Android TV devices. It comes with predefined device types called AVDs that define specific, common Android devices that can be installed for your use, and you can create your own device definitions and emulator skins. The AVD Manager is used to create and manage the AVDs. To create an AVD emulator, follow the steps below that refer to Figures 2.14 and 2.15.

1. Click on the *Device Manager* on the far-right side of the Android Studio window as circled in Figure 2.14.
2. Click on the *Create Virtual Device* icon denoted as a "+" symbol.
3. Select a device to serve as an emulator. In Figure 2.15, a *Pixel 3a* device in the *Phone* category has been selected. Click Next.

A system image must be downloaded for association with the chosen emulator as illustrated in Figure 2.16. It is usually best to select the latest API number identified for the system images. Once selected, click Next and then accept the license agreement as prompted in the dialog box that follows. The system image will then be downloaded and installed. This will take a few minutes to complete. Once installed, you will have the option of naming the AVD. Additional AVDs can be added as emulators to Android Studio anytime by following this process. You will most likely want to install an emulator from the *Tablet* category as well.

Anytime you run an app, you use an AVD created in this way. You always have the option of connecting an Android device to your computer to use it

FIGURE 2.14
Android virtual Device Manager.

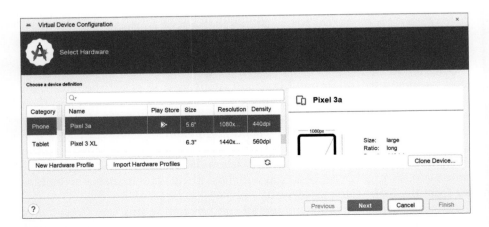

FIGURE 2.15
Selection of an AVD.

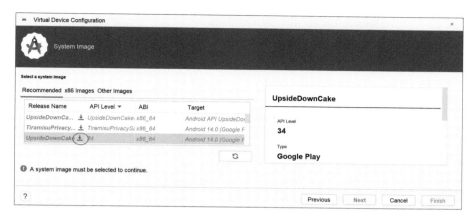

FIGURE 2.16
Selecting a system image for the AVD.

instead. Throughout this book, we utilize the AVDs as illustrated in Figure 2.17 by following these steps:

1. Make sure that the app is selected as shown in Figure 2.17.
2. Confirm the emulator (AVD) selection and click the green play button adjacent to the app designation as shown in Figure 2.17.

FIGURE 2.17
Running the app.

After clicking the green play button, the app is compiled, and if there are no errors, it is installed as an *apk* on the selected emulator, or AVD. An *apk* is an Android application package and is the file format that Android uses to both distribute and install apps. Once installed, the app is automatically executed, and the initial screen is displayed within the *Running Devices* window as illustrated in Figure 2.18.

FIGURE 2.18
App installed and launched on the AVD.

Congratulations! You have just created and run your first Android app!

Important Notes on the Emulator

The controls on the emulator toolbar can be very helpful when running apps. A brief explanation of the purpose of the more popular controls is provided in Figure 2.19.

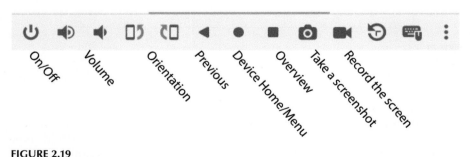

FIGURE 2.19
The AVD controls.

Running Your App on a Physical Android Device

It is also possible to download your app to a real Android hardware device, such as your personal Android phone. Your personal phone can be connected via USB or as a wireless device to the computer on which Android Studio is running. It may be important that you modify the security settings on your Android device by opening the device's *Settings* to select *Developer Options* to enable *USB debugging*.

Android Studio Emulator Device Orientation

One of the challenges Android app developers encounter is the myriad of different devices running the Android platform. This is something of which we will be mindful as we move through the various chapters in this book. An app can be developed for portrait or landscape orientation or portrait and landscape orientation. Developing for portrait and landscape orientation is nontrivial and discussed in a later chapter. Developing for portrait or landscape orientation is a less complicated effort. Portrait orientation is the default. In order to develop a simple app for landscape orientation, two things must be addressed: editing orientation and runtime orientation.

Android Studio App Editing Orientation

The layout orientation for a screen activity in Android Studio must be modified from its default portrait orientation to landscape orientation. To accomplish this task, we use the *Orientation for Preview* button as shown in Figure 2.20.

Changing Android Emulator Orientation

By default, an emulator starts in portrait orientation. It is easy to change the orientation of the emulator using the orientation controls shown in Figure 2.20. However, doing so will not necessarily adjust the orientation of the app's screen layout when launched on an AVD emulator. For this reason, it is sometimes necessary to modify the autorotation setting of the emulator device. To do so, use the *Home* button to launch the *Settings* app and locate the *Auto-rotate* setting associated with the display. An example is shown in Figure 2.21.

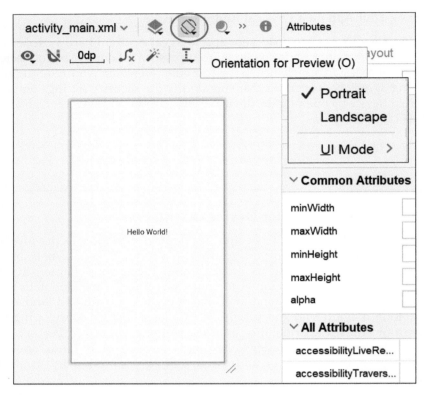

FIGURE 2.20
Layout editor orientation.

FIGURE 2.21
Enabling the AVD autorotation.

Closing an App to Return to the Welcome Screen

To gracefully exit the editor environment after working on an app, use the "Main Menu" identified by the hamburger menu in the upper right corner of the editing window. Then select *File → Close Project* as illustrated in Figure 2.22.

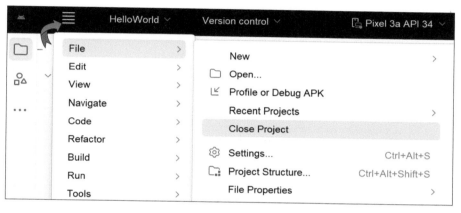

FIGURE 2.22
Closing the Android project.

Navigating Android Versions, Code Names, and API Levels

The following table illustrates the relationship among the Android mobile operating system's version numbers, code names, and respective API levels. The Android code names are fashioned after desserts (since it is said that Android devices make our lives sweeter) and ordered alphabetically. Each version represents enrichment of and improvements to the Android SDK. As the API number increases, so does the functionality. As was illustrated in the AVD setup, when configuring an app, both a minimum API level and a target API level are identified. The minimum API level designates the absolute minimum level required to run the application, whereas the target API identifies the optimal level for which the application has been coded.

Now that we have successfully created and run our first Android app, we are ready to add pizzazz with images and icons in Chapter 3.

Exercises

E2.1 Install Android Studio on the computer which you will be utilizing for the lessons covered in this book. Once Android Studio is installed, create a new Android project as discussed in this chapter. Then create two virtual device emulators, or AVDs as was discussed in this chapter. Be sure that one is a phone device, and the other is a tablet device. Run your Android project twice using each emulator for testing purposes.

E2.2 Until a short time ago, developers used Eclipse with the ADT (Android plug-in) to develop Android apps. In the last few years, however, Android Studio has become the Android app developer platform of choice. Use the Internet to explain the functionality of Android Studio. Who maintains and supports it? What is IntelliJ? What is IDEA?

E2.3 Use the Internet to briefly explain to what an Android "AVD" refers as it relates to Android app development.

E2.4 Use the Internet to briefly explain "Gradle" in terms of Android Studio app development.

E2.5 Use the Internet to explain to what the Android term *apk* refers.

E2.6 To what unit of measurement does each of the following refer and when should it be used:

a. dp   b. sp

E2.7 Why should an Android developer never use px as a unit of measurement?

E2.8 On which is the Android OS (operating system) based? Windows/Mac OS/Linux

3

First Image Impressions and Launcher Icons

Learning Outcomes:

- ✓ *Successful inclusion of images as drawable resources within project folder hierarchy.*
- ✓ *Successful specification of images as background property values.*
- ✓ *Successful use of the Android ImageView widget.*
- ✓ *Understanding of the Design and Blueprint views within the Activity Design mode.*
- ✓ *Ability to generate a customized launcher icon.*
- ✓ *Awareness of the app's Android Manifest file and the specification of an app's launcher icon within it.*
- ✓ *Ability to manipulate emulator orientation.*

DOI: 10.1201/9781003286325-3

In the previous chapter, you successfully installed the Android Studio IDE and created your first Android app. This first Android app is a very simple "Hello World" program. And while it is exciting the first time you successfully execute it, it loses its luster exponentially with each subsequent run. That's because as you expand your ability to code on your Android devices, two extraordinary things happen. First, your ability to transfer what your mind has created to a phone screen expands in proportion to your awareness of what apps are available. Second, your speed to produce exceptional products, simple or complex, is enhanced allowing you to do more. This means that the graphic design and implementation of apps for your projects become an ever-evolving journey of interlinking ideas and codes. Simply put, the more you learn about constructing apps, both basic and advanced, the more exciting the experience.

In this chapter, we begin to consider the inclusion of images in our apps. We'll look at static image usage and discuss the essential considerations of which app developers need to be aware regarding images and icons. The discussion that follows addresses the specification of a screen background image, individual areas of the screen where images can be placed, and the creation of a launcher icon for an app.

Background Images

A background image by convention is an image that covers the mobile screen background. An image is considered a project resource and as such its filename must consist of only lowercase letters. The mechanism to specify a background image is an easy two-step process. To illustrate, let's open the "Hello World" project created in Chapter 2. The easiest way to open a previously created project is to select it from the list of projects previously created in the Android Studio Welcome Screen as shown in Figure 3.1, by simply clicking on the entry.

FIGURE 3.1
Re-launching Android Studio.

If for some reason the project you wish to open is not listed, click the "Open" at the top of the window and then navigate to the project through the file manager on your computer system.

In order to open properly, you will want to see the Android Studio logo icon displayed next to the app project name. If no such icon is displayed, you will need to select the "Import project" menu option instead and then select the *"build.gradle"* file.

Once the app project is open in Android Studio, follow the steps below to include a background image within your activity layout.

Step 1: Drag the background image file (.png) to the app project's sub-folder named *drawable*, which is found in the app's *res* folder as illustrated in Figure 3.2. An image file named *worldimage.png* will appear in the project's *res/drawable* folder after a "Refactor" approval of the move.

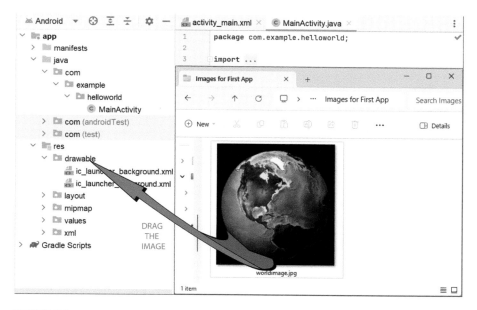

FIGURE 3.2
Dragging an image from the File Explorer.

Step 2: Once the image file exists in the *drawable* folder, it can be referenced within the app. To make the image the screen's background image, it needs to be assigned to the *background* property for the screen layout. So, here are the sub-steps required to set the screen's background property:

Step 2.a: Open the *activity_main.xml* file if it is not already open.

Step 2.b: In the Design view, click on the *ConstraintLayout* in the Component Tree and then scroll down to "All Attributes" in the Attributes panel. Doing so results in a listing of all of the eXtensible Markup Language (XML) properties associated with the *ConstraintLayout* component.

Step 2.c: Scroll to the background property and click in the adjacent cell.

Step 2.d: Then click on the background value "Pick a resource" icon shown on the right as an ellipsis image and circled in Figure 3.3.

This opens the "Pick a Resource" dialog window as shown in Figure 3.4.

FIGURE 3.3
Assigning a background image resource.

Step 2.e: Then click on the Drawable tab to make sure it is selected. Doing so identifies a list of file names associated with the app project Drawable resources. The world image file appears because it was previously stored in the *res/drawable* folder in Step 1. So, click on the *worldImage* drawable resource to select it.

Step 2.f: Click OK.

Run the app, and a screen similar to that shown in Figure 3.5 should be displayed.

Graphics that can be drawn to the screen are considered *drawables* in Android development. An image is more specifically considered a bitmap drawable resource. There are several different types of "drawables", including bitmap files, nine-patch files, layer lists, shape *drawables*, scale *drawables*, and others. For the most part, we will be working with the bitmap file category

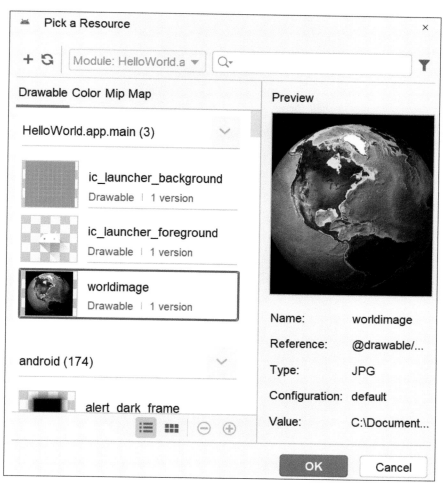

FIGURE 3.4
Selecting the background image file.

of *drawables* which includes graphic files of type .png, .jpg, or .gif. The png format is used in a majority of apps, as it is a lossless format, meaning that compression does not compromise its quality and that it has the greatest support for transparency and supports interlacing.

You may have noticed that the "world" portrayed in the image in the Resources dialog window Preview and that portrayed in the Android Emulator smartphone device window look a little "squished". But if you were to render the same background image on an Android tablet with a larger screen size, such as a Nexus 9 emulator device, the image would appear perfectly proportional.

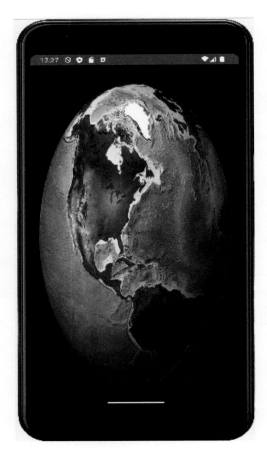

FIGURE 3.5
Running app with background image.

As documented on the Android Developer website, Android by default
scales bitmap "drawables" so that they render at the appropriate physical
size on a device. They therefore recommend that you format your images so
that such scaling will render an appropriate appearance, or that you specify
alternative versions of your image to accommodate the different resolutions
of different screens. In this sense, several different versions of an image
may need to be included and specified for different device screen sizes and
dimensions. For our purposes here, the scaling modification is not too upset-
ting, and we accept it. But if we are developing an app for a general audience,
especially if we plan to charge for its use, we will want to be far more concerned with the inclusion of multiple versions of our images to ensure perfec-
tion of rendering on various screens. Therefore, a more detailed discussion
of this important issue will be addressed in Chapter 6 after we have more
experience in developing Android apps.

ImageView Widgets

It is often desirable to include an image on the screen that is not a background image. The easiest way to display an image on an app screen is to first save the image file in the *res/drawable* subfolder within the Android project, as was previously done for the background image. But the difference is that after doing so, the container on the screen that is used to display it takes the form of an *ImageView* widget that is placed in the screen layout.

So, there are three steps involved.

Step 1: Make sure that the file specifying the image to be displayed on the screen has been moved to the *drawable* subfolder. For example, in the discussion that follows, an image file named *planeinflight.png* has been moved to the *drawable* subfolder within the sample app.

Step 2: Drag an *ImageView* widget from the Design Palette to the location in the screen layout (*activity_main.xml* in this example) where the image is to be displayed, as shown in Figure 3.6. Note that this also opens the "Pick a Resource" dialog window prompting for the image file to be loaded into the *ImageView* widget.

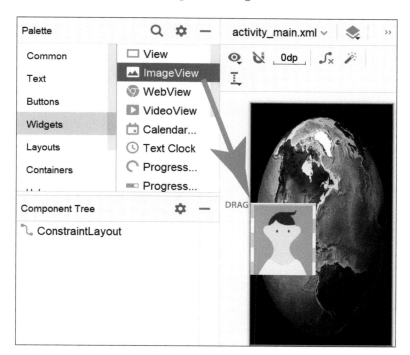

FIGURE 3.6
Drag an *ImageView* widget onto the layout.

Step 3: Select the image to be displayed in the *ImageView* as shown in Figure 3.7 and then click OK. The image will now display in the screen layout.

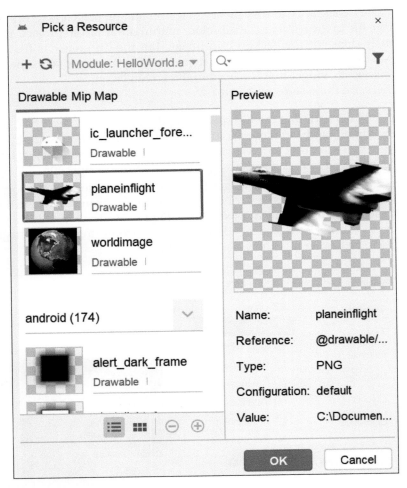

FIGURE 3.7
Select an image resource for the *ImageView*.

There are several things to note at this point. First, the *layout_height* and *layout_width* of an *ImageView* component can be specified in dp units rather than as *wrap_content* if the situation warrants. However, such size or dimension specifications should be "externalized" in accordance with Android development practices. The topic of externalization is discussed in the next chapter.

Second, an error has been flagged for the *ImageView* as indicated by the red error signal shown in Figure 3.8.

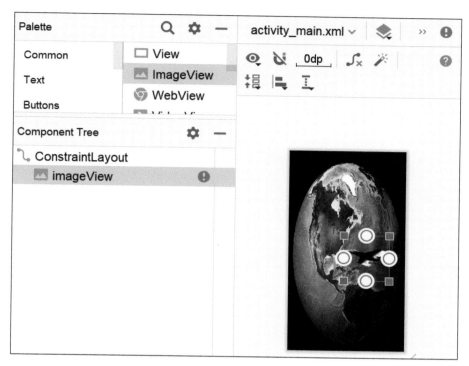

FIGURE 3.8
Error indicating missing constraints.

Clicking the error signal informs us that there is a constraint error. Because our screen layout is a *ConstraintLayout*, all widgets added to the screen must be "constrained" within the layout. All widgets placed within the screen confines must be *constrained* both vertically and horizontally. Failure to constrain a widget such as this *ImageView* will result in erratic placement when the app runs. In other words, this image may appear virtually anywhere on the screen of the target device when the app runs. And if there are multiple unconstrainted widgets, they may all stack on top of one another when the app runs.

Therefore, the solution is to constrain the widget by dragging the circles defined along its horizontal and vertical borders to either other constrained widgets or the borders of the layout (i.e. parent) itself. Open circles denote missing constraints. The image in this case also needs to be resized. This can be accomplished by dragging inward one of the solid blue colored square corner borders shown in Figure 3.9.

Drag from each of the open circles to the respective border (top, bottom, left, and right) of the screen layout to constrain the image and then size the image appropriately.

Solid circles denote successful constraints. Once constrained, you can still relocate the image within the screen layout. Notice that the error indicator has now changed to a warning indication signaled as a yellow triangle symbol also shown in Figure 3.9.

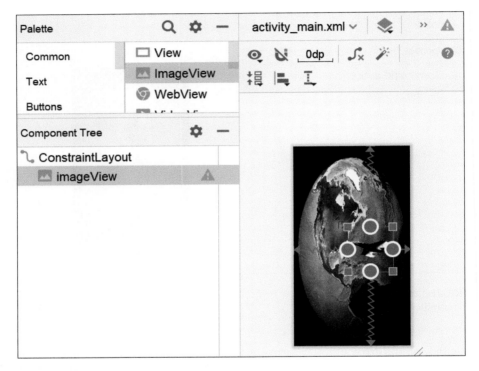

FIGURE 3.9
Constraint anchors are circles, and squares are for sizing.

Clicking on the yellow warning symbol badge produces the explanation for this very important warning. The explanation reads that the image is provided without a "contentDescription", which is one of the attributes of an *ImageView* widget. A "contentDescription" is extremely helpful to the visually impaired who have screen readers installed, since it enables the screen reader to describe the image. The "contentDescription" attribute is also important to people who have graphics disabled on their mobile device, since it conveys an important content item on your screen on which they would otherwise completely miss out. So, it is very important to always provide a content description for your images via the "contentDescription" attribute.

To easily do so, simply specify a value for the "contentDescription" attribute in the "Common Attributes" section of the Attributes panel. In this case, the content description entered is "plane flying across globe" as shown in Figure 3.10.

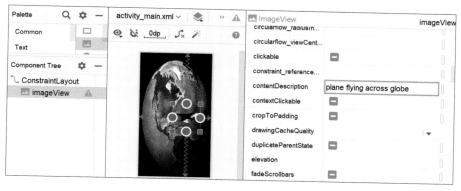

FIGURE 3.10
Assigning a "contentDescription".

And just when you thought you might be finished, you notice that there is still a warning indicator symbol. If you click on this symbol, the warning is explained as shown in Figure 3.11.

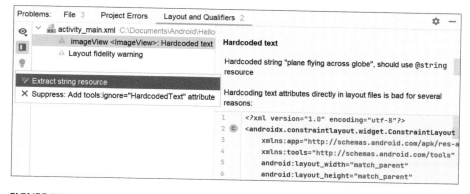

FIGURE 3.11
Warning explanation and quick fix for hardcoded text.

The reason for this warning is that all string values are meant to be "externalized" in Android apps. Typing a text value as an attribute is considered "hardcoding text" and is severely frowned upon. This topic is explained in significant detail in the next chapter. In the meantime, just click on the "light bulb" for the "Quick Fix" option to extract the string resource and select the first option, which reads "Extract string resource" as shown in Figure 3.11. This opens a dialog window as shown in Figure 3.12 that offers the opportunity to save the string value as an externalized resource, so click OK.

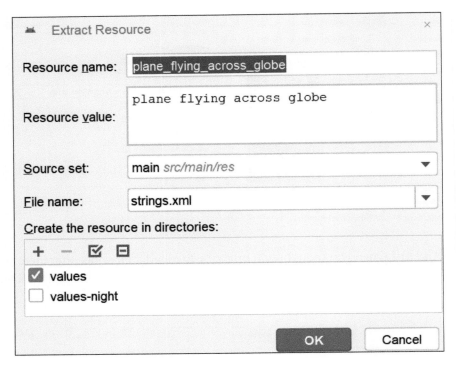

FIGURE 3.12
Externalizing a string resource.

Now, finally, no error or warning should be displayed.

Customizing an App Launcher Icon

An app's launcher icon is a graphic that helps a user to identify your app on his or her device's home screen. According to the Android Developers site, one of the goals of an application launcher icon is to assist with brand promotion. Since user home screens differ widely in terms of screen sizes, resolutions, and densities, Android provides an "Image Asset Studio" to facilitate the adaptation of an image for use as a launcher icon.

As documented on the Android Developer's Image Asset Studio site, you may utilize the Image Asset Studio by doing the following:

1. Make sure that the Android view is selected in the Project window. Right-click the *res* folder and select *New > Image Asset*.

2. From the *Asset Studio* window as shown in Figure 3.13, specify the following:

   a. Select the Icon Type: *Launcher icons (Adaptive and Legacy)*

   b. Select the *Image* as the Asset Type

   c. Name your launcher icon.

   d. Navigate to the image file by clicking the folder icon in the *"Path:"* input specification as shown below.

   e. Be certain to do so in BOTH Foreground Layer and Background Layer tabs!

   f. Click Next.

   g. Click Finish.

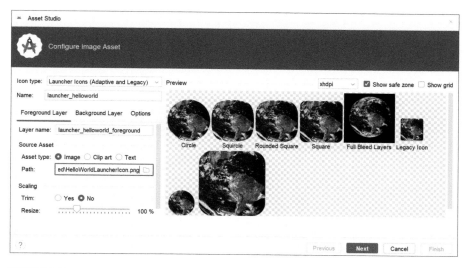

FIGURE 3.13
Assigning a launcher icon to your app.

The *Image Asset Studio* has created a variety of launcher icons in various formats that conform to the myriad of Android devices on which your app may be installed. In order for the launcher icon to be associated with your app when installed on a device, however, there is one more task that must be performed. You must also make the necessary modifications to the *AndroidManifest.xml* file. The *AndroidManifest.xml* file is located in the Android Project's manifests folder as shown in Figure 3.14.

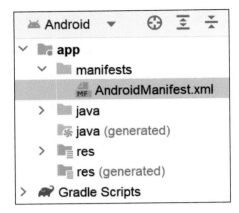

FIGURE 3.14
Locating the *AndroidManifest* file.

The modifications that you will make to the manifest file consist of changes to the default launcher icon filenames as shown in lines 9 and 11 in Figure 3.15.

FIGURE 3.15
Modifying the manifest file to identify the launcher icon.

Design Issues

There are several ways to include images in an app. One of the easiest methods as discussed earlier in this chapter is to include a *drawable* image referenced by file name from the app's *drawable* resource folder. As earlier stated, Android by default scales bitmap "drawables" so that they render at the appropriate physical size on a device. As we saw in the case of the world globe background image, this can result in a disproportional scaling of an image. App developers need to be aware of this possibility when working with images in apps. As previously noted, a resolution of this problem is to save different versions of an image within the app so that the appearance of the image will not be compromised. This is a nontrivial task, however, and a little more app development experience will be helpful before tackling this issue later in the text.

When working with *drawable* resource images in Android apps, it is best to use the .png format.

When developing apps, changes and modifications to code, values, and image files are a natural course. In order to keep the Android Studio development environment abreast of such changes, you may need to "Clean" the project from time to time. To do so, from the Android Menu Bar, select Build → Clean Project as shown in Figure 3.16.

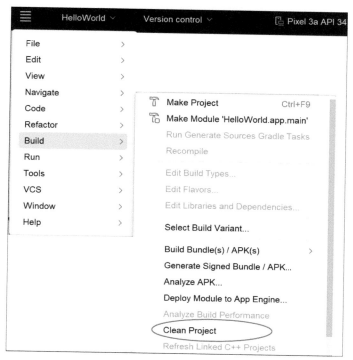

FIGURE 3.16
Clean the android project.

Exercises

The exercises below set up an initial screen that will be incrementally enhanced in subsequent chapters to eventually implement an attractive and complete functional app. You can download royalty-free images from the web to use as image files and launcher icons or use those which have been provided for download for each app described in the exercises that follow. Remember that filenames for drawable and mipmap resources <u>must</u> always be in lower case. And a launcher icon image is expected to be 512 px square. Images of the .png format are preferred.

E3.1 Create a new Android project named *FloorTilesCalc* for a smartphone mobile app that assists in the calculation of the number of floor tiles required to cover the floor in a rectangular room. Use any smartphone platform such as the Pixel 3a AVD. The specifics of the final version of this app are detailed in subsequent chapters. This is just the first phase. For now, the purpose of this exercise is limited to the setup of a customized launcher icon and a screen background. Use the images provided as download from this text website or download a royalty-free image to use as the screen layout background and a launcher icon. Leave the "Hello World" text component on the screen for now. We will address this text component in the beginning of the next chapter. Run the app to make certain that the background image appears correctly. A sample output screen is provided online in the supplementary resources for this book.

E3.2 Create a new Android project named *Inches2Meters* for a smartphone mobile app that assists in the conversion between inches and meters. Develop for any phone device of your choice, such as the Pixel 3a or Nexus 6 as examples. The specifics of the final version of this app are detailed in subsequent chapters. This is just the first phase. For now, the purpose of this exercise is limited to the setup of a customized launcher icon and a screen background. Use the images provided as download from this text website or download a few royalty-free images to use as the screen layout background and a launcher icon. Leave the "Hello World" text component on the screen for now. We will address this text component in the beginning of the next chapter. Run the app to make certain that the background image appears correctly. A sample output screen is provided online in the supplementary resources for this book.

E3.3 Create a new Android project named *DivingApp* for a tablet mobile app. Your good friend Sky Waters is a diving enthusiast and has asked you to code an Android app that will run on a tablet device and can be used to estimate how long a diver's air supply will last on a deep dive in salt water. The specifics of the final version of this app are detailed in subsequent chapters. This is just the first phase. For now, the purpose of this exercise is limited to the specification of a launcher icon, the use of a screen background image, and the placement of an additional image. Use the images provided as download from this text website or download a few royalty-free images to use instead. Leave the "Hello World" text component on the screen for now. We will address this text component in the beginning of the next chapter. Run the app to make certain that the background image appears correctly. A sample output screen is provided online in the supplementary resources for this book.

E3.4 Create a new Android project named *PlanBoatTrip* for a tablet mobile app that assists in basic planning for a self-navigated boat trip. Use the Nexus 9 or some similar tablet device. When designing and running the app, use landscape mode. The specifics of the final version of this app are detailed in subsequent chapters. This is just the first phase. For now, the purpose of this exercise is limited to the specification of launcher icons, the use of a screen background image, and the placement of an additional image. Use the images provided as download from this text website or download a few royalty-free images to use as the screen layout background and image on the screen layout and a launcher icon. Leave the "Hello World" text component on the screen for now. We will address this text component in the beginning of the next chapter. Run the app to make certain that the background image appears correctly. A sample output screen is provided online in the supplementary resources for this book.

E3.5 Create a new Android project named *BeautifulBalloon* for a smartphone mobile app. Use any phone device of your choice for the design and emulator. You are anxious to "land" a summer internship at the *BeautifulBalloon* hot air balloon ride fairground. The job will be yours if you are able to code an Android app that will be used by the staff to determine the correct mix of environmental conditions and mechanical values required to safely grant hot air balloon rides to the public. The specifics of the final version of this app are detailed in subsequent chapters. This is just the first phase. For now, the purpose of this exercise is limited to the specification of launcher icons, the use of a screen background image, and the placement of an additional image. Use the images provided as download from this text website or download a few royalty-free images to use as the screen layout background, and image on the screen layout and a launcher icon. Leave the "Hello World" text component on the screen for now. We will address this text component in the beginning of the next chapter. Run the app to make certain that the background image appears correctly. A sample output screen is provided online in the supplementary resources for this book.

4

Externalizing Resources: Strings, Colors, and Sizes

Learning Outcomes:

✓ *Successful eternalization of string resources.*
✓ *Successful externalization of color resources.*
✓ *Successful externalization of dimension resources.*
✓ *Understanding of when to use dp and sp and why not to use px units.*
✓ *Understanding of the role of the res/values/strings.xml file and how string resources for the app are stored in XML.*
✓ *Understanding of the role of the res/values/colors.xml file and how color resources for the app are stored in XML.*

                    DOI: 10.1201/9781003286325-4

✓ Understanding of the role of the res/values/dimens.xml file and how size specifications for widgets of the app are stored in XML.

✓ A basic understanding of screen design issues in terms of the use of color, styles, and themes.

✓ Successful handling of TextView components and their externalized attribute values.

We began to work with app resources in the last chapter, where we discussed the use of images and launcher icons. Now that we have begun to work with images in our apps, it is time that we address other app resources. For example, you may have wanted to enlarge the default "Hello World!" string displayed in the app examples in the last chapter. Or you may have wished to change the color of this text string so that it was more noticeable on the screen's background image. Furthermore, we won't want to see "Hello World!" on most of our apps but will instead want to see different text displayed.

Specifying a color or changing the size of displayed text is not as simple as simply typing a color name or a numeric value. In fact, the correct means of adding color and specifying font sizes and spacing dimensions requires that we externalize these attributes as resources. In addition, any text displayed on our mobile app screen will need to optimally be defined as an externalized string value resource. The technique for externalizing resources and the benefits and advantages of doing so are covered in significant detail in this chapter.

The externalization of resources is such an important issue in the development of Android apps that an entire project subfolder is dedicated to the storage and representation of these resources. To illustrate, let's launch Android Studio and open the *HelloWorld* project created in Chapter 2 and with which we worked in Chapter 3.

Note that if your app project does not appear in the "Projects" window of the Android Studio welcome screen, you can open the project using the "Open" option on the top of this window, as was previously noted in Chapter 3.

Once the project is opened, expand the *app* folder in the Project panel. Then expand the *res* subfolder. Something like that shown in Figure 4.1 will be displayed if the *values* subfolder is also expanded.

The *res* folder organizes the app's resources. As displayed above, the *res* folder contains four subfolders namely *drawable, layout, mipmap*, and *values*. Briefly, the *layout* folder is used to organize the screen layouts for app activities. The *drawable* and the *mipmap* folders were used in the previous chapter to store image files and the launcher icons for the app, respectively. And the other two subfolders will be addressed in this chapter. The *values* subfolder is actually the basis of most of the discussion in this chapter. This is where string and color and size resources are defined. It should be noted here that sizes are included in what Android development categorizes as "dimension" resources.

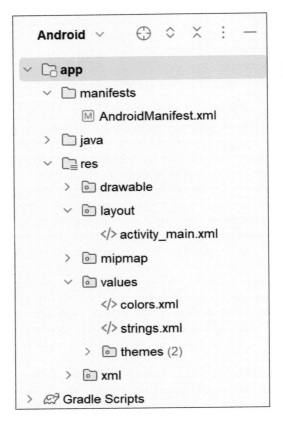

FIGURE 4.1
Android project resources.

Overview of Externalized Resources

When we expand the *values* subfolder, we see the files listed in Figure 4.1. The files listed in the *values* subfolder are XML files and are named in accordance with the types of values defined in each file.

The text strings, color specifications, text sizes, margin and padding offsets, and other dimension specifications are stored in these files so that they may be referenced by name anywhere in the app's code. This can be quite advantageous to use for code reuse purposes. In addition, if we name a color coding its value only once but using its name in multiple places within our app, we need make only one change if we decide on a different color value.

We take a closer look at each resource file category in this chapter.

Externalizing String Resources

As noted in Chapter 3, the *strings.xml* file defines the string values used in our app by associating an identifier with a constant string value. Let's open the *strings.xml* file by simply double-clicking on the file name. The contents of this file from our introductory project are displayed in Figure 4.2.

</> strings.xml ✕

```
1    <resources>
2        <string name="app_name">HelloWorld</string>
3        <string name="plane_flying_across_globe">plane flying across globe</string>
4        <string name="greetings">Greetings</string>
5    </resources>
```

FIGURE 4.2
Example of a *strings.xml* resource file.

As observed in Figure 4.2, two string constants have been externalized as string resources at this point in our app. Externalization means that the identifier name defined can be used by the identifier name anywhere in the app code. Recall that *plane_flying_across_globe* was used in Chapter 3 as the identifier for the value for the *ImageView* element's "contentDescription" attribute. This was done in response to the warning message received after we added *ImageView* to the layout. The suggested fix for this warning back in Chapter 3 was to add a value for the "contentDescription" attribute, which was then converted to an externalized resource.

It is important to note that the name of the app as identified on the Android device is also stored as a string resource within the *strings.xml* file identified as the *app_name* as listed in line 2 in Figure 4.2.

In Chapter 3, when working with the screen layout identified by file name *activity_main.xml*, we worked exclusively with the Android Studio Editor's Design mode. But beginning in Chapter 4, it can often be very helpful to be able to alternatively switch to the "Code" mode, when working with the screen activity layout. The difference is that the Design mode works with screen components in the screen's Component Tree and in the screen's visual layout in a Graphical User Interface (GUI) context. Code mode, on the other hand, explicitly lists the XML code that implements the Design mode representation.

To illustrate, double-click on the *res/layout/activity_main.xml* file displayed in the Android Project panel. By default, it opens in Design mode. To switch to the Code mode view, click the Code button as shown in Figure 4.3.

```
</> activity_main.xml  ✕                                          ≡  ≡◻  ▣        ⋮

  1      <?xml version="1.0" encoding="utf-8"?>
  2 ©    <androidx.constraintlayout.widget.ConstraintLayout xmlns:android="http://schemas.android.com/apk/res/android"
  3          xmlns:app="http://schemas.android.com/apk/res-auto"
  4          xmlns:tools="http://schemas.android.com/tools"
  5          android:layout_width="match_parent"
  6          android:layout_height="match_parent"
  7 ▣        android:background="@drawable/worldimage"
  8          tools:context=".MainActivity">
  9
 10      <ImageView
 11          android:id="@+id/imageView"
 12          android:layout_width="159dp"
 13          android:layout_height="165dp"
 14          android:contentDescription="plane flying across globe"
 15          app:layout_constraintBottom_toBottomOf="parent"
 16          app:layout_constraintEnd_toEndOf="parent"
 17          app:layout_constraintHorizontal_bias="0.746"
 18          app:layout_constraintStart_toStartOf="parent"
 19          app:layout_constraintTop_toTopOf="parent"
 20          app:layout_constraintVertical_bias="0.521"
 21 ▣        app:srcCompat="@drawable/planeinflight" />
 22
 23      </androidx.constraintlayout.widget.ConstraintLayout>
```

FIGURE 4.3
The code representation of the layout.

To further appreciate the *strings.xml* externalization of string values, such as that associated with the *ImageView's* "contentDescription" attribute, pay particular attention to line 14 in the code listing of Figure 4.3. Note that the externalized string resource is used as the value for the *"android:contentDescription"* attribute. If you click on the string value, the attribute value specification changes to the values stored for the @string resource name in the *strings.xml* file. The right-hand side of this attribute is the value "@string/plane_flying_across_globe", where @string denotes that the value is a string resource defined in the *strings.xml* file.

This may seem like a lot of work, especially for string values that will most likely be used only once in an app. The merit of this effort, however, lies in the fact that it enables constant values such as strings to be maintained independently from the code that utilizes them. And in addition, it facilitates the ability to accommodate different languages and locales. Furthermore, with the increase in screen sizes and resolutions, an optimal string value of longer length can be more easily accommodated in the future, which would be more likely the case for a string prompt for input.

Add a *TextView* widget to the layout. To do so, return to Design mode and click on the *TextView* widget in the Palette as shown in Figure 4.4 and drag it onto the layout.

The red error flag will not disappear until the *TextView* is constrained in all four directions, as indicated by the four open circles. Constrain it. As a result, the red error flag is replaced with a yellow warning flag. This is once again

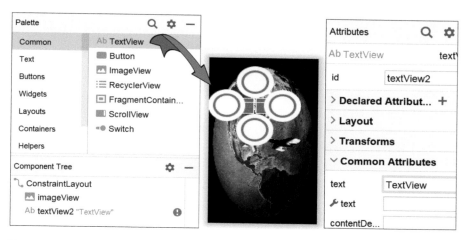

FIGURE 4.4
Dragging a *TextView* widget onto the layout.

due to the fact that the *text* attribute value has not been externalized. Since you do not wish for the value to remain "TextView", replace it with a different text value such as "Greetings". To do so, simply click in the *text* value box as shown in Figure 4.5 and type the new value over the old value. Upon doing so, the yellow warning flag appears, as displayed in Figure 4.5. The reason for this warning is because our new string value has not been externalized. To remedy, you can simply click on the warning symbol to display the suggested fix and then select and follow the "light bulb" hint to fix this issue, which is once again "Extract string resource" as was the case in Chapter 3.

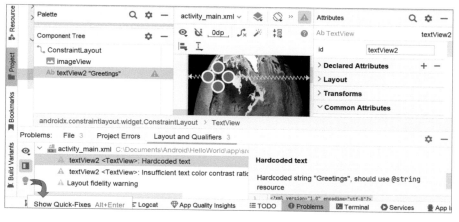

FIGURE 4.5
Selecting a Quick Fix for a text value specification.

There are still two warnings displayed in Figure 4.5. One such warning identifies an "Insufficient text color contrast ratio", which will be addressed by the creation of a new color resource in the next section. The other warning identifies a "Layout fidelity warning", which you may or may not see as it depends on the Android API with which your project is created. This warning, if it does appear, can be ignored.

When the "Extract string resource" is selected to fix the "Hardcoded text" warning, an "Extract Resource" dialog box appears as displayed in Figure 4.6.

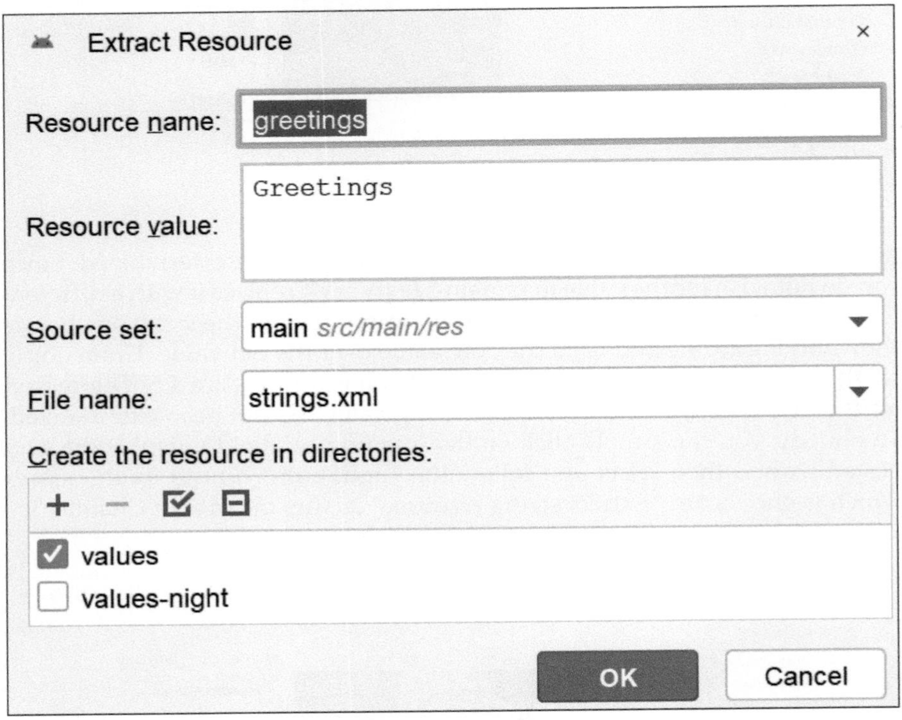

FIGURE 4.6
Extract string resource dialog window.

Click OK to save the "Greetings" string value as an externalized string resource in the *strings.xml* file in the *res/values* subfolder. A look at the attributes panel in the editor window confirms the saving of the string resource, and for final proof of this externalization effort, take a peek at the *strings.xml* file results.

The purpose of the *strings.xml* file is to collect identifier associations with string constant values, as was illustrated in this example. In a later chapter, we'll see how string arrays are defined in this same file in a similar fashion. In addition, if a string value is desired to span multiple lines, you will need to add the escaped newline "\n" character within your externalized string value.

Externalizing Color Resources

The *colors.xml* file is where identifiers are associated with color specifications. Since design etiquette dictates that colors should generally be the same across the different screens in an app, it stands to reason that the same color specifications will be utilized within the individual screen layout code files. Therefore, it makes perfect sense to define the color specification once in a central location and then utilize it by identifier name in the multiple appropriate layouts. Furthermore, externalizing the color resources by specifying them in the *colors.xml* file also makes it significantly easier and more consistent to change the color scheme across the various screens that compose the app.

Now that we have made the case for color externalization, let's explore how it is accomplished. To start, open the *colors.xml* file by double-clicking on this filename in the *values* subfolder within the *res* folder in the Project. A listing like that shown in Figure 4.7 should be displayed.

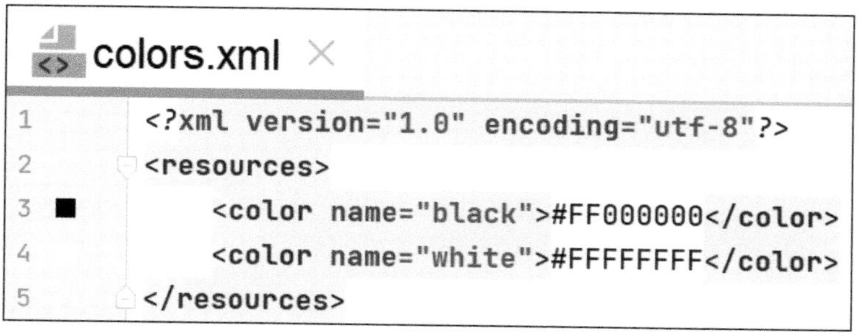

```
colors.xml ✕
1    <?xml version="1.0" encoding="utf-8"?>
2    <resources>
3 ■      <color name="black">#FF000000</color>
4        <color name="white">#FFFFFFFF</color>
5    </resources>
```

FIGURE 4.7
Example of a *colors.xml* resource file.

The color specification value is represented in hexadecimal Red-Green-Blue (RGB) notation. It is possible to specify the color value in any of the formats specified in Table 4.1.

As illustrated in Figure 4.7, Android Studio displays the color rendering of the RGB hexadecimal value specified by each XML color tag pair in the outer margin in the *colors.xml* file. A name for the color is required along with the hexadecimal representation for the desired color.

TABLE 4.1

The Range of Specifications for Color Resources

#RGB	*where*	*R represents the Red factor in hexadecimal notation*
#ARGB		*G represents the Green factor in hexadecimal notation*
#RRGGBB		*B represents the Blue factor in hexadecimal notation*
#AARRGGBB		*A is the opacity setting represented as a hexadecimal value*

As an example, let's add the yellow color to the app. To do so, click on the *TextView* element in the layout design or alternatively in the Component Tree and then click on the "Pick a Resource" button in the value field for the *"text-Color"* attribute as shown in Figure 4.8.

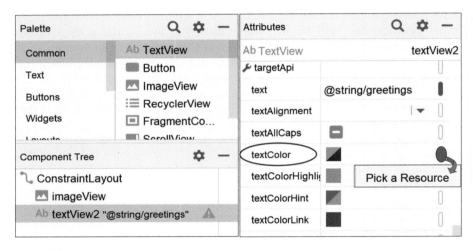

FIGURE 4.8
Creating a color resource for a widget.

Clicking this button opens the "Pick a Resource" dialog window, where you can click on the Color resource category as shown in Figure 4.9. All color resources that have been externalized appear under the "Project" heading. Under these appear other color resources that are built-in Android colors and themes. Note the "plus" sign in the upper portion of the window.

Clicking the circled "plus" symbol is a way to create a new color resource. Click the "plus" symbol and then select "Color Value", as shown in Figure 4.10. A dialog box for a new color value resource then appears prompting for a name for the new color and an eyedropper icon enabling you to select the desired color from a palette. Click on the eyedropper, and select a shade of yellow from the color palette. Then click OK.

The new yellow color has been added to this project as a color resource and can be specified as a color value for any appropriate widget. To select it as the text color for our *TextView* that reads "Greetings", just click on it as illustrated in Figure 4.11. Then click OK.

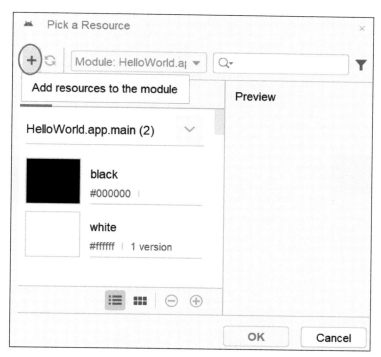

FIGURE 4.9
Adding an additional resource.

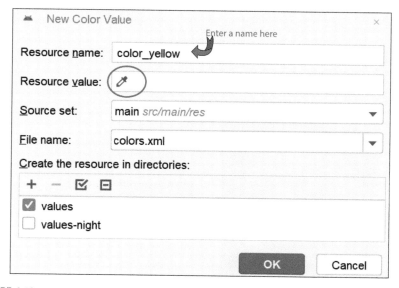

FIGURE 4.10
Defining a new Color Value resource.

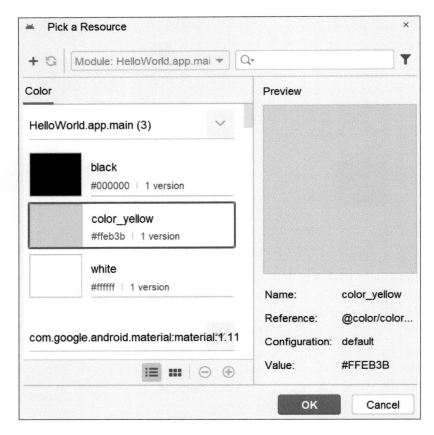

FIGURE 4.11
Assigning the new color resource as an attribute value.

As Figure 4.12 illustrates, our *TextView* widget's color has been modified.

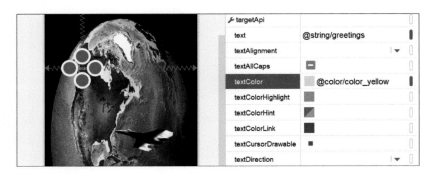

FIGURE 4.12
Color attribute value updated.

This very same set of steps can be used to change the color of any screen layout component, including the background property. In Chapter 3, the background property was set to a "Drawable" resource rather than a "Color" resource, but it is easy to define a color resource in *colors.xml* and then utilize the color as a background property value by subsequently selecting it from the Resources dialog window.

Note that many properties of UI components can be colored, including the background color of a button, the color if its text, the background color of an input element, just to name a few. It is easy to see all of the properties of each of these UI elements by simply clicking on them in either the Component Tree or Design View, and then scrolling through the "All Attributes" section displayed in the Attributes panel.

Now that we know how to add color to our apps, let's discuss resizing elements. For example, our "Greetings" text is really much smaller than it should be.

Externalizing Size Alias Dimension Resources

A dimension in Android is a unit of measure. A dimension value is specified as a number with a unit type. For example, 12 px, 18 dp, 1 in, and 32 sp are examples of dimension values.

You almost never want to use absolute pixels (px units) to define sizes or relative measures. The reason being that different screens have different pixel densities. This means that a specific number of pixels (px) will render differently on different devices, dependent upon their pixel densities. Screens render graphics in terms of screen size and screen density. Screen size refers to the actual physical size of the screen as measured by the diagonal. Screen density refers to the number of pixels in a physical area of the screen, usually as the number of dots per inch (dpi). But a px specification is absolute. A px is a dot. Using px, which is an absolute value, in an app that will render on different screen densities (dpi) will produce unreliable results.

A "dp" (or dip), on the other hand, is a density independent pixel. It is a virtual unit. An Android device transparently scales dp units to screen pixels. Therefore, when specifying dimensions, always use dp units, with the exception noted below. A dp is a density-independent pixel that corresponds to the physical size of a pixel at 160 dpi. The Android device will employ a formula translation when rendering a dp specification on non-160 dpi devices.

The exception to the rule that you should always use dp units is with regard to the display of text. The "sp" unit should be used for text size units.

An sp is the same base unit but is scaled by the user's preferred text size (it's a scale-independent pixel), so you should use this measurement unit when defining text size and use dp for all other size units.

Should you find yourself in a position where you need to convert px, dp, sp, and other units, there are various online sites that provide calculators to assist you. For example, the calculator found at the URL http://angrytools.com/android/pixelcalc/ can be very helpful.

To illustrate the declaration and use of a dp and sp unit measurement, let's enlarge the text in our "Hello World!" app. Let's create a dimension resource unit measurement to be used for this purpose. We will change the size of the "Greetings" message to a larger sp unit. To do so, we select the *TextView* widget in the Component Tree and then scroll through the "All Attributes" list until we see the *textSize* attribute as shown in Figure 4.13. The default value that is displayed has not been externalized. It is best to create a dimension resource value for all size attributes for reasons that become clear in later chapters as app development gets more sophisticated rather than to use the drop-down list of values.

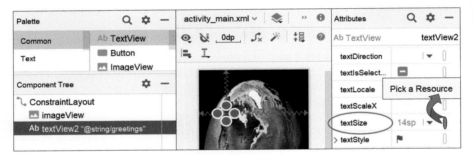

FIGURE 4.13
Preparing a dimension resource specification.

Click on the "Pick a Resource" button to the right in the value field to open the Resources dialog window. Click the plus sign on the left as shown in Figure 4.14 and select "**Dimension Value**". Then enter a Resource name and Resource value as indicated in Figure 4.15 and click OK.

Notice several things have happened. First, the size of the text is significantly enlarged. Second, a new file has been added within the *values* subfolder of the project. The new file is named *dimens.xml* as illustrated in Figure 4.16. Click on the *dimens.xml* file to open it. It should display content similar to that shown in Figure 4.17.

Should you decide that you would prefer a different value than 42 sp, you may change it by simply editing this *dimens.xml* file and then save the file.

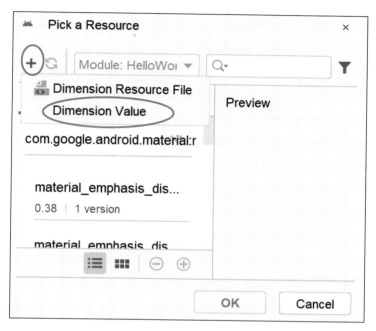

FIGURE 4.14
Creating a new Dimension Value.

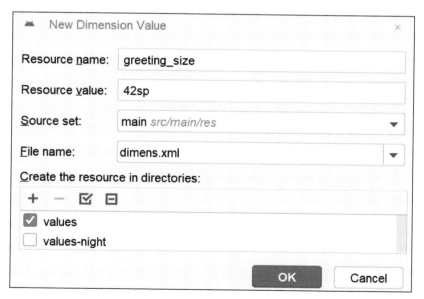

FIGURE 4.15
Specifying a Dimension Value resource.

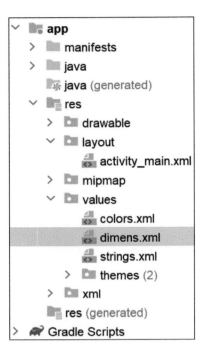

FIGURE 4.16
A new dimens.xml file has been created.

```
</> dimens.xml    ×

1    <?xml version="1.0" encoding="utf-8"?>
2    <resources>
3        <dimen name="greeting_size">42sp</dimen>
4    </resources>
```

FIGURE 4.17
Contents of the newly created file.

The new size will be automatically applied to every widget for which you have specified *greeting_size* as its size specification.

Note the relevant *TextView* widget now displays the following as its *textSize* value as is illustrated in Figure 4.18.

Run the app. You should see the text displayed in a larger size now.

As previously noted, Android app developers should specify sizes in terms of dp and sp units, whenever possible. The sp unit, as illustrated above, is best utilized as a scalable font size for text. The dp unit should be utilized for

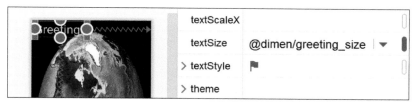

FIGURE 4.18
Dimension resource applied to a widget.

all other size specifications. Distance offsets, margins, lengths, and widths are a perfect use for the dp unit. In fact, if we look closely at the Code mode view of the *activity_main.xml* layout file, we see that the dp unit is used extensively as the default unit for several specifications, as illustrated in Table 4.2.

TABLE 4.2

The *activity_main.xml* Layout File Illustrating Dimensions and Resources

```xml
<?xml version="1.0" encoding="utf-8"?>
<androidx.constraintlayout.widget.ConstraintLayout
xmlns:android="http://schemas.android.com/apk/res/android"
 xmlns:app="http://schemas.android.com/apk/res-auto"
 xmlns:tools="http://schemas.android.com/tools"
 android:layout_width="match_parent"
 android:layout_height="match_parent"
 android:background="@drawable/worldimage"
 tools:context=".MainActivity">

 <ImageView
    android:id="@+id/imageView"
    android:layout_width="159dp"
    android:layout_height="165dp"
    android:contentDescription="@string/plane_flying_across_globe"
    app:layout_constraintBottom_toBottomOf="parent"
    app:layout_constraintEnd_toEndOf="parent"
    app:layout_constraintHorizontal_bias="0.746"
    app:layout_constraintStart_toStartOf="parent"
    app:layout_constraintTop_toTopOf="parent"
    app:layout_constraintVertical_bias="0.521"
    app:srcCompat="@drawable/planeinflight" />

 <TextView
    android:id="@+id/textView2"
    android:layout_width="wrap_content"
    android:layout_height="wrap_content"
    android:text="@string/greetings"
    android:textColor="@color/color_yellow"
    android:textSize="@dimen/greeting_size"
    app:layout_constraintBottom_toBottomOf="parent"
    app:layout_constraintEnd_toEndOf="parent"
    app:layout_constraintHorizontal_bias="0.043"
    app:layout_constraintStart_toStartOf="parent"
    app:layout_constraintTop_toTopOf="parent"
    app:layout_constraintVertical_bias="0.005" />
</androidx.constraintlayout.widget.ConstraintLayout>
```

As an app developer, you are free to modify the number of dp units in any displayed usage above, but to do so in accordance with Android developer standards will require externalization. In addition, as you develop more complex apps, you will find yourself introducing height and width dp specifications, as well as dp offset alignment distances. Again, you will most likely do so by externalizing these dp specifications as named dimension resources. Doing so will lead to easier and more mistake-free modifications for future screen enhancements and universal consistent modifications across an app. In addition, externalizing dimension resources will make it easier to accommodate different screen sizes and resolutions.

Overview of Styles and Themes

The externalization of styles is most productive in apps with multiple screens, as each screen layout XML file can use style inheritance to adopt consistent component colors, font sizes, and other style options. This topic is examined in significant detail in a subsequent chapter after the topic of multiple screen apps has been discussed later in this book.

So far, we have applied custom values to the attributes of various widgets, including *TextView* and *ImageView* components. But as our apps improve in function and features, it will often be the case that such customization will need to be applied to multiple widgets within our application. For this reason, Android makes style classes available to developers. Themes are also available and differ from styles in that they are applied to an entire ap or activity rather than an individual view or widget.

Styles that are applicable to multiple widgets within an app are generally collected within a file named *styles.xml* in the *values* subfolder of the *res* folder. A style is generally a grouping of attributes that specify values for properties such as font color, font size, or background color to name a few. The style as a collection of attribute values can then be applied by a simple name reference to any number of widgets in a layout or across multiple screen layouts.

A theme on the other hand describes a collection of resources that can be referenced by name and applied to widgets or styles or entire layouts. Themes are created in the same way that styles are created. But themes are applied differently utilizing a theme attribute within the Android manifest file.

Much more is discussed regarding styles and themes in a later chapter, while just a brief introduction has been provided here. For those readers who are more advanced or ambitious, please see Chapter 12 for the treatment of styles and themes.

Screen Design Issues

As an app developer, you should be aware of common industry-accepted screen design rules that are relevant to the use of color and units of dimension within mobile apps. There is a plethora of websites that explain complementary color schemes.

In addition, you will also want to be aware of any Android device-specific color rendering problems or issues before making your app available for download.

With regard to dimension design issues, there are several things that you can do as an app developer to address different screen sizes and resolutions. An excellent source for insight on this topic is the Android Developer site. More advanced topics to be covered in later chapters include the use of Size Qualifiers, Smallest-width Qualifiers, Layout Aliases, and Orientation Qualifiers. In the meantime, you can benefit from the following dimension specification tips:

➢ Focus more on the spacing between elements rather than the size of elements themselves.

➢ View layouts within the Android Studio editor by using different "Device for Preview" settings.

➢ Utilize other *dimens.xml* files for landscape mode and wide screen devices.

➢ Use the "wrap_content" and "match_parent" property values wherever appropriate. The "wrap_content" specification sets the width or height of the component to the minimum size necessary to fit its container. The "match_parent" specification expands the component to match the size of its parent container.

➢ Use the Constraint Layout or an alternative flat layout whenever possible. Additional layouts are described in Chapter 6.

What's Next?

Now that the basics of externalized resources have been addressed, we can develop apps with appropriately sized and spaced elements in color. So, in the next chapter, we will begin to add user interface (UI) components to our apps that will enable the user to interact with the app in terms of inputs and outputs to provide functionality to our apps.

Exercises

The exercises below build on the initial app screens developed in the exercises in Chapter 3. These exercises are limited as we do not have too many components to work with yet, but they do provide practice with the topics discussed in this chapter. So, we continue to incrementally enhance these apps in this and subsequent chapters to eventually implement attractive and fully functional apps. Be sure to specify content descriptions for all images.

E4.1 Modify Exercise E3.1, the *FloorTilesCalc* app, where you set up an initial screen layout for a smartphone app that assists in the calculation of the number of floor tiles required to cover the floor in a rectangular room. Modifications to color and size dimensions must be externalized resources, and strings must not be hardcoded but are to be externalized as resources within the *strings.xml* file (so if hardcoded, be sure to "Quick Fix" them). The screen background is to be a light brown color that could be said to resemble a wood shade of oak or pine. A *TextView* widget is to be used to specify a heading. The color of this heading text is to display as a dark brick red on a background of a light tan color. This text should prompt the user to "Calculate the number of floor tiles required" and is to be displayed on two lines. Use a dimension resource in scalable units to set the size of the text label. The exact specification should be appropriately large enough to be readable but not so large that it proves harmful to the screen design. Be mindful of the spacing of the text within the background color. The additional *TextView* elements asking for floor length, floor width, length of a tile, and "How many tiles are required?" are to be of the same text color as the dark brick red text color for the heading. Find a royalty-free image online and display it in the layout. The image must have a content description specification. A sample output screen is provided online in the supplementary resources for this book. In a later chapter, we will build on this assignment to implement a fully functional app.

E4.2 Modify Exercise E3.2, the *Inches2Meters* app, where you set up an initial screen layout for a smartphone app that assists in the conversion between inches and meters. Additions of string values and modifications to color and size dimensions must be externalized resources and are to minimally include the following. A heading reading "Inches and Meters Conversion" is to be the assigned value in a *TextView* widget, the text color of which is a true black. Modify the background color of this *TextView* component to be that of a pale blue color. Use a dimension resource in scalable units to set the size of the text. The exact specification should be appropriately large enough to be readable but not so large that it proves harmful to the screen design. Be mindful of the spacing of the text within the background color. An additional *TextView* element is to ask for a value to be converted (the conversion will take place in a later chapter assignment), and a third *TextView* widget is to serve as a label for the conversion result. Both are to be of the same text color as the pale blue background color for the heading, with a background color of true black. A sample output screen is provided online in the supplementary resources for this book. In a later chapter, we will build on this assignment to implement a fully functional app.

E4.3 Modify Exercise E3.3, the *DivingApp*, where you set up an initial screen layout for a tablet device app that can be used to estimate how long a diver's air supply will last on a deep dive in salt water. Additions of string values and modifications to color and size dimensions must be externalized resources and are to minimally include the following. All text is to be of color bright white on a true black background. The heading is to read "HOW LONG CAN I STAY DOWN?". Be mindful of the spacing of the text within the background color. The TextView components may need to be slightly relocated in the layout to accommodate the background. Use dimension resources in scalable units to set the size of all text elements. The exact specification should be appropriately large enough to be readable, but not so large that it proves harmful to the screen design. A sample output screen is provided online in the supplementary resources for this book to give an idea as to how the final screen might appear at this stage in this evolving app. In a later chapter, we will build on this assignment to implement a functional app.

E4.4 Modify Exercise E3.4, the *PlanBoatTrip* app, where you set up an initial screen layout for a Nexus 9 tablet or a similar tablet device app that assists in the basic planning for a self-navigated boat trip. The app will run in landscape mode. Additions of string values and modifications to color and size dimensions must be externalized resources and are to minimally include the following. All text is to be of color gold on a background color of midnight blue. The heading is to read "PLANNING A BOATING EXCURSION". Use scalable units as dimension resources to set the text sizes. The exact specification should be appropriately large enough to be readable, but not so large that it proves harmful to the screen design. Be mindful of the spacing of the text within the background color. Find a free, no copyright image online and display it in the layout. The image must have a content description specification. Add a *TextView* widget with an externalized text value that reads "Specify these trip parameters:". Then add additional TextView widgets that specify text prompts for "Trip Speed:", "Trip Distance:", and "Engine Horsepower:". A sample output screen is provided online in the supplementary resources for this book to give an idea as to how the final screen might appear at this stage in this evolving app. In a later chapter, we will build on this assignment to implement a functional app. For now, just build an attractive app with the widgets as stated above.

E4.5 Modify Exercise E3.5, the *BeautifulBalloon* app, where you set up
an initial screen layout for a smartphone mobile app that assists
with parameters and calculations involved in floating a hot air balloon. Additions of string values and modifications to color and size
dimensions for *TextView* widgets must be externalized resources
and are to minimally include "Barometric reading", "Envelope
Volume", "Air Temperature", and "Lift Weight". All text is to be
of a color shade of yellow. A *TextView* widget heading is to read
"HOT AIR BALLOON RIDES" and have an orange background.
Use scalable units as dimension resources to set the text sizes.
The exact specification should be appropriately large enough to
be readable but not so large that it proves harmful to the screen
design. Be mindful of the spacing of the heading text within the
background color. Find a suitable, free, no copyright image online
and display it in the layout. The image must have a content description specification. A sample output screen is provided online in the
supplementary resources for this book to give an idea as to how
the final screen might appear at this stage in this evolving app. In
a later chapter, we will build on this assignment to implement a
functional app.

5

Interacting with Users via Keyboard and Buttons

Learning Outcomes:

- ✓ Successful incorporation of Button components and assignment of onClick attributes.
- ✓ Specification of onClick method code within the activity .java file.
- ✓ Successful referencing of UI components within Java code.
- ✓ Deeper awareness of concerns regarding apk size and the minimal footprint of an app due to individual class import practice.

DOI: 10.1201/9781003286325-5

In the previous chapters, we created a simple Android app and then discussed adding images, color, and dimension specifications to it. A lot went into this first app example. But it does not do much, except to look pretty. And so, it is with Android apps: you need to include a lot to do a little. Always keep in mind that your audience is in essence desensitized due to over stimulation provided by emerging technologies, demanding eye-catching graphics in social media and video.

In this chapter, we are ready to begin to interact with our app users. There are many different ways to interact with mobile apps. Some of the more elaborate means include swiping, pinching, and other touch methods. We can also offer voice input. These more elaborate methods of input are covered in later chapters. We interact with apps in more basic ways using the keyboard with input fields and clickable buttons. While not as exciting, these basic means of interaction are critical and essential. Therefore, the latter are the subject of this chapter, as we need to cover the basics first.

Screen Elements for Basic User Interaction

Let's consider a simple but useful app that will convert temperature values between Fahrenheit and Celsius equivalents. The simple interface we would like to create in this app is shown in Figure 5.1.

FIGURE 5.1
Demo app for this chapter.

The basic function of this app is to convert a specified number to either Celsius or a Fahrenheit equivalent temperature. So, minimally, we will need an input field for the value to be converted and two buttons. The input field will take the form of a text box that Android refers to as an *EditText* component, which is an editable subclass of the *TextView* component. One button will read "Convert to Celsius" indicating a desire to convert the given temperature from Fahrenheit to Celsius, and the other button will read "Convert to Fahrenheit", indicating the desire to convert from Celsius to the equivalent Fahrenheit temperature.

To get started, create a new Android project for phone target devices. Select the "Empty Views Activity" as we did in our previous project (*we will be using the Empty Views Activity template until further notice*). When customizing the activity, stay with the defaults unless you want to change the location in your environment where the project is to be stored. Be certain to select Java as the language.

Android Studio will create the new project and build the Project Gradle information. Recall that if the activity_main.xml file is not open, you can find it by expanding the (Project) project folder structure and then expand the res and layout folders to double-click on the *activity_main.xml* file to open it in the Editor.

As is the case with any new project, by default, a *TextView* widget with string value "Hello World!" was automatically created when the project was created. This *TextView* component can be modified to suit our purpose, or we can delete it and drag a new *TextView* widget from the Palette onto the Design mode display when needed. If we take the minimalist approach, we can just modify the default element that was automatically created.

So, while in Design mode, click on the *TextView* element in the Component Tree. This will open the attributes panel on the right, displaying the most popular attributes for the selected *TextView* element. In the Attributes panel on the right, there is a *text* property and in the adjacent cell, its value "Hello World!" is displayed. Chapter 4 taught us how to externalize string values. The easiest means of doing so is to simply type over the default value with the string value, "Enter a temperature value:" without the quotes. As we saw in Chapter 4, upon doing so, a warning message appears indicating one error/ warning. Recall that you can click on the warning indicator to open a dialog box to remedy the problem by selecting the "light bulb quick fix hint" and then "Extract string resource". Upon successfully externalizing the string, the Component Tree will contain a specification for an @string resource and the warning symbol disappears.

Adding Input Capability to Our Screen Layout

The Android Studio editor provides a plethora of controls that you can drag and drop onto the screen design layout. Focusing on the Palette when in Design mode, you can scroll through all of the available user interface widgets. Under the "Text" heading are several input box types shown as shown in Figure 5.2. There are text fields for plain text input, password input, date and time input, and several different types of numeric input. For our purposes, since we are interested in a numeric user input representing a temperature value, we will be selecting the "Number (Decimal)" *Text* element.

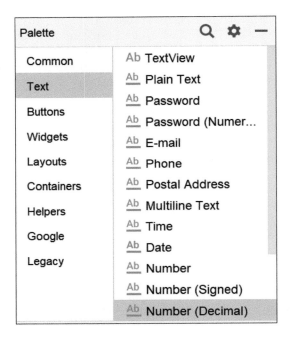

FIGURE 5.2
Variety of input types available.

Click on the "Number (Decimal)" widget and drag it onto the layout so that it appears under the *TextView* component. The result should appear as shown in Figure 5.3. Also, it helps to know that when the app is run and the focus moves to this input text component, Android will display a numeric mode keyboard for the user since the input type is a number.

As indicated in Figure 5.3, there are subsequent errors and warnings to resolve. One such error is due to the fact that we have not yet constrained this new widget horizontally and vertically. Since it is meant to be associated logically with the prompt for the user to enter an input value, we can anchor it to the *TextView* widget. Alternatively, we can instead anchor it to the layout's borders, or we can anchor it with a mixture of both.

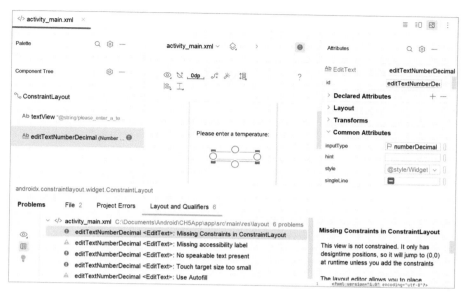

FIGURE 5.3
Errors and warnings for a new widget.

The constraint layout's component elements, referred to by the Android Developer site as "child views", are constrained in positions that may be relative to each other or to the layout (parent). In this way, each "child view" is assigned a position in relation to its parent, or in relation to the position of one of its "sibling" elements. The ultimate "parent" is the constraint layout itself, and so if a component is positioned relative to it, you will see alignment specifications such as *app:layout_constraintBottom_toBottomOf="parent"*. If a component is positioned relative to a sibling, then you will see words such as *"layout_constraintEnd_toEndOf"* or *"layout_constraintTop_toBottomOf"* with a specified *id* of the sibling.

In later chapters, we will use other layout alternatives to the constraint layout. The constraint layout is the default because it is a flat layout, as opposed to a nested layout, and so generally yields better performance than some of the other layouts. Android Studio only recently introduced the *ConstraintLayout*, and it became popular because it grants much more control than do the other layouts.

In the meantime, we also need to address the other warnings and errors indicated. Table 5.1 provides a description of how we may successfully address each of the indicated warnings and errors commonly associated with editable text widgets.

TABLE 5.1

Common Errors and Warning for Editable Text Widgets

Errors/Warnings for EditTextNumberDecimal	Remedy/Solution
No speakable text present	Assign text to the hint attribute
Touch target size too small	Enlarge the input text box component by dragging corner(s)
Missing constraints in ConstraintLayout	Establish top, bottom, left, and right constraints in layout relative to parent layout itself or a child
Use autofill	Click the "light bulb quick fix" and select set option
Missing accessibility label	Is addressed by the hint attribute setting

Also of note is that the input text box for the numeric decimal has been assigned the *id* "editTextNumberDecimal". This can be confusing to work with later, so change this *id* value to *usertemperatureVal* as shown in Figure 5.4.

FIGURE 5.4
Assigning ids to widgets.

Upon doing so, a pop-up dialog box displays asking if you wish to rename this component throughout the project files. The vast majority of the time, you will respond by selecting "**Refactor**". Examining the error flag, there is an indication that *"No speakable text is present"* for the editable input. Remedy this by specifying a *hint* attribute value explaining the properties for the input required.

Adding Buttons to the Layout

Almost everyone knows that a button on a display screen is a clickable or "pressable" element that causes some action to occur. In Android Studio layout design mode, the button control is available as a Widget control from the Palette at the top of the list of Widgets, as shown in Figure 5.5.

To add a button, make certain that you are back in Design mode and drag the Button widget from the Palette onto the displayed layout while positioning it appropriately with suitable constraints.

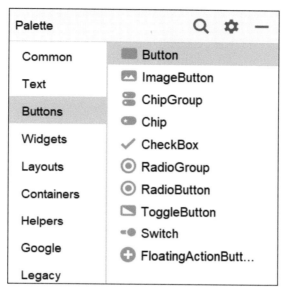

FIGURE 5.5
Types of Button widgets.

The layout should afterward contain a *Button* widget, as shown in Figure 5.6. When the button object is selected, its attribute list will be displayed. So, scroll to its *text* property and click in the cell adjacent to type the new value "CONVERT TO CELSIUS". Then create a new string resource on demand by clicking the warning indicator and its "Quick Fix" to externalize the string resource as detailed in Chapter 4 and as you did previously with the *TextView* prompt in this project. Buttons require *onClick* property assignments as well, which will be discussed shortly.

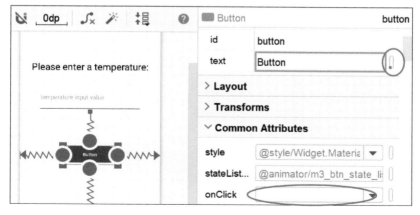

FIGURE 5.6
Button widgets need text and *onClick* values.

Create a second button in the same way by dragging a second Button widget from the Palette to the layout. Assign the value "CONVERT TO FAHRENHEIT" to its *text* property and then externalize the value as a string resource.

At this point, we would absolutely want to apply further styles and colors, as was addressed in Chapter 4. Perhaps we could also include an image as an *ImageView* component or as a background image, as was demonstrated in Chapter 3. It is understood that to properly introduce a color necessitates that we define an externalized color resource, and any image inclusion requires the physical addition of an image file in the file structure of the project app's *res/drawable* subfolder.

It appears that it would also be quite desirable to enlarge the *TextView* that displays the "Enter a temperature value:" text prompt. To follow proper Android coding etiquette, this size alteration requires the use of an externalized dimension resource. Again, the methods by which an externalized dimension value can be created were previously discussed in Chapter 4.

Figure 5.7 displays a styled running app after the addition of a drawable image and a few color, size (dimen), and string externalized resources.

FIGURE 5.7
Running app thus far.

When running the app, try clicking the buttons. Nothing happens. This is because button functionality necessitates the use of Java code. Before we add this code, let's add one more component to the screen. The component required is a *TextView* widget which will be used to display the calculated temperature value equivalent computed from the input value specified by the user.

So, drag another *TextView* widget onto the layout for the result and constrain it below the second button. Android Studio has initialized the text property value of this new addition to the string value, "textView". We do not wish to see an initial value as it is meant to display the result calculated after the user clicks the appropriate button. Since this component should have no text display value when the app is run until the user clicks one of the buttons, delete the value for its text property. The result is shown in Figure 5.8. Be sure to also assign an id value of the result so that we can easily reference this widget later to display the result of our calculation(s).

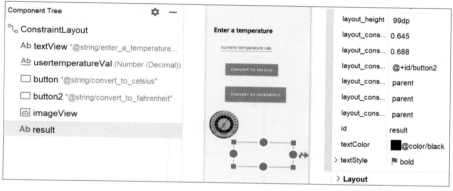

FIGURE 5.8
TextView ready to receive a computed result.

And now, we are finally ready to add Java code to our app to compute a Celsius or Fahrenheit temperature equivalent.

Java Gives Life to Your Buttons

Coding the action for a button requires two primary tasks. The first is to specify a Java method name for the *onClick* property for the button in the activity xml layout file. The second task is to actually code the Java method in the activity's java file.

Connecting a Button Click Event to Java Code

A button usually displays a label describing the action that will take place when the button is clicked or pressed. The action is a response that is affected in a Java-coded method. This Java method is placed in the activity layout's corresponding Java file. For example, consider the app's Android Studio project organization shown in Figure 5.9. The *java* folder and the *res/layout* folder have been expanded. By default, when the Android app is launched, the *java/MainActivity.java* file executes. One of its purposes is to load the screen defined by the *layout/activity_main.xml* file.

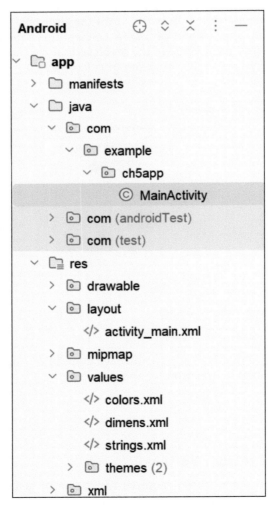

FIGURE 5.9
Location of the main activity Java code file.

Figure 5.10 provides a look at the default code presently contained within the *MainActivity.java* file for the temperature conversion example app that has been our focus in this chapter, and since no modification has yet been made to this file, it is representative of any project created as type *Empty Views Activity*. The import statements for "EditText" and "TextView" are not always present.

```java
package com.example.inclassexample;

import androidx.appcompat.app.AppCompatActivity;

import android.os.Bundle;

import android.widget.EditText;
import android.widget.TextView;

public class MainActivity extends AppCompatActivity {

    @Override
    protected void onCreate(Bundle savedInstanceState) {
        super.onCreate(savedInstanceState);
        setContentView(R.layout.activity_main);
    }
}
```

FIGURE 5.10
Default Java code for a main activity.

The default contents of the Java activity file define an *onCreate* method, whereby the default action is to create the activity and display its eXtensible Markup Language (XML) layout.

Any code referenced by the components of the activity_main.xml UI layout file is sought in the *MainActivity.java* file. So, the events associated with a button in the layout file are identified by property names, such as *onClick*. And the value assigned to this property name is sought as a method name within the activity's corresponding Java file.

To illustrate using our temperature conversion app, open the *activity_main.xml* file. Select the button labeled "CONVERT TO CELSIUS" from either the Component Tree or the Design mode of the layout. Then in the list of attributes, navigate to the *onClick* property for this button. The default value for the *onClick* property is nothing. Change this *onClick* property value to "convertCelsius". Follow the same procedure to change the *onClick* property for the button labeled "CONVERT TO FAHRENHEIT" to "convertFahrenheit" (without the quotes). These *onClick* property values will serve as the method names for the button click actions coded in the activity .java file. A warning indicator may appear after the *onClick* property is assigned a value. The future direction is to code an *onClick Listener* as the alternative to this property. This listener event handler is discussed later in the book. So, for now, we will ignore this warning. As Figure 5.11 illustrates, an error flag is indicated for each button since the *onClick* Java code has not yet been defined.

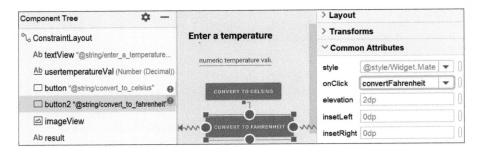

FIGURE 5.11
Assigning a Java method name to a button *onClick* property.

Coding the Java onClick Method

Now that the *onClick* property for each button has been assigned a value, the next task is to code a Java method corresponding to each *onClick* property specification. So, two Java methods need now be coded: one is to be named "convertCelsius" and the other is to be named "convertFahrenheit". Both are to be coded within the *MainActivity.java* file. The skeletal outline for these methods within the *MainActivity.java* file is displayed in Figure 5.12 in lines 15 through 22.

As noted, there is an issue with the mandatory *View* parameter type for the two buttons' click event methods. But the good news is that Android is offering a solution. The hint displayed in Figure 5.12, indicated by the snapshot, is instructing us to press the Alt and Enter keys together to remedy the error. An import statement is added so that the *View* class is defined to the application.

The Java code required for each method action must now be added. In determining the logic of this code, let's consider the conversion to Celsius first. To convert to Celsius, we must obtain the user input from the *"editText"* component in the screen layout.

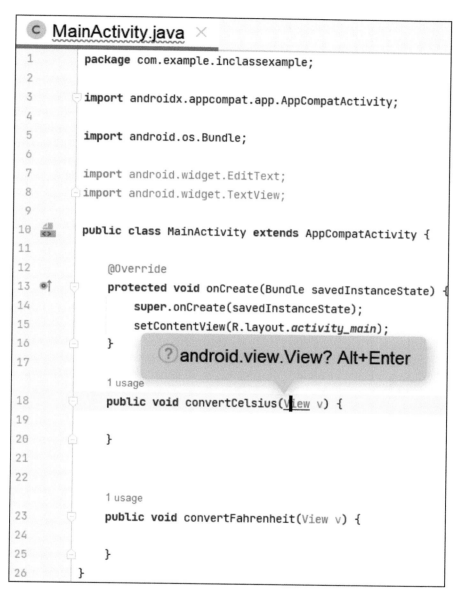

```
1   package com.example.inclassexample;
2
3   import androidx.appcompat.app.AppCompatActivity;
4
5   import android.os.Bundle;
6
7   import android.widget.EditText;
8   import android.widget.TextView;
9
10  public class MainActivity extends AppCompatActivity {
11
12      @Override
13      protected void onCreate(Bundle savedInstanceState) {
14          super.onCreate(savedInstanceState);
15          setContentView(R.layout.activity_main);
16      }
17
    1 usage
18      public void convertCelsius(View v) {
19
20      }
21
22
    1 usage
23      public void convertFahrenheit(View v) {
24
25      }
26  }
```

FIGURE 5.12
Signatures for the *onClick* methods.

Recall that a bit earlier we assigned an id of *"usertemperatureVal"* to the input box, so we have a means to retrieve it from the screen. All screen input is of string type, however, and so must be converted to be used as a numeric value. Therefore, we will parse the input to treat it as a Java "double" type of value, convert the number to Celsius, as the button indicates, and then display the result.

Also recall that there is a *"TextView"* component in the *activity_main.xml* layout to contain this result, for which we previously assigned an *id* value of "result". Since we have the necessary component's ids defined, we can continue with our Java code for the *onClick* button actions. Both methods, namely "convertCelsius" and "convertFahrenheit", are void methods that accept one parameter of type *"View"*. The *"View"* parameter is actually the button instance that has been clicked. This enables you to share *onClick* methods among buttons, which we will look at in a later chapter. For now, we will simply code two separate methods, one for each button. The code for these two *onClick* button methods will be similar.

Let's look at the code for the "convertCelsius" method for the "CONVERT TO CELSIUS" button first. The first task within the method is to obtain the user input value. To obtain the user input value, we must first reference the *"EditText"* component programmatically. We do so by coding the Java statement:

```
EditText userinput = (EditText)
findViewById(R.id. usertemperatureVal);
```

An error will appear since *EditText* cannot be recognized. In fact, the error message will look similar to that displayed in Figure 5.13. Holding down the Alt key while pressing the Enter key will cause the appropriate import statement to be added to the code file.

FIGURE 5.13
Import statement is required for *EditText* class.

The *findViewById* method is used to reference a widget component of type *"View"* on the screen layout. Most of the elements on the screen layout are of base class *"View"* including buttons, textboxes, checkboxes, and *"TextViews"*. The input text value of the *EditText* widget that we have referenced above as "userinput" can next be loaded into a string variable. Although it is a numeric field, the input from text box is of string type and must be converted to a number in a subsequent Java statement. The Java statement to retrieve the actual value from the input textbox is as follows:

```
String inputval = userinput.getText().toString();
```

The string value in the variable named "inputval" can now be converted to a Java variable of type "double":

```
double tempval = Double.parseDouble(inputval);
```

Since the user clicked the button to convert the input value to a Celsius temperature, the next program statement within the method computes the equivalent Celsius temperature:

```
double celsiusequiv = (tempval - 32) * 5.0 / 9.0;
```

We can finally now display the Celsius equivalent temperature for the user input. To do so, however, requires two Java statements. The first Java statement references the *TextView* component of the screen where the result is to be displayed. Earlier, we assigned an id of "result" to this *TextView* component. So, the next Java statement references it:

```
TextView result = (TextView) findViewById(R.id.result);
```

Again, an error occurs, and if you click on the red text, you will be instructed to hold the Alt key down while pressing the Enter key, as has occurred now anytime we have referenced a widget component class for which a Java *import* statement has not yet been declared. Executing the *Alt+Enter* key sequence results in the addition of the following import statement:

```
import android.widget.TextView;
```

And now that we have a programmatic reference to the screen component that will be used to report the result, we can assign to it a string to display with the Java statement:

```
result.setText("Celsius equivalent is " + celsiusequiv);
```

Note that it is perfectly acceptable to break this statement up into two Java statements, which may even be desirable since it is easier to read:

```
String msg = "Celsius equivalent is " + celsiusequiv;
result.setText(msg);
```

The code to be executed when the user clicks the other button to convert to Fahrenheit in this example is very similar. In fact, the most significant change is in the conversion calculation itself. Table 5.2 lists the code for both Celsius and Fahrenheit temperature conversion methods displayed in the final *MainActivity.java* file.

The comment lines have been added as an explanation of the Java statements required to perform the conversions. Note that the Java code programmatically references the components in the screen layout using the method *findViewById* and the parameter specified with syntax *R.id.componentsAssignedIDvalue*.

TABLE 5.2

Java Code to Operationalize the Button Click Events

MainActivity.java

```java
package com.example.inclassexample;
import androidx.appcompat.app.AppCompatActivity;
import android.os.Bundle;
import android.view.View;
import android.widget.EditText;
import android.widget.TextView;
public class MainActivity extends AppCompatActivity {
    @Override
    protected void onCreate(Bundle savedInstanceState) {
        super.onCreate(savedInstanceState);
        setContentView(R.layout.activity_main);
    }

    public void convertCelsius(View v) {
        // To obtain user input value, we must first reference the EditText
        component
        EditText userinput = (EditText) findViewById(R.id.inputTemp);

        // Load the text value from the EditText component into a Java string
        variable
        String inputval = userinput.getText().toString();

        // Convert the string input to a number of Java type double
        double tempval = Double.parseDouble(inputval);

        // Convert the value to a Celsius temperature from an assumed
        Fahrenheit value
        double celsiusequiv = (tempval - 32) * 5.0 / 9.0;

        // Programmatically reference the TextView component to display the
        result
        TextView result = (TextView) findViewById(R.id.result);

        // Set the text property of the result TextView component to a string
        message
        String msg = "Celsius equivalent is " + celsiusequiv;

        result.setText(msg);
    }

    public void convertFahrenheit(View v) {
        // To obtain user input value, we must first reference the EditText
        component.
        EditText userinput = (EditText) findViewById(R.id.inputTemp);

        // Load the text value from the EditText component into a Java string
        variable
        String inputval = userinput.getText().toString();

        // Convert the string input to a number of Java type double
        double tempval = Double.parseDouble(inputval);

        // Convert the value to a Fahrenheit temperature from an assumed
        Celsius value
        double fahrenheitequiv = (tempval * 9.0 / 5.0) + 32;

        // Programmatically reference the TextView component used to display
        the result
        TextView result = (TextView) findViewById(R.id.result);

        // Set the text property of the result TextView component to a string
        message
        String msg = "Fahrenheit equivalent is " + fahrenheitequiv;

        result.setText(msg);
    }
}
```

Note that two additional import statements were added to support the *EditText* and *TextView* types used in the Java statements. As in the case of the *View* required import, these may also be added using the *Alt+Enter* (*Option+Enter* on the Mac) keystrokes when prompted by Android Studio. You will notice that Android Studio prompts you for individual class imports as necessitated by the class objects referenced in your code. This is a very different paradigm from the import references Java programmers tend to make in desktop applications, where an entire class hierarchy tends to be imported regardless of how much of it is actually referenced in the program code. On the mobile platform, the goal is to create an app footprint that is as small as possible, thereby reducing the size of the *apk* downloaded to the Android device. Therefore, it makes perfect sense that only the code specifically referenced by the application should become part of the *apk*. So, individual targeted import statements such as those shown below are specified rather than "*android.widget.*;*" which is commonly specified in desktop Java applications.

Run the app. If a "*Build failed*" error message is displayed, be sure to correct all errors that may occur due to mistakes in your Java statements. Test the app with a few inputs. A pair of sample runs is displayed in Figure 5.14. Recall

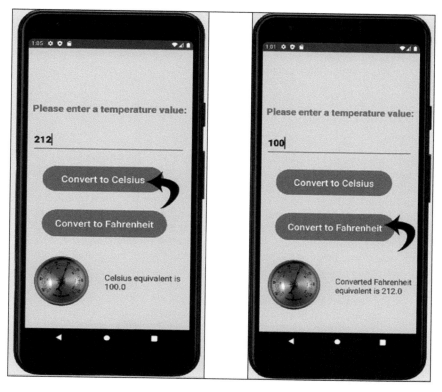

FIGURE 5.14
Sample execution runs of our completed app.

that when we added the input text widget, we specified its "inputType" as "numberDecimal". For this reason, when we click in the input box when the app is running, the numeric keyboard is automatically provided for input.

When running the app, note that the order of the *EditText* components in the Component Tree influences the natural order in which the user input is solicited with the tab key when the app is run.

Mobile Screen Design Issues

The example in this chapter was designed for a smartphone. Later examples will sometimes be designed for tablets. While there is a capability to design for smartphone devices and tablets within the same app, the early app examples in this textbook will indicate a design for one or the other, but generally not both. Later, however, we will look at designing a single app for a variety of devices, including both mobile and tablet platforms.

A design issue pertinent to the UI controls covered in this chapter would draw attention to the dimensions of the *TextView*, *EditText*, and *Button* controls. As an app developer, you will want to make certain that the font sizes are large enough to make the text on the screen easily readable. In addition, the size of the buttons and the spacing between elements must be adequate to accommodate the size of your users' fingers. You always want to ensure that your user experience is as positive as possible.

Exercises

The exercises below build on the initial app screens developed in the exercises in Chapter 3, to which initial externalized resources were added in the corresponding exercises in Chapter 4. We are now adding additional components to these apps to accommodate user interaction and we are adding Java code to complete functionality as well, resulting in attractive and completely functional apps. Not to say that there is still not room for improvement, which is the reason for some of the follow-up questions. Be sure to specify "hints" for all input fields and content descriptions for all images.

E5.1 Modify Exercise E4.1, the *FloorTilesCalc* app, to complete the implementation of a smartphone mobile app that assists in the calculation of the number of floor tiles required to cover the floor in a rectangular room. Your parents had decided to contract with a handyman to tile the unfinished basement in their home. You were startled as to how much they were actually willing to pay this handyman and informed them that you can do just as good a job. After all, you have watched two how-to videos on the subject.

Now, you want to be sure to acquire and have your parents pay for the correct number of floor tiles required. Your buddy has asked to help as his parents are also considering a total redo of their tiled kitchen floor. Given what looks to be a multi-job effort, you are ready to code a mobile app to assist with the materials planning, particularly with the precise estimation as to how many floor tiles to acquire. From the "how to" videos you watched, you learned that it is wise to calculate a "waste" component in determining the number of tiles required to accommodate for broken tiles and partials tiles. So, you are adding the components identified below that are required to accomplish this task. For the sake of this example, all floor tiles are assumed to be square in shape.

Three decimal input values are required for (a) the length of the room in inches, (b) the width of the room in inches, and (c) the length in inches of an individual floor tile. All *TextView* prompts for inputs were created in Exercise 4.1.

All text input fields are to use as their background color the externalized tan color resource created in Exercise 4.1. Furthermore, all of the input fields are of type "Numeric (Decimal)" and include a hint property with value "specify inches".

There are two buttons, both of which are to have as their background color the same externalized yellow color resource previously mentioned. The color of the text label values on the buttons are to be the same externalized dark brown color resource utilized for the *TextView* components.

One button is to be labeled with the externalized string resource value "With 5% waste" and when pressed is to invoke the *onClick* method named "calcWastePercent5", which calculates the number of floor tiles required for the area of the room (length × width) divided by the floor tile length squared and then adds a 5% number of extra tiles. The second button is to be labeled with the string resource value "With 10% waste" and when pressed is to invoke the *onClick* method named "calcWastePercent10", which calculates the number of floor tiles required for the area of the room (length × width) divided by the floor tile length squared and then adds a 10% number of extra tiles. In either case, the final answer is to be rounded up to the nearest integer value and is to be displayed in the same dark brown color as the other *TextView* components with the same yellow color background as the two buttons.

Screenshots for two sample runs are provided online in the supplementary resources for this book.

Follow-up Questions:

➤ The Java code statements that implement the "WITH 5% WASTE" button and those that implement the "WITH 10% WASTE" button are very similar. How might the code for these two buttons be combined?

➤ What would be required to implement the same functionality with just one button?

➤ How might we make the screen layout "less busy" but still interesting? Base your answer on what you know as an app user rather than on the material we have covered so far.

E5.2 Modify Exercise E4.2, the *Inches2Meters* app, to complete the implementation of a smartphone mobile app that has a very simple but important function, which is to convert measurements between inches and meters. Your sister is studying to be an architect. Architectural objects are generally very large. Just think of the *Burj Al Arab* in Dubai, or *The Absolute Towers* in Canada, or *The Guggenheim Museum* in Spain, or *The Minerva Building* in London. It is impossible to make drawings of these buildings in full size. Therefore, scales are used to draw floor plans and denote elevations and architectural details of buildings. The notation for the reduction or enlargement of a drawing is referred to as the scale of the drawing. According to the American National Standards Institute (ANSI), the International System of Units (SI) linear unit commonly used on drawings is the millimeter or meter. But in many drawings, the inch is used as the linear unit. Your sister is having trouble moving between inches and meters. So, you have come to the rescue with a user-friendly Android app.

This app requires the addition of an input text component of type "Number (Decimal)", and two buttons positioned as shown in screenshots for two sample runs that are provided online in the supplementary resources for this book.

The new input component is required for the user input, and its background is to use the same pale blue externalized color resource as previously mentioned. Supply a hint such as "Enter a number".

One of the buttons should be labeled "Convert to Inches" and the other button should be labeled "Convert to Meters". Note the text placement within the buttons. The "Convert to Inches" button when clicked assumes the input value is in inches units and converts it to the equivalent value in meters. The "Convert to Meters" button when clicked assumes the input value is in meters units and converts it to the equivalent value in inches.

The *TextView* component previously added for the display of the result is already present but will need to concatenate the calculated result. Be sure to round the numeric value in the result to a maximum of four decimal places and watch the padding influenced positioning as displayed in the screenshots for two sample runs that are provided online in the supplementary resources for this book.

It is helpful for the calculations to know that:

One meter is equivalent to 39.3701 inches.
One inch is equivalent to 0.0254 meters.

Follow-up Questions:

➤ The Java code statements that implement the "CONVERT TO INCHES" button and those that implement the "CONVERT TO METERS" button are very similar. How might the code for these two buttons be combined?

➤ What would be required to implement the same functionality with just one button?

➤ What would be required to add versatility to this app so that additional units such as feet, yards, centimeters, and millimeters could also be converted? What might be a design alternative to simply adding additional buttons?

E5.3 Modify Exercise 4.3, the *DivingApp*, in which an initial screen layout for a tablet device was created. Your good friend Sky Waters is a diving enthusiast and has asked you to code an Android app that will run on a tablet and can be used to provide a rough guesstimate as to how long a diver's air supply will last on a deep dive in salt water. Researching the code requirements for such an app, we have determined that five input values are required for the calculations necessary to make such a guesstimate. The five inputs are detailed below.

Each input should consist of a "Number (Decimal)" text type component that displays a hint on a white background. A Button to compute the result and an additional *TextView* component is required to display the result of the calculations. The Button is to have a white background tint and a black text color, using the colors that have been externalized for the input labels or prompts. The result must be rounded to one decimal place, is to appear as white text on a black background, also using the same externalized colors and text size as were used to create the input prompts.

A detailed explanation of the inputs follows, along with the calculations that must be performed when the user "presses" the button provided below.

Inputs required:

a. The individual's **RMV** rate

This is the Respiratory Minute Volume rate for the diver. Each person has their own rate. It is the volume of breathing gas that a diver consumes in one minute and is measured in liters per minute. It is an individual's constant rate moving at a moderate rate at the surface.

An example would be 20 liters per minute, or 20 liter/min.

b. The **Tank volume**

The size of the air tank or the air tank volume that is the amount of air in the tank.

This is measured in liters. An example would be a 12-liter tank.

c.   The **starting air pressure** in bars.

d.   The planned dive **depth** in feet. Input feet and then later convert to meters.

e.   **Reserve pressure** in bars. This is the tank pressure at which the diver wishes to begin ascent back up to the surface.

Here is the series of calculations the app must do internally to estimate how long your air supply will last on a dive:

1. Calculate your SAC in bars/min:

Surface Air Consumption Rate = RMV Rate/Tank Volume

For example: SAC rate = (20 liters/min)/(12 liters)
                                = 1.6666667 bar/min.

2. Calculate the pressure for the depth at which you will be diving:

Pressure = (depth in meters)/10 + 1

1 foot is equivalent to 0.3048 meters.

So, if depth is 68 feet, equivalent meters is 21 meters

So, Pressure = 20.7264/10 + 1 = 3.07264 ata

3. Determine the air consumption rate in psi/min at the planned depth:

Air consumption rate = SAC * Pressure

So, for example, Air consumption rate
      = 1.6666667 bar/min * 3.07264 ata = 5.121067 bar/min

4. Determine how much air you will have available:

Available air pressure = Starting air pressure – Reserve pressure

For example, 200 bar starting pressure
– 50 bar reserve pressure = 150 bar

5. Calculate how long the air will last in minutes:

Time in minutes = (Available air pressure)/(Air consumption rate)

For example, (150 bar)/(5.121066667 bar/min) = 29.3 mins

NOTE: As complex as these equations are, they are NOT reliable to use for an actual diving application! So please be aware that this app is meant for coding practice only! Do NOT go diving with it!

A screenshot for a sample run is provided online in the supplementary resources for this book.

Follow-up Questions:

- ➢ What design alternative might you suggest to lessen the number of simultaneous inputs required on the screen?
- ➢ From your experience with mobile apps, how might this app be redesigned to lessen the need to use the keyboard so frequently to specify the inputs?

E5.4 Modify Exercise 4.4, the *PlanBoatTrip* app, where you set up an initial screen layout for a tablet app that assists in the basic planning for a self-navigated boat trip in calm water. The app will run in landscape mode. This version of the app requires that the user enters three input values. The Number (Decimal) widgets for these input values are to all specify an appropriate hint for a (double) value. These are the required input values:

- ✓ Speed in knots for the trip
- ✓ Distance in nautical miles of the trip
- ✓ Engine horsepower

The app will then compute and display the trip duration in minutes and the minimum number of fuel gallons required for the trip. These calculations are determined by these formulas:

$$Time\ in\ minutes = (60 * Distance\ in\ nautical\ miles) \div Speed\ in\ knots$$

$$Fuel\ required = ((0.50 * horsepower)/6.1)/60 * Time\ in\ minutes$$

A *TextView* widget needs to be added to display the trip calculated results. The results are to be communicated in a red text color which of course must be externalized as a color resource. Make sure that results are displayed without any decimal positions.

A screenshot for a sample run is provided online in the supplementary resources for this book.

Follow-up Question:

- ➢ *This version of the app requires that the input speed be specified in knots, the distance in nautical miles, and the time in minutes. But what if we wanted to add flexibility to the app to permit the user to specify different units, for example speed in miles per hour or time in hours? How could the input units be made more flexible?*

E5.5 Modify Exercise E4.5, where the initial screen layout began for the *BeautifulBalloon* smartphone mobile app. Based on the screen design so far, you are still in the running to "land" a summer internship at the Beautiful Balloon hot air balloon rides fairground. The job will be yours if you are able to modify this Android app so that the staff can utilize it to determine the "envelope temperature" required for the balloon payload lift. Here is some background information to explain the relevant terminology and the mathematical equations and input necessary for the required computation.

A hot air balloon consists of a bag called the "envelope" that is capable of containing heated air and so is the portion that actually looks like a balloon. Beneath the envelope is a wicker basket, which carries passengers and usually a source of heat, in most cases a burner and propane tanks. The envelope of a hot air balloon does not have to be sealed at the bottom since the air near the bottom of the envelope is at the same pressure as the air surrounding.

This app will display the minimal "envelope temperature" in Fahrenheit. The formula to calculate the minimal "envelope temperature" T_{env} will need to be converted to Fahrenheit prior to display since it is computed in Kelvin degrees as:

$$T_{env} \,^{\circ}K = [(P_{alt} * V)/R_s]/[(P_{alt} * V)/(R_s * T_{amb}) - L]$$

where the R_s is assumed to be the constant 287.058 representing dry air density, and all remaining variables on the right-hand side of this equation are all inputs and represent the following:

P_{alt} is the atmospheric pressure at the altitude of the fairground's location represented in pascal units. However, it must be input as a more user-friendly barometric pressure in Hg representing inches of mercury in US units and then converted in the Java code to pascal units for use in the formula. To assist in this conversion, note that 1 Hg = 3386.38866667 pascals.

V is the volume of the envelope (balloon open-ended expanded to max size) represented in cubic meters (m^3). However, it must be input in a more user-friendly US cubic feet (ft^3) measurement and then converted in the Java code to cubic meters.
To assist in this conversion, note that 1 ft^3 = 0.0283168 m^3.

T_{amb} is the ambient temperature, which is the current air temperature reading expressed in the formula in Kelvin degree units. However, it must be input as a more user-friendly Fahrenheit temperature and then converted in the Java code to Kelvin.
To affect this conversion, use the equation:
Kelvin = (Fahrenheit + 459.67) * 5.0/9.0.

L   is payload lift (weight) requirement in units of kilograms (kg). However, it must be input as a more user-friendly US pounds (lbs) value and then converted into Java code to kilograms for use in the formula.

To assist in this conversion, note that 1 lb = 0.453592 kg.

Note that the input value for L will need to include the 250 lbs weight of the envelope (balloon), 140 lbs weight of the passenger basket, 50 lbs weight of the double burner, 450 lbs weight of the fuel tank and propane content, and the total weight (lbs) of the passengers. Management at Beautiful Balloon has asked that the 890 lbs identified here be added to the passenger weight as input rather than hardcoded in the app to accommodate variance of equipment that may be used on any given day.

If the calculated value for T_{env} exceeds 490°F, the app should display a warning message instead of the T_{env} value, indicating that the envelope (balloon) material may be dangerously compromised by the heat.

Each input text component is to have a light yellow (externalized resource) color and includes a hint message as shown below.

The Button widget is to use the externalized orange color as its background color and the externalized yellow color resource.

Screenshots for two sample runs are provided online in the supplementary resources for this book. The first computes the envelope temperature to lift the balloon off the ground, given the indicated input values. The second example illustrates the output that should be displayed if the calculated envelope temperature is too hot and poses a dangerous situation. In both examples, the input barometric pressure is 29.91 Hg. The input envelope volume is the same value since the same balloon is used, and it has a specific volume of 100,000 cubic feet. The air temperature in the two examples differs as does the lift weight.

Follow-up Question:

➢ How might we make the screen layout "less busy" but still interesting? Base your answer on what you know as an app user rather than on the material we have covered so far.

6

More on Layouts and Living without Constraints

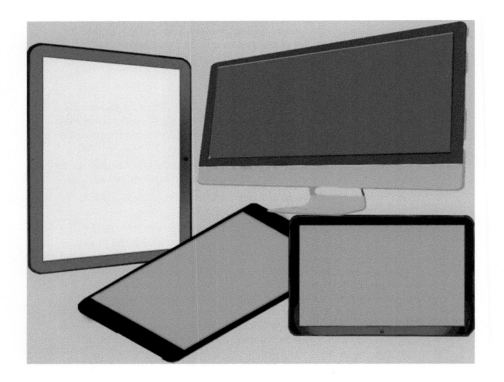

Learning Outcomes:

- ✓ Understanding of the dp unit in relation to screen pixel dimensions (px) and screen densities (dpi).
- ✓ Successful use of the smallest width layout as a design strategy for accommodating different screen sizes and densities.
- ✓ Understanding of the mapping of different sized versions of an image to different screen sizes and densities and successful utilization of different drawable folders.
- ✓ Successful accommodation for device orientation within an app.

  DOI: 10.1201/9781003286325-6

✓ *Understanding of how to programmatically force the orientation of a device to portrait or landscape orientation when necessary.*

✓ *Understanding successful utilization of alternative values folders and resource files.*

✓ *Understanding of the logic and use of the Linear Layout and Table Layout managers.*

✓ *Enabling a vertical scrolling feature for a screen.*

As has been observed thus far, layouts organize the components placed on an activity screen. There are several layouts from which to choose when designing user interface screens, the *ConstraintLayout, LinearLayout,* and *TableLayout* being some of the more popular layouts. The *ConstraintLayout* manager has been used throughout the text thus far, and so a major focus of this chapter is a study of other layout managers. However, before doing so, it is important to note that these other layouts are going to present the same basic challenge that the *ConstraintLayout* has posed thus far, which is the challenge of creating a screen layout that looks attractive on all screen devices, with their assortment of varying characteristics. Therefore, a strategy for addressing this basic challenge is discussed first, prior to looking more closely at some of the alternative layout managers to the *ConstraintLayout* that has been used thus far.

Designing for Different Screen Characteristics

An app screen, or user interface, also referenced as an activity, is structured in terms of a "layout". A layout is officially consisted of a hierarchy of what are termed *"ViewGroup"* and *"View"* objects. The *ConstraintLayout* is an example of a *ViewGroup*. We have worked with a few View objects already, including the *TextView, ImageView,* and *Button* widgets. The *ConstraintLayout* was used in all apps discussed in the previous chapters, both within the text and in the various exercises. There are several explanations for this. First, it is a "flat" layout, which means it lends itself to performance advantages over many other layouts. Second, the bias percentage value that we use to position screen components in terms of horizontal and vertical offset lends well to positioning across different screen densities and sizes.

However, there are so many different sized screen devices of such varying screen densities that it is very naïve to think that one screen layout is going to render attractively on every possible device screen. Therefore, before discussing different layouts, which all have the same difficulties rendering attractively on different sized screens, we will discuss a strategy popular at this time for addressing the attractive rendering of a screen layout on the myriad sizes and densities of today's Android devices.

When reviewing a layout in edit mode, the layout is rendered according to the "Device for Preview" setting found on the eXtensible Markup Language (XML) editor toolbar as shown in Figure 6.1.

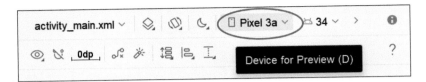

FIGURE 6.1
Device for Preview selector.

For example, let's look again at the temperature convert app that was coded in the previous chapters. Experiment with the "Design for Preview" editor feature to select different options as illustrated in Figure 6.2 to view this layout on other devices to check how it renders similarly or differently across these devices. Be sure to select at least one phone and at least one tablet device.

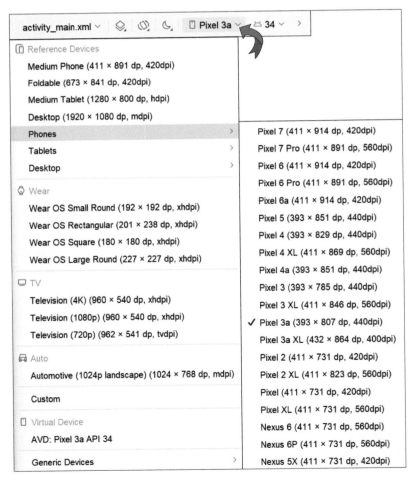

FIGURE 6.2
Device for Preview options.

However, when the selected device's screen is significantly larger, such as the Nexus 10 as shown in Figure 6.3, the screen real estate offered by the device is not used as effectively. In most cases, it is very important for an app to render attractively on many different devices. This necessitates a strategy for addressing the attractive rendering of an app's screen layout across devices of varying screen resolutions and densities. One such strategy is to create multiple screen layouts and designate a distinct layout for each different category of screen size. A popular strategy to address this motive is known as the "smallest width" design, and it involves the creation of several resources corresponding to the minimum width in dp units of a device.

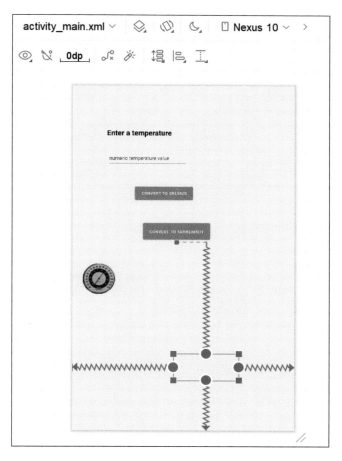

FIGURE 6.3
Layout designed for mobile phone rendered on tablet device.

Designing Layouts for Smallest Width

The popular strategy known as the "smallest width" design can be implemented with multiple layout designs targeted for specific screen width
devices. This involves the creation of several layouts corresponding to the
minimum width in dp units of categories of devices. Consider the table displayed in Figure 6.4. The first column represents the device model. The second column represents the width in pixels of the screen provided by the
device model. The fourth column is the density classification of the device,
and the last column is the calculated "smallest width" dp. This is the value
that we can use as the cut-off for a category of devices to address with a
customized layout.

DETERMINING SMALLEST WIDTH DP FOR CUSTOMIZED LAYOUTS

Device	Width_px	*160	density	= dpi_density	smallest width dp = (Width_px * 160) / dpi_density
Nexus S	480	76800	hdpi	240	320
Galaxy Nexus	720	115200	xhdpi	320	360
Nexus 7	1200	192000	xhdpi	320	600
Nexus 9	1536	245760	xhdpi	320	768
Nexus 6	1440	230400		560	411

FIGURE 6.4
Information required to determine smallest width values.

Considering the information in Figure 6.4, it is obvious that we need a
smallest width of 768 dp units (sw768dp) in order to customize a layout for
the Nexus 9. While not shown in the table, this is also the smallest width
specification that we can use to address a customized layout for the Nexus
10 tablet. The "beauty" of the table information is that anyone can calculate
the smallest width dp specification for any device. All that is required is the
identification of the pixel width and the density rating. Density rating and
corresponding dpi value were presented in Chapter 3. Device pixel widths
and dpi densities can be discovered with a web search. Knowing the pixel
width of the device and the dpi density rating allows one to calculate the
smallest width specification using the formula:

Smallest width $(swdp) = ((\text{width in pixels}) * 160)/(\text{dpi density})$

So, for the Nexus 9 and Nexus 10, a specification of sw768dp is required. But for the Nexus 7, we need an sw600dp specification.

So, let's define a 600 dp smallest width layout to accommodate all three of these devices. If it does not yield satisfactory results for the Nexus 9 and Nexus 10, then we have the option of defining a third layout with an sw768dp, but in this sample app, we most likely will not need to do so.

The convention is to use the default layout, *res/layout/main_activity.xml*, for the smaller screen devices and then define a second layout for the other devices. When you select an alternative Device for Preview, as illustrated in Figure 6.2, Android Studio creates an alternative layout for you that matches the smallest screen width of the selected alternative device. This is illustrated by the creation of a second layout file named activity_main. xml(sw600dp) after the Nexus 10 preview device is selected as shown in Figure 6.5.

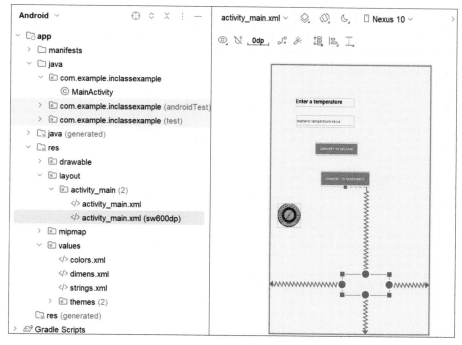

FIGURE 6.5
Creating an alternate resource directory.

If this second layout is not automatically created, we can create it manually by following the steps identified below. Either way, the multiple layouts will be included in the app's *apk* and automatically utilized for larger screen devices. To create this second layout, if it is not automatically created, follow the steps below.

Step 1: Create a second layout directory in the *res* folder by right-clicking on the *res* folder in the Project Structure within Android Studio and then selecting *New → Android Resource Directory* as shown in Figure 6.6.

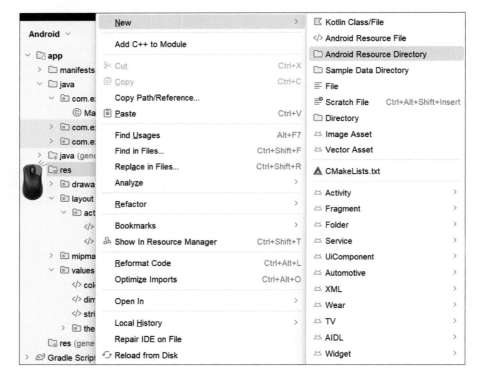

FIGURE 6.6
Upon selecting a different Device for Preview a second layout is created.

Step 2: In the dialog box that appears, specify that the "New Resource Directory" is to implement a smallest width design for 600 dp by selecting the "Smallest Screen Width" qualifier on the left and clicking the $\boxed{>>}$ button. Then type 600 (no dp) in the "Smallest screen width" box prompt as shown below. It is very important to make certain that the "Resource type" is Layout using the drop-down arrow highlighted in Figure 6.7. The remaining fields are automatically filled in as shown in Figure 6.7.

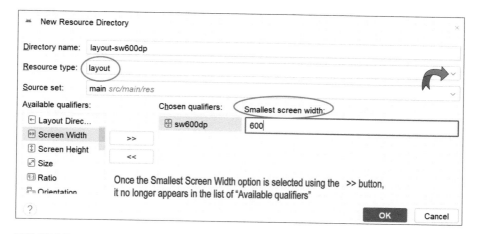

FIGURE 6.7
If the second layout is not automatically created, we need a new Resource Directory.

Step 3: Click OK. Now that we have created the new resource directory, we can create the new layout file. So, create the new layout file to be stored in the new directory by right-clicking on the *res* folder again, but this time select *New → Android Resource File* as shown in Figure 6.8.

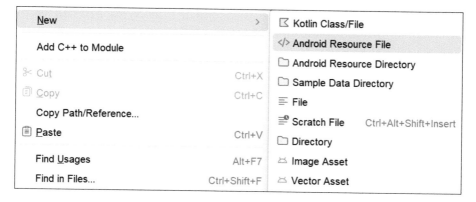

FIGURE 6.8
Creating an alternative layout file as needed.

Step 4. Complete the process of file creation by naming the file and specifying the correct folder as shown in Figure 6.9. It is important to note that the file name is still *activity_main.xml* since this is meant to be an alternative layout for the same activity. It is essential that the alternate layout files have the **same name**. Note that the "Directory name" is the very one created in the previous step, and the Resource type must be specified as *Layout*. So, your input specifications are as highlighted in Figure 6.9.

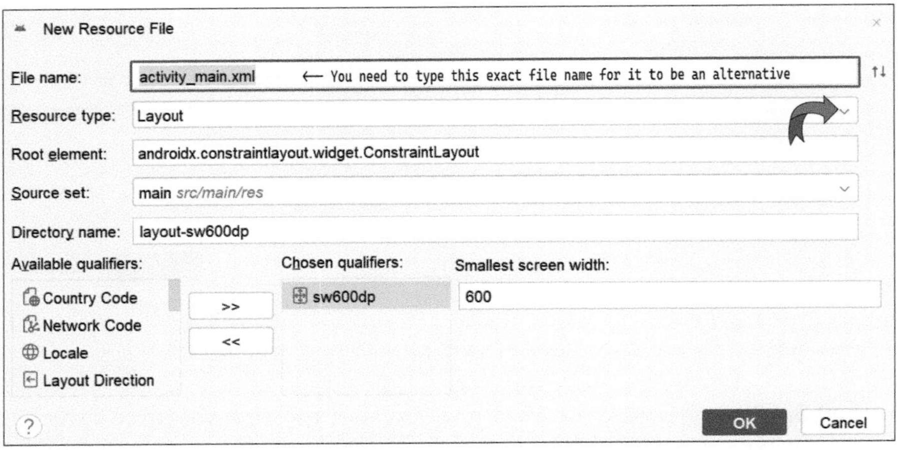

FIGURE 6.9
Creating an *activity_main.xml* file version for a tablet.

As previously mentioned, these four steps are only necessary if Android Studio did not automatically create the alternate *activity_main.xml* file when the alternate preview device was selected. Either way, the Project structure is now updated to reflect this second layout file. And now, this alternative layout can reflect an entirely different design appropriate for the alternate screen sizes and densities supported. So, the alternative layout specification is completed as appropriate for a tablet device. The idea is that our layout specifications for *activity_main* will now render attractively on different screen sizes and densities.

The very "cool thing" is that the device will select between the two layouts when the app is launched on it. So, a tablet device will select the second layout. An example of two such alternative layouts is shown in Figure 6.10. The particular layout resource is chosen based on the smallest width of the host device's screen characteristics.

It is important to note that when coding an app, the size of the *apk* installed on the device increases with each additional layout. As a developer, you can specify any number of additional layouts to match different device characteristics, but achieving the delicate balance between rendering correctly on different screen devices and generating a reasonably sized *apk* can be challenging.

Later in this chapter, we will look at how we can specify alternate dimension values and image sizes in a similar way to how we just created an alternate layout.

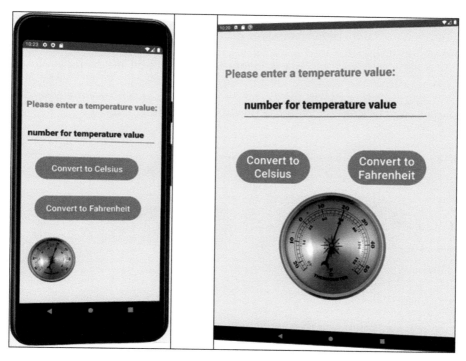

FIGURE 6.10
Appropriate layout auto selected by running device.

Designing Specifically for Portrait and Landscape Modes

The last section discussed the use of the "smallest screen width" property in designing appropriate screen layouts. The "smallest screen width" property is a fixed, static attribute of the device. This is in contrast to the "screen width" property that refers to the current actual width of the screen device as presently oriented. In other words, the screen width property changes when the screen's orientation is altered between portrait mode and landscape mode. The "smallest screen width" property, on the other hand, is not influenced by the orientation state of the device.

As an Android app developer, you can also create layouts specific to screen width. To do so, follow the steps identified in the previous section but substitute "screen width" for "smallest screen width" when creating a new Android resource file.

It is very common for a layout to be attractive in one orientation, portrait or landscape, but to lose its attractiveness when viewed in the alternate orientation. For example, a layout designed for portrait orientation may "waste" the right half of the screen when viewed in landscape orientation. Such an experience can seriously detract from an app. For this reason, developers will often create distinct layouts for different orientations, as well as different screen sizes.

It is relatively easy to view a layout in the different orientations. To do so, one utilizes the "Orientation for Preview" tool option when working in the Design view of the editor as shown in Figure 6.11. This tool enables the Design view to alternate between portrait and landscape modes.

FIGURE 6.11
Orientation for Preview tool.

Sometimes you'll find that you develop an app layout for a tablet device but realize that you want to accommodate smartphone device users as well. In some cases, a tablet portrait layout can rather easily be adapted as a landscape layout on a smartphone device. In such a circumstance, it is often possible to use Java code to force landscape orientation when the layout is displayed on a smartphone device as opposed to a tablet.

The Java statements that can be coded to force a smartphone (non-tablet) device to landscape orientation involve (a) an interrogation of the screen layout size and (b) the setting of the screen orientation to landscape mode. These Java statements are relatively few and have been organized below.

The interrogation of the screen layout size is performed by calling an activity method named "isTabletDevice" that you can code to return a boolean value of true or false as shown here:

```
public boolean isTabletDevice() {
    if(getResources().getConfiguration().isLayoutSizeAtLeast(
      Configuration.SCREENLAYOUT_SIZE_LARGE))
      return true;
    else
      return false;}
```

Then, within the default *onCreate* method in the Java activity code, a call to this method is added, and if it returns true, then the screen orientation is forced to landscape while executing this activity as shown in Table 6.1.

TABLE 6.1

Java Code Forcing Landscape Orientation

```java
//MainActivity.java
import androidx.appcompat.app.AppCompatActivity;

import android.content.pm.ActivityInfo;
import android.content.res.Configuration;
import android.os.Bundle;
import android.view.View;
import android.widget.EditText;
import android.widget.TextView;

public class MainActivity extends AppCompatActivity {

public boolean isTabletDevice() {
   if(getResources().getConfiguration().isLayoutSizeAtLeast(
                           Configuration.SCREENLAYOUT_SIZE_LARGE))
        return true;
   else
        return false;
}
@Override
protected void onCreate(Bundle savedInstanceState) {
 super.onCreate(savedInstanceState);

 if (!isTabletDevice()) {
   // force landscape orientation

  this.setRequestedOrientation(ActivityInfo.SCREEN_ORIENTATION_LANDSCAPE);
 }

      setContentView(R.layout.activity_main);
  }
```

As a separate issue, to force the orientation on all devices to portrait, in the *onCreate* method, before the "setContentView" method call, simply specify the statement:

```
this.setRequestedOrientation
(ActivityInfo.SCREEN_ORIENTATION_PORTRAIT);
```

The use of Java statements to force the screen orientation can be helpful. But there will be times when this method is not preferable to simply defining an alternative landscape layout. So, to define an alternative landscape layout, you again follow the same three steps required to define an alternative smallest screen width with modification as follows:

1. Right-click on the *res* folder in the Project pane and select *New* → *Android Resource Directory*. In the dialog window that opens, select *Orientation*, click the ⟩⟩ button, and then select *Landscape*. Be certain to specify the "Resource type" as *layout*, as shown in Figure 6.12, before clicking the OK button.

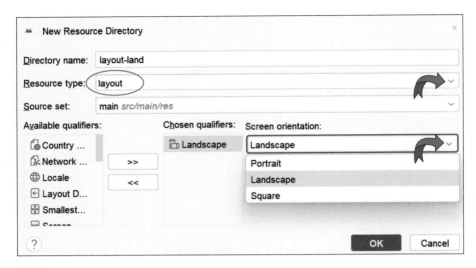

FIGURE 6.12
New "res" subdirectory for Landscape Orientation Layout.

2. Create the new layout file to be stored in the new directory by right-clicking again on the *res* folder in the Project pane and then select *New → Android Resource File*. In the dialog window that opens, scroll down the list of "Available qualifiers" to find and select *Orientation*. Then click the >> button and complete the specifications as shown in Figure 6.13.

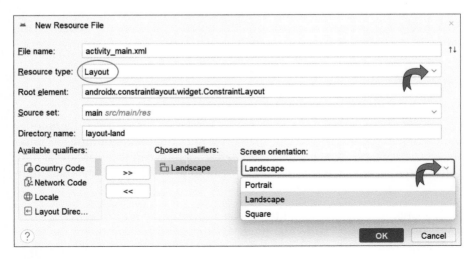

FIGURE 6.13
New "res" file for Landscape Orientation Layout.

3. Code the layout file for the landscape orientation. We will look at coding layout alternatives to the *ConstraintLayout* later in this chapter.

It is also possible to code a layout that is both a smallest screen width **and** alternative landscape orientation layout. To do so, select **both** the *Orientation* and the *Smallest Screen Width* qualifiers from the list of "Available qualifiers" on the left side of the dialog box and then go on to assign the number of width units and the portrait or landscape orientation.

Figure 6.14 illustrates an app that contains several layouts for the same activity to accommodate several screen devices and different orientations, illustrating that as many of these alternate layouts as is necessary can be created. The code file behind all of these alternate layouts is the single file named *MainActivity.java*.

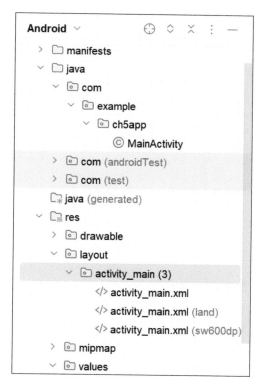

FIGURE 6.14
Three alternative layouts for main activity.

Again, remember that every additional layout increases the size of the *apk*, so striking a balance between *apk* size and different device accommodation can be compromising.

Designing with Different Image Sizes

Previously when specifying the alternative layout design for the larger tablet devices, we simply utilized the image of the weathered thermometer twice in order to occupy more space on the larger screen. But we could instead actually utilize a larger version of the image in our layout alternative for larger dp value screen widths. To do so, a second larger version of the image is required and once available is placed in a second drawable folder that is specifically identified for use to accommodate a larger screen. In other words, the larger version of the image is placed in a new folder created with the folder name *res/drawable-sw600dp*. It is important that the image file name be **exactly** the same as the image file name in the *res/drawable* folder.

The creation of this alternate drawable folder is done in a very similar manner to that which was previously used to create an alternate layout folder. Basically, when creating the new "Android Resource Directory", use the "Resource type" drop down arrow to select drawable, which may require scrolling up in the list. The exact steps for incorporating an alternate drawable resources folder are specified below. Note however that while the smallest screen width qualifier is selected in the example below, we could just as easily select the orientation qualifier if, in the future, we wished to specify an alternate image when the device switched to landscape mode.

So, for example, in the temperature conversion app referenced previously equipped with a *res/layout-sw600dp* folder, we now add a *res/drawable-sw600dp* folder by again right-clicking on the *res* folder in the Project pane of the editor and then selecting *New → Android Resource Directory* following the same exact steps that we did for the alternate layout directories as shown previously.

To then create the actual drawable-sw600dp folder using the "New Resource Directory" dialog window, as shown in Figure 6.15, select "Smallest Screen Width" but this time, select the "drawable" Resource type.

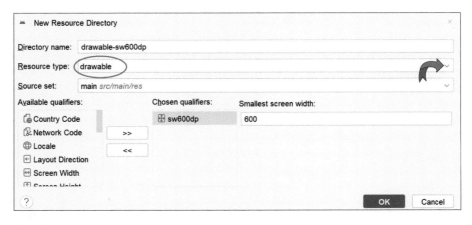

FIGURE 6.15
Specifying a new drawable resource directory.

Nothing usually appears in the Android view in the Project pane as a result of this directory creation. But in the next step when the filename of the alternate image is specified, we must make certain that the filename is exactly the same as the filename in the older *drawable* folder. As an example, if we are adding a larger temperature gauge image for use on tablets but wish to retain the smaller version of the image on phone devices, in this example, we would name **BOTH** files *tempgauge.png* (or both some similar filename). This "**same name**" scheme is very important. The next step is to move the larger version of the image into this new drawable folder. You can do so by dragging the second version of the image onto the NEW *drawable-sw600dp* folder in the Project pane or within the file app of the operating system (e.g. Windows File Explorer). Figure 6.16 illustrates the target location of the tablet version of the *tempgauge. png* file. Note, however, that "Project" rather than "Android" has been selected as the view as illustrated in Figure 6.16.

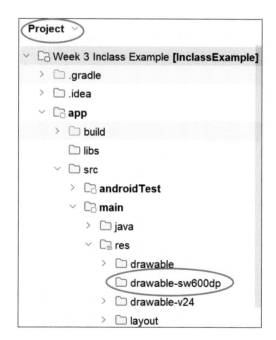

FIGURE 6.16
Target subfolder for the tablet image in project view.

Once the alternate tablet version of the image file is moved to the app project's *drawable-sw600dp* folder, the "Android" view within the Project pane in Android Studio refreshes to reflect the existence of two versions of the drawable image as shown in Figure 6.17.

FIGURE 6.17
Two versions of drawable image.

Now that an alternate version of the image is available for screens matching the smallest width of 600 dp, let's re-run the app on the Nexus 9 (or Nexus 10) emulator device. The launched app selects the most appropriate image as specified by the drawable resource files as shown in Figure 6.18.

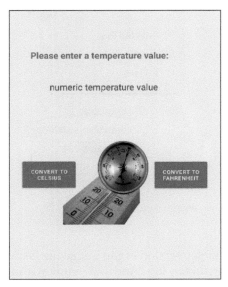

FIGURE 6.18
Alternate tablet image selected as drawable file.

As was the case with the smallest width 600 dp qualifier for the main layout, Android chooses the drawable resource that is closest to the device's "smallest width", without being larger, when the app runs on the target device. The advantage here is that we do not need to create different layouts but can use different sizes of an image within the same layout on different devices. We should note however that it is possible and even desirable sometimes to use both different layouts and different sizes of an image.

If your intention is to provide the same screen layout across the spectrum of device displays available, then you will want to be mindful of the relationship among dpi, image pixels, and pixel ratios. Table 6.2 illustrates the image scale ratios relevant to drawable images across the range of devices and their respective density ratings.

TABLE 6.2

The Range of Density Ratings and Relevant Image Scale Factors

Device density rating:	MDPI	HDPI	XHDPI	XXHDPI	XXXHDPI
In dpi units:	160	240	320	480	640
Image scale factor:	1x	1.5x	2x	3x	4x

Designing with Various Values Subfolders

When creating a new Android resource directory and a new Android resource file, you likely noticed that the default selection for the directory name was "values:". Just as we previously created *layout* folders and *drawable* folders, and *layout* files and *drawable* files for different screen characteristics, so too can we create different *values* folders and files as well. For example, it may often be desirable to specify larger text sizes for tablets than for smartphones. Furthermore, it would often be most desirable to use the same layout for both categories of devices but specify different *"dimens"* values for heights, widths, and other size specifications. This can often be accomplished most efficiently by using one set of dimension resource names in the layout but specifying two different sets of values for these dimensions. The specification of two different sets of dimension values for the same dimension resource name is achieved by creating alternate *"values"* resource directories and alternate *"dimens.xml"* files within these directories.

This is accomplished by using the same sequence of steps we took to create alternate drawable resources in the previous section. Specifically:

1. Right-click on the *res* folder in the Project pane and select *New →
   Android Resource Directory*. In the dialog window that opens, select whatever qualifier is appropriate, such as "Smallest Screen Width" or "Orientation" or both. Be certain to specify the "Resource type" and Directory name as "values" before clicking the OK button.

2. Right-click on the *res* folder in the Project pane and select *New* →
   Android Resource File. In the dialog window that opens, again select
   whatever qualifier is appropriate. Be certain to specify the "Resource
   type" and Directory name as "values", and for the file name specification, you should enter *"dimens.xml"* (or *"colors.xml"*, *"strings.xml"*,
   etc.) before clicking the OK button.

3. Code the second set of values to be used for the alternate screen
   characteristic(s) using the same **exact** names as in the original values
   file. This is critical as Android will automatically decide which of the
   two named values is appropriate for the current device on which it
   is running.

Illustrations of alternate dimension resource files will be encountered in
future examples.

The Linear Layout

The *LinearLayout* is a view group that orders its child components in a single
horizontal or vertical direction. This direction is specified using the orientation attribute. The *LinearLayout* ensures that a horizontal orientation consists
of only one row. When a vertical orientation is specified, each row will contain only one child component ensuring a single column. For this reason, the
LinearLayout is often nested within another layout and is used to organize a
row or column type of arrangement within its parent layout. It can be very
helpful with positioning of items within groups, for example, as a group of
checkboxes or radio buttons, which are discussed in a later chapter.

As an example, let's specify a *LinearLayout* with vertical orientation for a new
activity. To begin, locate the *"LinearLayout* (vertical)" *ViewGroup* in the Layouts
category of the Palette panel within the Android Studio Editor and drag the vertically oriented *LinearLayout* to the screen editing area as shown in Figure 6.19.

Note there is an error indicator after the *LinearLayout* is positioned. The error
message indicates that the *LinearLayout* is missing constraints. This makes sense
since the *LinearLayout* has been positioned within the default *ConstraintLayout*
and therefore needs to be constrained both vertically and horizontally as is
every other *View* or *ViewGroup* within a *ConstraintLayout*. This is indicated by the
four open circle "handles" displayed in Figure 6.19. We can drag these handles
to the margin boundary of the parent container to constrain the *LinearLayout*.
When constrained, the open circles again transition to solid circles.

Components that we now add to the *LinearLayout* are positioned in a linear
fashion rather than a constrained fashion. This is technically due to the fact
that the *LinearLayout* is a "child" element of the *ConstraintLayout*, but components added to the *LinearLayout* are "child" elements of the *LinearLayout*. To
illustrate, let's add a few components to the *LinearLayout*.

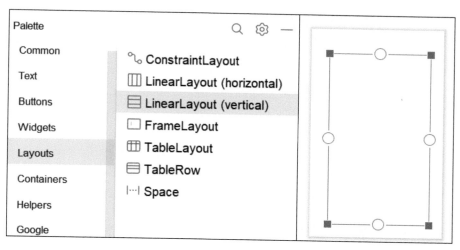

FIGURE 6.19
Adding a linear layout within a constraint layout.

Recall that this particular *LinearLayout* is vertically arranged. Let's add a *TextView* widget to the new *LinearLayout* and assign a text value of "Linear Item 1" and a text size of *36sp* and a "gravity" of "center" so that the text is displayed center aligned. To do so, we simply drag a *TextView* component from the Palette "Text" category and modify its attributes as we have done so frequently in previous examples. Drag another *TextView* widget and assign a text value of "Linear Item 2" to it. The results are displayed in Figure 6.20.

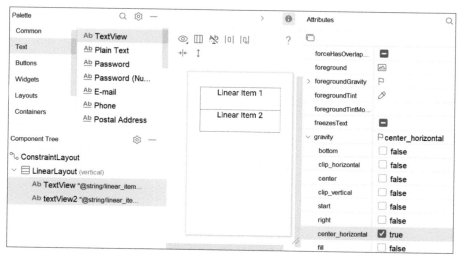

FIGURE 6.20
Positioning widgets within a linear layout.

Let's examine the code listed in Table 6.3 that has been generated after the externalization of resources is completed.

TABLE 6.3

The Layout File Code Illustrating a Vertical Linear Layout within a Constraint Layout

```xml
<?xml version="1.0" encoding="utf-8"?>
<androidx.constraintlayout.widget.ConstraintLayout
 xmlns:android="http://schemas.android.com/apk/res/android"
    xmlns:app="http://schemas.android.com/apk/res-auto"
    xmlns:tools="http://schemas.android.com/tools"
    android:layout_width="match_parent"
    android:layout_height="match_parent"
    tools:context=".MainActivity">

    <LinearLayout
        android:layout_width="393dp"
        android:layout_height="602dp"
        android:orientation="vertical"
        app:layout_constraintBottom_toBottomOf="parent"
        app:layout_constraintEnd_toEndOf="parent"
        app:layout_constraintHorizontal_bias="0.307"
        app:layout_constraintStart_toStartOf="parent"
        app:layout_constraintTop_toTopOf="parent"
        app:layout_constraintVertical_bias="0.496">

        <TextView
            android:id="@+id/textView"
            android:layout_width="match_parent"
            android:layout_height="wrap_content"
            android:gravity="center"
            android:text="@string/linear_item_1"
            android:textColor="@color/redtext"
            android:textSize="@dimen/TextviewItems"
            android:textStyle="bold" />

        <TextView
            android:id="@+id/textView2"
            android:layout_width="match_parent"
            android:layout_height="wrap_content"
            android:gravity="center"
            android:text="@string/linear_item_2"
            android:textColor="@color/redtext"
            android:textSize="@dimen/TextviewItems"
            android:textStyle="bold" />
    </LinearLayout>
</androidx.constraintlayout.widget.ConstraintLayout>
```

Examining the code, we see that the *LinearLayout* is indeed nested within the *ConstraintLayout* and that the *TextView* widgets are nested within the *LinearLayout*. While the *LinearLayout* includes attributes for constraints, the *TextView* widgets do not and instead include layout height and width attributes. Since the layout is a vertically oriented linear layout, the layout widths of the widgets contained within have value *"match_parent"*, thus specifying the width of the parent container, the *LinearLayout*.

So, since the *TextView* widgets have been added to a vertical *LinearLayout*, they are automatically positioned in a sequential downward fashion within the layout. By default, there is no vertical spacing between them. A fairly easy way is to use the padding attributes associated with each of the widgets within the layout. For vertical spacing, the appropriate attributes are the *padding-top* and *padding-bottom* properties. Note that the padding is considered part of the widget element, as illustrated in its selection outline in Figure 6.21 where padding has now been added to the top and bottom of the first *TextView* widget.

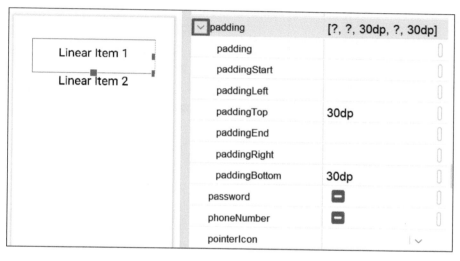

FIGURE 6.21
Assignment of padding to a layout widget.

Adding five more *TextView* components with padding specifications to the two already present results in the screen render displayed in Figure 6.22 when the app is run.

But the seventh *TextView* component is missing from a tablet device, and even more of the components are missing from a mobile phone device. Try scrolling to see the missing items. There is no way to see them. Scrolling does not happen without the use of a *<ScrollView>* wrapper around the *LinearLayout*, or any other layout for that matter. The use of a *ScrollView* wrapper that will enable scrolling is outlined in the code listing of Table 6.4.

Rerun the app and scroll through all of the items now.

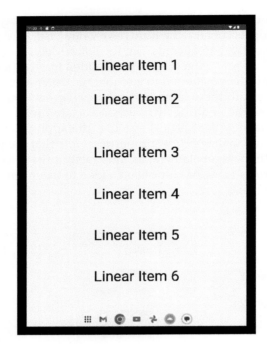

FIGURE 6.22
"Linear Item 7" is missing from view.

TABLE 6.4

Use of a *ScrollView* Container to Enable Vertical Scrolling of Screen Components

```
<?xml version="1.0" encoding="utf-8"?>
<androidx.constraintlayout.widget.ConstraintLayout
    xmlns:android="http://schemas.android.com/apk/res/android"
    xmlns:app="http://schemas.android.com/apk/res-auto"
    xmlns:tools="http://schemas.android.com/tools"
    android:layout_width="match_parent"
    android:layout_height="match_parent">

 <ScrollView
  android:layout_width="match_parent"
  android:layout_height="match_parent" >
    <LinearLayout …

        <TextView … />
          …
    </LinearLayout>

    </ScrollView>

</androidx.constraintlayout.widget.ConstraintLayout>
```

The *ScrollView* Container

As previously demonstrated, Android layouts do **not** automatically scroll. It is possible that a portion of your layout may require the user to scroll, especially on a device with a screen height less than that which you are using for design. In order to enable the user to scroll your layout, you need to enclose your layout in a *ScrollView*. As observed in Table 6.4, a *ScrollView* is relatively simple to use and contains your layout within it, by enclosing your layout with *<ScrollView></ScrollView>* tags.

It is important to note that the *ScrollView* is found in the "Container" category within the Palette, and it may contain only one direct child. So, for example you cannot place a *TextView* and an *ImageView* directly within a *ScrollView*. Instead, you must place the *TextView* and *ImageView* within a layout that is then in turn placed within the *ScrollView* container.

A horizontal scroll view container is also available for those who are interested in implementing horizontal scrolling capability. Such a feature should be reserved for specific applications as horizontal scrolling is discouraged in all but very rare circumstances and so is not discussed in detail in this book.

The Table Layout

The *TableLayout ViewGroup* is an alternative to the previously discussed layouts. It arranges its child components into rows, and the rows consist of columns. Its primary arrangement is as a series of *TableRow* elements, each of which defines a row in the table and each row has zero or more cells. A cell is defined to contain one component. The number of columns in the table is determined by the row with the maximum number of cells. Cell components must be added to a row in increasing column order, and it is possible to specify a layout column number for the cell using the *layout_column* property. Column numbers within a row begin with zero. A table can leave cells empty. Empty cells are considered empty columns and are most obviously specified by skipping a column number. Cells can also span columns using the *layout_span* property.

It is often necessary to specify the following for a *TableLayout*:

```
android: stretchColumns = "*"
android: shrinkColumns = "*"
```

To illustrate the *TableLayout* manager, drag a *TableLayout* from the *Layout* category within the Palette panel onto the *ConstraintLayout* in the screen editing window. It is often helpful to size the *TableLayout* within the *ContstraintLayout* so that a padding exists around it.

Add a *TableRow* to the *TableLayout* by dragging a *TableRow* from the Palette. Then proceed to drag widgets into the row in the order desired. An examination of the Component Tree verifies the widgets contained within each row. Note that properties such as margin, padding, and gravity may need to be set in order to align the components properly within a row.

Design Issues and Considerations

Several layout managers have been discussed, namely the *ConstraintLayout*, *LinearLayout*, and *TableLayout*. While each of them can be uniquely advantageous in certain situations, the *ConstraintLayout* is the latest of the layout managers made available by Google. Per the Android Developer website, the *ConstraintLayout* was made available as an improved layout manager for Android developers and was designed in conjunction with the layout editor. As a serious Android app developer, it would be wise to utilize it as often as appropriate since its purpose includes performance improvements as a newer technology.

One of the goals of an app developer in general is the delivery of an app that will attract and retain as many users as possible. The popularity of an app naturally depends on its ease of use, attractive design, and reliable results. Therefore, an app developer's goal includes the attractive and reliable rendering of the app on as many devices as possible. Such a universal appeal usually demands that the app developer code more than one activity layout corresponding to one or more device screen properties, such as smallest screen width, screen width, and orientation. In conjunction with layouts, the *res/values* files can prove very helpful in addressing different screen sizes and densities. For example, the *res/values/dimens.xml* file can be stored in multiple versions corresponding to screen characteristics. In addition, graphic images may need to be stored as multiple versions in an assortment of *drawable* folders within the app package but all with the same filename.

Likewise, as we will see in a later chapter, when coding multiple layouts to address different devices' screen characteristics, screen components are generally assigned the same id and properties, including *onClick* method names, across the different layout files. This facilitates the use of one Java code file per activity.

When alternate files are created, especially for drawable resources, it may be necessary to "Clean" the project by clicking the menu item *Build → Clean Project* to update the layout components.

Exercises

These exercises modify the apps coded in the previous chapter. The modifications focus on the use of alternate layouts and resources to accommodate different screen characteristics. It is important to note that the Java code from the respective previous assignment should NOT change at all. Be sure to specify "hints" for all input fields and content descriptions for all images.

E6.1 Modify Exercise E5.1, the *FloorTilesCalc* app that was developed as a smartphone mobile app so that it will now render attractively on a larger screen tablet device in portrait mode. Code any alternate layouts (such as sw600dp) or values resource files required so that it will also render appealingly in both portrait and landscape mode on a smartphone and a tablet device. If an alternative layout is required, make use of one of the layouts discussed in this chapter as your choice of layout manager. Now that you are familiar with the vertical scrolling feature, it would be wise to utilize it.

E6.2 Modify Exercise E5.2, the *Inches2Meters* app that was developed as a smartphone mobile app so that it will now render attractively on a larger screen tablet device in portrait mode. Code any alternate layouts (such as sw600dp) or values resource files required so that it will also render appealingly in both portrait and landscape mode on a smartphone and a tablet device. If an alternative layout is required, make use of one of the layouts discussed in this chapter as your choice of layout manager. Now that you are familiar with the vertical scrolling feature, it would be wise to utilize it.

E6.3 Modify Exercise E5.3, the *DivingApp* app that was developed as a tablet app so that it will now render attractively on a smaller screen smartphone device in landscape mode. Code any alternate layouts or values resource files required. In addition, use the Java code discussed in this chapter to force the orientation of the device to landscape mode. If an alternative layout is required, make use of one of the layouts discussed in this chapter as your choice of layout manager. Now that you are familiar with the vertical scrolling feature, it would be wise to utilize it.

E6.4 Modify Exercise E5.4, the *PlanBoatTrip* app that was developed as a tablet app so that it will now render attractively on a smaller screen smartphone device. Code any alternate layouts or values resource files required. In addition, use the Java code discussed in this chapter to force the orientation of the device to landscape mode. If an alternative layout is required, make use of one of the layouts discussed in this chapter as your choice of layout manager. Now that you are familiar with the vertical scrolling feature, it would be wise to utilize it.

E6.5 Modify Exercise E5.5, the *BeautifulBalloon* app that was developed
as a smartphone mobile app so that it will now render attractively
on a larger screen tablet device. Code any alternate layouts (such as
sw600dp) or values resource files required so that it will also render appealingly in both portrait and landscape mode on a smartphone and a tablet device. If an alternative layout is required, make
use of one of the layouts discussed in this chapter as your choice of
layout manager. Now that you are familiar with the vertical scrolling feature, it would be wise to utilize it.

7

Improving the UI with Selection Inputs and Dynamic Content

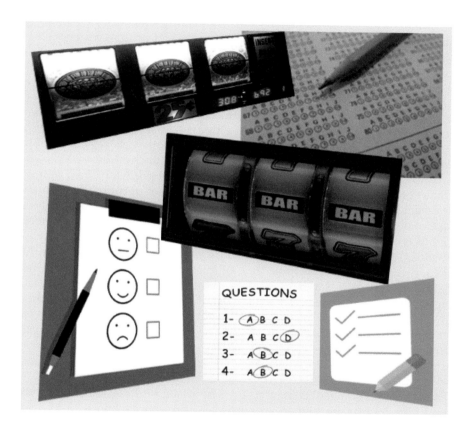

Learning Outcomes:

✓ Successful implementation of a spinner control with static input and programmatic retrieval of the selected item.

✓ Successful retrieval of user selection from a spinner control.

✓ Successful implementation of checkboxes and programmatic retrieval of checkbox input values.

DOI: 10.1201/9781003286325-7

✓ *Successful implementation of radio button groups and programmatic retrieval of radio button input.*
✓ *Successful implementation of image buttons.*
✓ *Understanding of visibility issues and how to dynamically alter screen content with Java code and visibility settings.*
✓ *Changing image source files programmatically to effectively display different images while an app is running.*
✓ *Implementing multiple buttons that share a common Java event method handler.*

Thus far, in terms of input, our apps can accept and process user specification from *EditText* fields. While these inputs are useful for free form values, it is more user-friendly if, whenever possible, an app provides a selection list of some kind to the user for the specification of input. The idea is that input from a mobile device is easier for a user to specify, if he or she can do so by clicking on an item rather than free form typing out a value on a keyboard, which many people find awkward to manipulate on a mobile device.

This chapter discusses the most popular types of such selection inputs which include the spinner control, radio buttons, and checkboxes. The spinner control is Android's term for a drop-down list of predetermined options. A radio button is an input that is selected from a set of mutually exclusive inputs where exactly one choice can be selected. A checkbox is an input that is optionally selected as a sort of "extra". Each of these very popular modes of input is covered in detail in this chapter.

In addition, each of these inputs can be dynamically configured. In other words, it is sometimes desirable that a list of input options be determined by information in a database or data obtained from a web server. This chapter, however, focuses on the static list of input options for each of these forms of selection input and so lays the foundation for utilization of selection inputs in an app. Later chapters may revisit the creation of such inputs using database or webserver information when these latter technologies are covered. Still, the foundation as covered in this chapter will prove invaluable to such efforts.

To provide meaningful context in the discussion of these selection inputs, we will implement them in an app example. The sample app is used by an HR department to manage the recertification efforts of their employees. Employees are required to attend one seminar a year in order to keep certification up to date. The registration for these seminars is to be made available in an Android app. The app is to run on mobile phone devices or on mobile tablets. To register, employees are required to select a seminar, a time of day, and indicate preferred locations of attendance. The seminar selection within the app will take the form of a spinner control. The time of day will be selected from a set of radio buttons. And the possible locations will be designated using checkboxes. A look at the screen we are building in this chapter to support this app is shown in Figure 7.1.

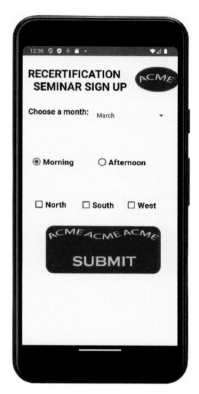

FIGURE 7.1
Sample app building in this chapter.

One related input specification to be covered in this chapter is that of the image button. An example of an image button is also provided in this sample app and is labeled with the text "submit" as seen in this screenshot.

So, create a new Android app project in Android Studio of type "Empty Views Activity" with a Java language specification. This sample app will utilize a *ConstraintLayout* to organize the activity.

Activating a Spinner Widget

The spinner control in an Android app is analogous to the drop-down list on a web page. A list of values is presented from which the user may select one. In our sample app, the spinner control is to present the employee user with a month selection list. The list consists of the months of March, April, May, June, October, and November. Therefore, these are the static values to be loaded into our spinner control. In order to implement a spinner control of options and a recognition of the user selected value in an Android app, three things must occur:

1. The list of static options is specified as an eXtensible Markup Language (XML) string array.
2. A spinner widget is dragged from the Palette in Android Studio onto the screen layout, and its entries property is set to point to the XML string array.
3. Java code is executed to respond to the user selection.

Before we address these three necessary actions for our sample app, let's consider the spinner control we are building. When it is loaded with the appropriate values, it will provide a drop-down list of options that will look something like that which is shown in Figure 7.2.

FIGURE 7.2
Choices for Spinner selection.

This example is used below to implement the steps identified for incorporating a spinner in an Android app.

Setting Up the String Array for the Spinner Static Options

So, the first action identified above states that the list of static options is to be specified as an XML string array. Therefore, open the *res/values/strings.xml* file in this app project in the Android Studio editor. Then define the string array named *seminar_months* that will contain the list of month options as shown here. The *seminar_months string-array* is defined as shown in Table 7.1 by enumeration of its *item* components.

TABLE 7.1

Defining the Spinner Entries in a String Array in the *strings.xml* File

---
strings.xml

```
<resources>
    <string name="app_name">SelectionInputsChapter7</string>
    <string name="recertification_header">RECERTIFICATION
             \u000A\u000D
             SEMINAR SIGN UP</string>
    <string name="choose_a_month">Choose a month:</string>
    <string name="acme_company_logo">ACME company logo</string>

    <string-array name="seminar_months">
        <item>March</item>
        <item>April</item>
        <item>May</item>
        <item>June</item>
        <item>October</item>
        <item>November</item>
    </string-array>
</resources>
```

Connecting the String Array to the Spinner Control in the Layout

Next, open the *layout/activity_main.xml* file in the Android Studio editor. Drag a *Spinner* widget from the Containers category in the Palette panel onto the layout as shown in Figure 7.3. The *TextView* component should also be included to serve as a descriptive prompt for the spinner control.

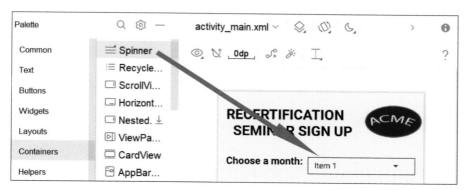

FIGURE 7.3
Dragging Spinner widget from Containers category.

Size the spinner appropriately and set the constraints for the spinner instance. Assign the choices for its drop-down list by scrolling to "All Attributes" in the Attributes panel when the spinner is selected and scroll to the "entries" property. Specify the name of the string array, *seminar_months*, as the *entries* property value as shown in Figure 7.4.

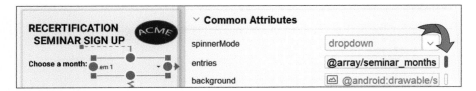

FIGURE 7.4
Link the Spinner entries to a string-array resource.

Run the app as constructed thus far. The list of month choices should be displayed when the spinner control drop-down arrow is selected as shown in Figure 7.5. Click on one of the months to select it and notice how the month now appears in place of the drop-down list of options.

FIGURE 7.5
User interaction with a Spinner widget.

Retrieving the User Selection from the Spinner Control at Runtime

Now that we can incorporate a spinner widget in the screen layout and know how to statically initialize its entries, it becomes important to be able to retrieve the user's spinner item selection when the app executes. This selection retrieval occurs in Java code within the activity .java file. But let's first add a *Button* widget to trigger the retrieval of this value. Let's label the button with text string value "SUBMIT". Let's also add a *TextView* so that when the button is pressed/clicked, we can code a display of the spinner choice *TextView* component. This way, we will be able to test to make certain that the spinner input control is working correctly.

Next let's modify the Java code for the activity so that when the button is pressed/clicked, the spinner selection will be displayed in the *TextView* component on the bottom of the screen. In order to enable this to happen, we must assign the button component's *onClick* property a value. As discussed in Chapter 5, this *onClick* value then becomes the name of a method in the java activity file. For the sake of this example, let's assign the Button component's *onClick* property a value of "processInput". The Java code required to retrieve the user spinner selection then consists of the following:

1. A Java code reference to the spinner component on the screen layout. This requires that an id value be assigned to the spinner control within the Android Studio editor. For the sake of this example, the assigned *id* value is "chosenmonth". Whenever you assign an id to an existing layout component, if asked whether or not all relevant references should be updated, always click "Refactor". Once the spinner component has been assigned an id value in the screen layout, a Java code reference to the spinner component can be created in the .java activity file as:

```
Spinner monthChoice = (Spinner) findViewById(R.
id.chosenmonth);
```

2. Now "monthChoice" can be used to obtain its current value as:

```
String spinnerSelectedValue = monthChoice.
getSelectedItem().toString();
```

3. Since we are not yet ready to do anything with the spinner selection, just display it as shown here. Note that the *TextView* component at the bottom of the screen layout was never assigned an id value. We will assign it the id value "result" in the layout file.

Then, we will use it to display the spinner selection in the .java
file as:

```
TextView output = (TextView) findViewById(R.id.result);
output.setText("You chose the month of " +
spinnerSelectedValue);
```

The updated contents for both the layout file and the .java file are listed in
Tables 7.2 and 7.3, respectively.

Run the app. Select the June item from the drop-down list. Then click the
SUBMIT button. Something like that shown in Figure 7.6 should be displayed.

TABLE 7.2

Listing of the Code in the *activity_main.xml* File

activity _ main.xml

```xml
<?xml version="1.0" encoding="utf-8"?>
<androidx.constraintlayout.widget.ConstraintLayout
xmlns:android="http://schemas.android.com/apk/res/android"
    xmlns:app="http://schemas.android.com/apk/res-auto"
    xmlns:tools="http://schemas.android.com/tools"
    android:layout_width="match_parent"
    android:layout_height="match_parent"
    android:background="@color/logo_color1"
    tools:context=".MainActivity">

    <TextView
        android:id="@+id/textView"
        android:layout_width="275dp"
        android:layout_height="69dp"
        android:text="@string/recertification_header"
        android:textColor="@color/black"
        android:textSize="@dimen/header_size"
        android:textStyle="bold"
        app:layout_constraintBottom_toBottomOf="parent"
        app:layout_constraintEnd_toEndOf="parent"
        app:layout_constraintHorizontal_bias="0.117"
        app:layout_constraintStart_toStartOf="parent"
        app:layout_constraintTop_toTopOf="parent"
        app:layout_constraintVertical_bias="0.04"
        tools:ignore="TextSizeCheck" />

    <ImageView
        android:id="@+id/imageView"
        android:layout_width="wrap_content"
        android:layout_height="wrap_content"
        android:contentDescription="@string/acme_company_logo"
        app:layout_constraintBottom_toBottomOf="parent"
        app:layout_constraintEnd_toEndOf="parent"
        app:layout_constraintHorizontal_bias="0.466"
        app:layout_constraintStart_toEndOf="@+id/textView"
        app:layout_constraintTop_toTopOf="parent"
        app:layout_constraintVertical_bias="0.04"
        app:srcCompat="@drawable/acmelogo" />
```

(Continued)

TABLE 7.2   (*Continued*)

Listing of the Code in the *activity_main.xml* File

---

activity _ main.xml

```xml
    <TextView
        android:id="@+id/textView2"
        android:layout_width="158dp"
        android:layout_height="39dp"
        android:text="@string/choose_a_month"
        android:textColor="@color/black"
        android:textSize="@dimen/prompttext_size"
        android:textStyle="bold"
        app:layout_constraintBottom_toBottomOf="parent"
        app:layout_constraintEnd_toEndOf="parent"
        app:layout_constraintHorizontal_bias="0.063"
        app:layout_constraintStart_toStartOf="parent"
        app:layout_constraintTop_toBottomOf="@+id/textView"
        app:layout_constraintVertical_bias="0.055"
        tools:ignore="TextSizeCheck" />

    <Spinner
        android:id="@+id/chosenmonth"
        android:layout_width="195dp"
        android:layout_height="48dp"
        android:entries="@array/seminar_months"
        app:layout_constraintBottom_toBottomOf="parent"
        app:layout_constraintEnd_toEndOf="parent"
        app:layout_constraintHorizontal_bias="0.261"
        app:layout_constraintStart_toEndOf="@+id/textView2"
        app:layout_constraintTop_toBottomOf="@+id/textView"
        app:layout_constraintVertical_bias="0.054" />

    <Button
        android:id="@+id/button"
        android:layout_width="183dp"
        android:layout_height="64dp"
        android:onClick="processInput"
        android:text="@string/submit_label"
        android:textColor="@color/logo_color1"
        android:textStyle="bold"
        app:layout_constraintBottom_toBottomOf="parent"
        app:layout_constraintEnd_toEndOf="parent"
        app:layout_constraintHorizontal_bias="0.443"
        app:layout_constraintStart_toStartOf="parent"
        app:layout_constraintTop_toTopOf="parent"
        app:layout_constraintVertical_bias="0.679" />

    <TextView
        android:id="@+id/result"
        android:layout_width="329dp"
        android:layout_height="89dp"
        android:text="@string/debug_results"
        android:textSize="@dimen/prompttext_size"
        app:layout_constraintBottom_toBottomOf="parent"
        app:layout_constraintEnd_toEndOf="parent"
        app:layout_constraintStart_toStartOf="parent"
        app:layout_constraintTop_toTopOf="parent"
        app:layout_constraintVertical_bias="0.943" />

</androidx.constraintlayout.widget.ConstraintLayout>
```

TABLE 7.3

Listing of the Code in the *MainActivity.java* File

MainActivity.java

```
package com.example.selectioninputchapter7;

import androidx.appcompat.app.AppCompatActivity;

import android.os.Bundle;
import android.view.View;
import android.widget.Spinner;
import android.widget.TextView;

public class MainActivity extends AppCompatActivity {

    @Override
    protected void onCreate(Bundle savedInstanceState) {
        super.onCreate(savedInstanceState);
        setContentView(R.layout.activity_main);
    }

    public void processInput(View v) {
        Spinner monthChoice = (Spinner) findViewById(R.id.chosenmonth);
        String spinnerSelectedValue =
                        monthChoice.getSelectedItem().toString();
        TextView viewChoice = (TextView) findViewById(R.id.result);
        viewChoice.setText("User selection is " + spinnerSelectedValue);
    }
}
```

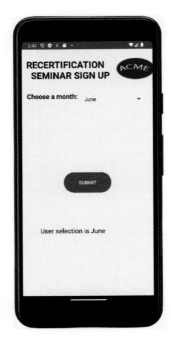

FIGURE 7.6
Results from running the app code thus far.

If you do not see the output that appears in response to the spinner selection of the June item, then compare your code to that listed in Tables 7.2 and 7.3 for the layout file and Java code file, respectively.

Tuning in with Radio Buttons

A radio button is an example of a two-state input: on or off, known in other words as checked or unchecked. The convention is to group radio buttons so that the selection of one of the radio buttons in the group precludes the selection of the others. As an example, a pet adoption center may present a form that asks its user searching for a pet to select the type of pet: cat or dog or horse. Such a form would present the users with three radio buttons, one and only one of which can be selected at any one point in time as shown in Figure 7.7.

FIGURE 7.7
Three radio buttons choice example.

In accordance, the time to include radio buttons in an Android app is when a desired input involves the selection of a group of mutually exclusive options. To incorporate radio button inputs in an Android app, three tasks must be completed:

1. The definition of a radio button group.
2. The identification of each radio button (two or more) belonging to the group.
3. The coding of Java statements to determine which radio button has been selected.

These tasks are addressed in detail below using our sample app for employee annual recertification. The radio buttons implemented in this example solicit the user's choice for "Morning" versus "Afternoon" time of day offerings.

Defining a Radio Button Group in Android

While it is possible to define a radio button group programmatically in the XML Code mode, our example here uses the Design mode within the Android

Studio editor. A radio button group component can be found in the Palette under the *Buttons* category as shown in Figure 7.8. Select the *RadioGroup* container in the *Buttons* category of the Palette and drag an instance to the screen layout as displayed in Figure 7.8. Assign to its *id* property the value "time_day".

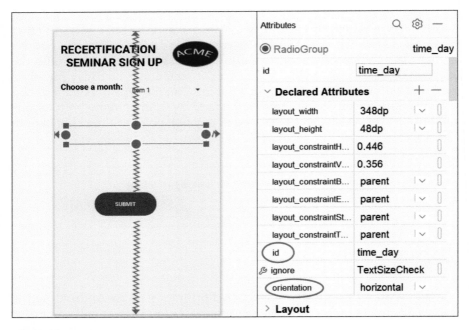

FIGURE 7.8
The *RadioGroup* widget found in the Buttons category.

Be mindful of the orientation property of the radio group. It has three possible values: horizontal for the case where the radio buttons are to be positioned across the same "row", vertical which means they should be placed underneath each other, and none which is the default and at present in turns defaults to vertical. In our example, we are looking for a horizontal orientation as noted in Figure 7.8.

Identifying Each Radio Button That Belongs to a Group

Drag a radio button from the *Buttons* group within the palette onto the radio group widget in the component tree. Note this may necessitate an increase in the width of the radio group in the layout. Drag a second *RadioButton* component from the Palette onto the *RadioGroup* within the layout. Again, some width adjustments may need to be made for the group and the individual buttons.

Radio button properties of particular interest include the *id* property and the *text* property, **both** of which should be explicitly set to their desired values. In our example, we will assign an *id* value of "morning" to the first radio button and a *text* value equivalent to the externalized string resource "Morning", as shown in Figure 7.9. Specify an *id* value of "afternoon" for the second radio button and an externalized string value of "Afternoon" to the *text* property. Adjust the text properties as desired.

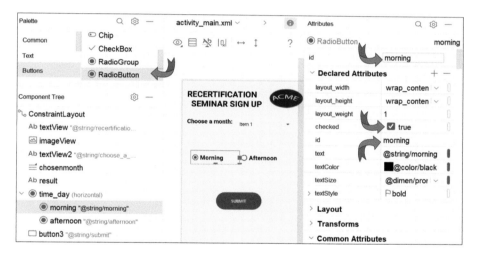

FIGURE 7.9
Radio buttons placed within the *RadioGroup* with unique id values.

One more thing to do that will ease the coding effort later is to make one of the radio buttons a default selection. This ensures that if the user skips this portion of the input, one of the radio buttons will still indicate a selection. After all, the rationale for using radio buttons as opposed to checkboxes is due to the fact that exactly one of the radio buttons must be selected. So, choose whichever button should be the default value and click on it in the Component Tree. Then scroll to its *checked* property and click the box provided. This is illustrated in Figure 7.9 where the morning option has been checked as the default selection.

**Java Statements Required to Determine Which Radio Button
Has Been Selected**

The Java coded steps necessary for determining which radio button the user
has selected are provided here.

1. Code a Java statement that references the radio group containing
   the various radio buttons. The general syntax for this statement is
   specified as:

   ```
   RadioGroup rg = (RadioGroup)findViewById(R.id.radiogroupassignedIDvalue);
   ```

2. Retrieve the id of the radio button checked from the group as indicated here:

   ```
   int checkedRadioButton = rg.getCheckedRadioButtonId();
   ```

3. Use the retrieved id value for the selected radio button in follow-
   up Java statements. Note that you **cannot** use a switch statement
   with *R.id* values. The switch statement requires constant values,
   and *R.id* values are not constant (the author found this out the
   hard way!).

   ```
   if (checkedRadioButton == R.id.assignedIDforRadioButtonA) {

           ...

   }

   else if (checkedRadioButton == R.id.assignedIDforRadioButtonB) {

           ...

   }
   ```

Previously, the Java code required to recognize the user selection for the
spinner component was added to the "ꜱᴜʙᴍɪᴛ" button's *onClick* method. In
this same app, the code for recognizing the radio button selected by the user
will also be placed in this same method. So, add the code highlighted in
Table 7.4 to the *MainActivity.java* file.

Run the app. Make a month selection and a time-of-day selection and then
click the Submit button. You should see screen content similar to that shown
in Figure 7.10. If any errors occur, go back and check your Java code to make
certain that it matches that provided in Table 7.4. In addition, the updated
contents of the *activity_main.xml* file is listed in Table 7.5. Sometimes, when

TABLE 7.4

Java Code Added for Handling the Radio Buttons

`MainActivity.java`

```
package com.example.selectioninputschapter7;

import androidx.appcompat.app.AppCompatActivity;

import android.os.Bundle;
import android.view.View;
import android.widget.RadioGroup;
import android.widget.Spinner;
import android.widget.TextView;

public class MainActivity extends AppCompatActivity {
    @Override
    protected void onCreate(Bundle savedInstanceState) {
        super.onCreate(savedInstanceState);
        setContentView(R.layout.activity_main);
    }
    public void processInput(View v) {
        Spinner monthChoice = (Spinner) findViewById(R.
        id.chosenmonth);
        String spinnerSelectedValue =
                        monthChoice.getSelectedItem().
                        toString();
        RadioGroup rg = (RadioGroup) findViewById(R.id.time_day);
        int checkedRadioButton = rg.getCheckedRadioButtonId();
        String whichRadioButton = "";  // to be determined next
        if (checkedRadioButton == R.id.morning) {
            whichRadioButton = "Morning";
        }
        else if (checkedRadioButton == R.id.afternoon) {
            whichRadioButton = "Afternoon";
        }
        else {  // so have a default checked
            whichRadioButton = "No time of day selected";
        }
        TextView output = (TextView) findViewById(R.id.result);
        output.setText("You chose the month of " +
        spinnerSelectedValue
                        + " and time of day " + whichRadioButton);
    }
}
```

creating the radio buttons, they are not added to the radio group correctly. So, if you are encountering errors, double check the screen layout XML code provided in Table 7.5 and make certain that the radio buttons are properly enclosed within the radio group.

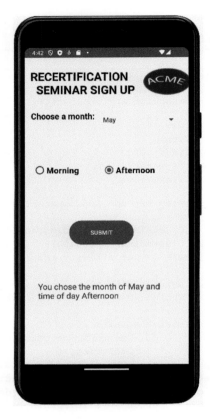

FIGURE 7.10
Running app results with radio button selection.

TABLE 7.5

Layout Code Listing with Radio Buttons

`activity_main.xml`

```
<?xml version="1.0" encoding="utf-8"?>
<androidx.constraintlayout.widget.ConstraintLayout
xmlns:android="http://schemas.android.com/apk/res/android"
    xmlns:app="http://schemas.android.com/apk/res-auto"
    xmlns:tools="http://schemas.android.com/tools"
    android:layout_width="match_parent"
    android:layout_height="match_parent"
    android:background="@color/logo_color1"
    tools:context=".MainActivity">
```

(Continued)

TABLE 7.5   (*Continued*)

Layout Code Listing with Radio Buttons

activity_main.xml

```
<TextView
    android:id="@+id/textView"
    android:layout_width="275dp"
    android:layout_height="69dp"
    android:text="@string/recertification_header"
    android:textColor="@color/black"
    android:textSize="@dimen/header_size"
    android:textStyle="bold"
    app:layout_constraintBottom_toBottomOf="parent"
    app:layout_constraintEnd_toEndOf="parent"
    app:layout_constraintHorizontal_bias="0.117"
    app:layout_constraintStart_toStartOf="parent"
    app:layout_constraintTop_toTopOf="parent"
    app:layout_constraintVertical_bias="0.04"
    tools:ignore="TextSizeCheck" />

<ImageView
    android:id="@+id/imageView"
    android:layout_width="wrap_content"
    android:layout_height="wrap_content"
    android:contentDescription="@string/acme_company_logo"
    app:layout_constraintBottom_toBottomOf="parent"
    app:layout_constraintEnd_toEndOf="parent"
    app:layout_constraintHorizontal_bias="0.466"
    app:layout_constraintStart_toEndOf="@+id/textView"
    app:layout_constraintTop_toTopOf="parent"
    app:layout_constraintVertical_bias="0.04"
    app:srcCompat="@drawable/acmelogo" />

<TextView
    android:id="@+id/textView2"
    android:layout_width="158dp"
    android:layout_height="39dp"
    android:text="@string/choose_a_month"
    android:textColor="@color/black"
    android:textSize="@dimen/prompttext_size"
    android:textStyle="bold"
    app:layout_constraintBottom_toBottomOf="parent"
    app:layout_constraintEnd_toEndOf="parent"
    app:layout_constraintHorizontal_bias="0.063"
    app:layout_constraintStart_toStartOf="parent"
    app:layout_constraintTop_toBottomOf="@+id/textView"
    app:layout_constraintVertical_bias="0.055"
    tools:ignore="TextSizeCheck" />

<Spinner
    android:id="@+id/chosenmonth"
    android:layout_width="195dp"
    android:layout_height="48dp"
    android:entries="@array/seminar_months"
    app:layout_constraintBottom_toBottomOf="parent"
    app:layout_constraintEnd_toEndOf="parent"
    app:layout_constraintHorizontal_bias="0.261"
    app:layout_constraintStart_toEndOf="@+id/textView2"
    app:layout_constraintTop_toBottomOf="@+id/textView"
    app:layout_constraintVertical_bias="0.054" />
```

(Continued)

TABLE 7.5 *(Continued)*

Layout Code Listing with Radio Buttons

activity_main.xml

```xml
<Button
    android:id="@+id/button"
    android:layout_width="183dp"
    android:layout_height="64dp"
    android:onClick="processInput"
    android:text="@string/submit_label"
    android:textColor="@color/logo_color1"
    android:textStyle="bold"
    app:layout_constraintBottom_toBottomOf="parent"
    app:layout_constraintEnd_toEndOf="parent"
    app:layout_constraintHorizontal_bias="0.443"
    app:layout_constraintStart_toStartOf="parent"
    app:layout_constraintTop_toTopOf="parent"
    app:layout_constraintVertical_bias="0.679" />

<TextView
    android:id="@+id/result"
    android:layout_width="329dp"
    android:layout_height="89dp"
    android:text="@string/debug_results"
    android:textSize="@dimen/prompttext_size"
    app:layout_constraintBottom_toBottomOf="parent"
    app:layout_constraintEnd_toEndOf="parent"
    app:layout_constraintStart_toStartOf="parent"
    app:layout_constraintTop_toTopOf="parent"
    app:layout_constraintVertical_bias="0.943" />

<RadioGroup
    android:id="@+id/time_day"
    android:layout_width="348dp"
    android:layout_height="48dp"
    android:orientation="horizontal"
    app:layout_constraintBottom_toBottomOf="parent"
    app:layout_constraintEnd_toEndOf="parent"
    app:layout_constraintHorizontal_bias="0.446"
    app:layout_constraintStart_toStartOf="parent"
    app:layout_constraintTop_toTopOf="parent"
    app:layout_constraintVertical_bias="0.356"
    tools:ignore="TextSizeCheck">

    <RadioButton
        android:id="@+id/morning"
        android:layout_width="wrap_content"
        android:layout_height="wrap_content"
        android:layout_weight="1"
        android:checked="true"
        android:text="@string/morning"
        android:textColor="@color/black"
        android:textSize="@dimen/prompttext_size" />

    <RadioButton
        android:id="@+id/afternoon"
        android:layout_width="wrap_content"
        android:layout_height="wrap_content"
        android:layout_weight="1"
        android:text="@string/afternoon"
        android:textColor="@color/black"
        android:textSize="@dimen/prompttext_size" />
</RadioGroup>

</androidx.constraintlayout.widget.ConstraintLayout>
```

Opting in with Checkboxes

As is the case with a radio button, a checkbox is a two-state input: on or off, or checked or unchecked. Unlike radio buttons that generally belong to a mutually exclusive group, a checkbox is an independent and optional input. On a form, checkboxes are often associated with the directive to check all that apply, which may result in zero or more checkbox selections. For example, a pizza order form may provide additional topping options as shown in Figure 7.11. Clicking on a checkbox indicates that the topping is desired. Clicking on one of the options does not preclude the selection of any of the others. And in fact, it is not necessary to select any additional toppings.

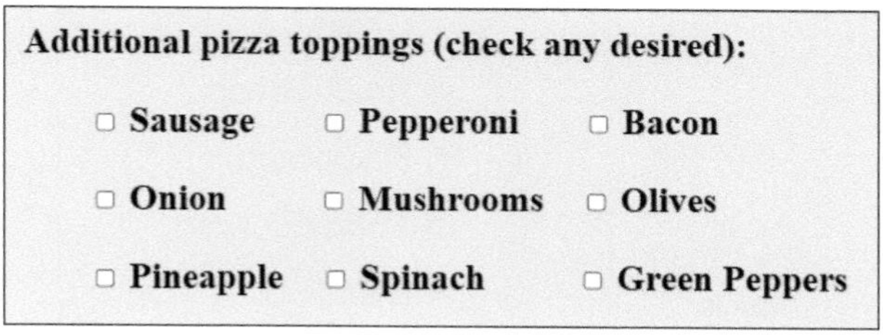

Additional pizza toppings (check any desired):

☐ **Sausage**   ☐ **Pepperoni**   ☐ **Bacon**

☐ **Onion**   ☐ **Mushrooms**   ☐ **Olives**

☐ **Pineapple**   ☐ **Spinach**   ☐ **Green Peppers**

FIGURE 7.11
Check box input example.

Checkboxes are implemented in an Android app in a similar way to radio buttons, except that there is no mutually exclusive grouping component. Of the three selection input elements discussed in this chapter, the checkbox is the simplest to implement.

Two steps are required to implement each checkbox in an Android app as described below.

1. A checkbox widget is incorporated into the screen layout, either explicitly by entering the XML code required for a checkbox specification or by dragging a checkbox widget onto the screen layout in the Design view of the Android Studio editor.
2. Appropriate statements are coded in the layout activity's Java file to recognize when the checkbox has been selected as an input.

Including a Checkbox UI Element in a Screen Layout

As mentioned previously, it is possible to keyboard type the <checkbox> XML code details in the activity screen's layout file. But since, as with the other components, the Design view prepares the XML code equivalent from the Graphical User Interface (GUI) specifications, it is easier to use the editor

Design view to create the checkbox component as illustrated in Figure 7.12. To do so, drag an instance of the Checkbox widget from the Design Palette to the screen layout.

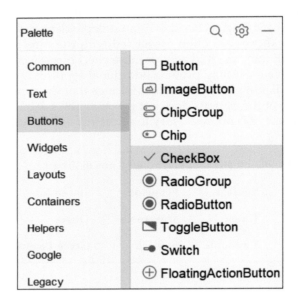

FIGURE 7.12
CheckBox widget located in the Buttons category of the palette.

In the sample app we are building in this chapter, three checkbox elements are required. These represent the possible locations to which the employee is able to commute to attend the seminar. The possible location options are to be labeled North, South, and West.

The screen layout displayed in Figure 7.13 illustrates that three checkbox widgets have been dragged onto the screen layout and labeled properly. In addition, as noted in the Component Tree, the id value of each of the checkboxes has also been modified to identify the location by name.

It can sometimes be difficult to set the baseline constraints between two elements in a layout. This is especially the case with the horizontal orientation of radio button groups and checkbox sets. So, don't forget that you can expand the "Declared Attributes" in the Attributes pane for an element as displayed in Figure 7.14.

Recognizing a Checkbox Selection in the Java Code

The Java statements necessary to determine whether a checkbox has been selected or not are relatively straightforward and consist of two statements: one to obtain a reference to the checkbox and a second to check the

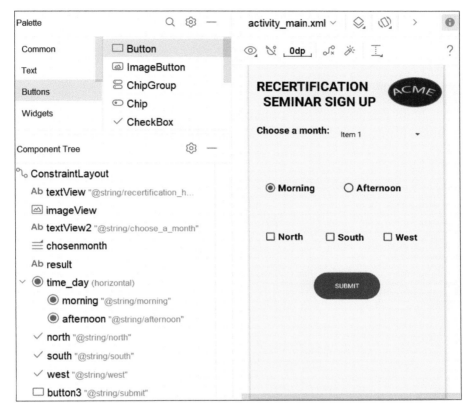

FIGURE 7.13
CheckBox widgets added to the layout.

Declared Attributes		
layout_width	109dp	
layout_height	48dp	
layout_constraintHorizontal_bias	0.092	
layout_constraintVertical_bias	0.155	
layout_constraintTop_toBottomOf	@+id/time_day	
layout_constraintBottom_toBottomOf	parent	
layout_constraintEnd_toEndOf	parent	
layout_constraintStart_toStartOf	parent	

FIGURE 7.14
Layout constraints for a widget under the Declared Attributes.

"isChecked" property value. In general terms, the two statements take the forms:

```
Checkbox checkboxVar = (Checkbox) findViewById(R.
id.checkboxId);
if (checkboxVar.isChecked) {… }
```

Applying this general syntax to our sample app, we have the following additional statements within the MainActivity.java file listed in Table 7.6.

TABLE 7.6

Java Code Processing CheckBox Input Values

MainActivity.java

```
package com.example.mpolk.chapterexampleapp;
import android.support.v7.app.AppCompatActivity;
import android.os.Bundle;
import android.view.View;
import android.widget.CheckBox;
import android.widget.RadioGroup;
import android.widget.Spinner;
import android.widget.TextView;
public class MainActivity extends AppCompatActivity {
    @Override
    protected void onCreate(Bundle savedInstanceState) {
        super.onCreate(savedInstanceState);
        setContentView(R.layout.activity_main);
    }
    public void processInput(View v) {
        Spinner monthChoice = (Spinner) findViewById(R.id.chosenmonth);
        String spinnerSelectedValue =
                monthChoice.getSelectedItem().toString();

        RadioGroup rg =
                (RadioGroup)findViewById(R.id.time_day);
        int checkedRadioButton = rg.getCheckedRadioButtonId();
        String whichRadioButton = "";
        switch(checkedRadioButton) {
            case R.id.morning :
            {
                whichRadioButton = " Morning ";
            }
            case R.id.afternoon:
            {
                whichRadioButton = " Afternoon ";
            }
        }  // end of switch
        CheckBox locationNorth = (CheckBox) findViewById(R.id.north);
        CheckBox locationSouth = (CheckBox) findViewById(R.id.south);
        CheckBox locationWest = (CheckBox) findViewById(R.id.west);
        String possibleLocations = "";
        if (locationNorth.isChecked())
            possibleLocations += "Possible location is North";
```

(Continued)

TABLE 7.6 (*Continued*)

Java Code Processing CheckBox Input Values

`MainActivity.java`

```
        if (locationSouth.isChecked()) {
            if (possibleLocations.length() ==0)
                possibleLocations += "Possible location is South ";
            else
                possibleLocations += " or South";
        }
        if (locationWest.isChecked()) {
            if (possibleLocations.length() ==0)
                possibleLocations += "Possible location is West ";
            else
                possibleLocations += " or West";
        }
        if (possibleLocations.length() == 0)
                possibleLocations = " No locations selected";
            TextView output = (TextView) findViewById(R.id.result);
            output.setText("You chose the month of " + spinnerSelectedValue
                    + " in the " + whichRadioButton  +
                    "\nand " + possibleLocations);
    }
}
```

Run the app. Make certain that all of the selection inputs are functioning correctly. Figure 7.15 provides an example of a sample run.

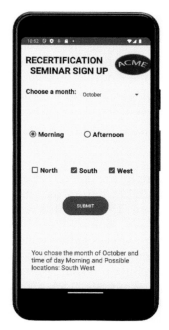

FIGURE 7.15
Sample run of app with a variety of selection inputs.

Working with Image Buttons

A possible fourth method of input selection is the image button, which is a graphical representation of an input specification. An image button can be thought of as a button that displays an image rather than text. Image buttons need not be a form of selection input since an image button can just be a more decorative representation of a submit button. But an image button can be used for input selection by providing a choice among an array of other buttons of equal status. For example, common image buttons include those displayed in Figure 7.16 and seen persistently for searching a site and linking to popular sites.

FIGURE 7.16
Common "image buttons" encountered in web activity.

To utilize your own image button in an Android app, you must complete three tasks:

1. Save the image that is to be used as a button in the appropriate *res/ drawable* folder within the Android project.
2. Drag an *ImageButton* widget from the Palette to the layout screen and select the appropriate drawable source when prompted to do so.
3. Code the *onClick* method to provide an action code sequence for the image button.

For example, in our sample annual certification app, let's replace the "SUBMIT" button with a similar button that has been prepared with the company logo imprinted on it. To utilize this custom image button, save it in the project's *res/drawable folder*. Remove the existing "SUBMIT" button that is to be replaced. Then drag an *ImageButton* widget from the "Buttons" category in the Palette panel to the layout screen as shown in Figure 7.17. When prompted, select the custom button resource. Once the new *ImageButton* has been located on the screen layout, the "Pick a Resource" dialog box shown below opens for the filename specification of the image. Select the appropriate image and click OK.

Next, with this new *ImageButton* selected, scroll down in the Attributes panel for the *ImageButton* and locate the *onClick* property. Then set its value to

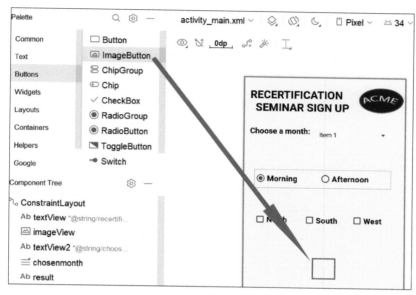

FIGURE 7.17
Replacing a button with an *ImageButton* widget.

the name of the Java method that has defined (or will define) the code statements to execute when the button is pressed. Recall in our example here that we previously coded a Java method named "processInput" to be executed when the button is pressed as illustrated in Figure 7.18.

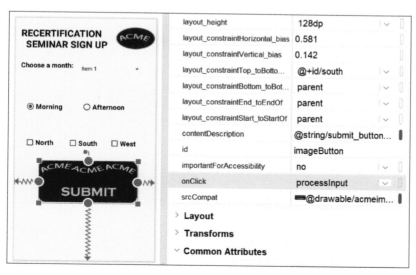

FIGURE 7.18
Setting the *onClick* property of the *ImageButton* widget.

Dynamically Altering Screen Content Beyond Text

It is often desirable to modify the screen content as an app is running. There are two popular means of doing so. One technique manipulates the visibility property of individual screen components. Another works with images to dynamically change the image source file property of an individual image component.

Modifying the Visibility Property of a Screen Component

You may have noticed by now that most of the components dragged to the activity layout have a visibility property. This visibility property has no specified value by default and can be set to "visible", "invisible", or "gone". The property can be set initially in the Attributes panel, and it can be set programmatically in Java. For example, a *TextView* component was dragged to the layout for the purposes of displaying output. The "visibility" property of this *TextView* component could be initially set to "invisible". But, when the user has specified the input values and clicks the submit button, the visibility property for this *TextView* result can be made visible when its value has been determined. To do this in Java is relatively simple as shown here.

```
TextView output = (TextView) findViewById(R.id.result);
output.setVisibility(View.VISIBLE);
output.setText("You chose the month of " +
spinnerSelectedValue
         + " in the " + whichRadioButton +
         "\nand " + possibleLocations);
```

To programmatically change the visibility property of a component, use the *setVisibility* method as shown above. The parameter specification for the method is an integer constant and it is best to use the predetermined constants *View.VISIBLE*, *View.INVISIBLE*, and *View.GONE*. The difference between *View.INVISIBLE* and *View.GONE* is that the latter removes the element completely from the layout so that it does not consume any space in the layout.

Modifying the Source File Property of a Screen Image Component

Sometimes it might be desirable to change the image held within an image container such as an image view or an image button while an app is running. To do so is relatively simple in the Java code within the activity .java file. To do so for an image view requires two Java statements. Assuming that the *id* of the image view, for example, is "myImageView", and the alternate graphic which we now wish to display is stored within the file named "*alternate_image.png*", and it has been saved in the *res/drawable* folder for the project, then just two Java statements are required, namely:

```
ImageView resetImagePicture = (ImageView) findViewById(R.
id.myImageVIew);
resetImagePicture.setImageResource(R.drawable.
alternate_image);
```

To change the image for an image button rather than an image view, the first statement above replaces *ImageView* with *ImageButton*. That is,

```
ImageButton resetImagePicture = (ImageButton)findViewById(R.
id.myImageButton);
resetImagePicture.setImageResource(R.drawable.alternate_image);
```

When Different Buttons Share the Same Method

Sometimes, especially with image buttons, two different buttons may require very similar Java code statements to affect their intents. In this case, as an efficient programmer, you may wish to code one *onClick* method and then account for the very minor differences in the button requirements within the single method, thereby sharing the very similar code. To do so necessitates that the *onClick* method be able to determine which button was clicked. This identification can actually be done using the View parameter of the *onClick* method and referencing its id property. An example illustrating how this can be accomplished is provided in a new app example.

Let's code an Android app that displays three image buttons. To keep the example as simple as possible, let's design it for a tablet device. Each image button is a picture of a certain type of duck. When the user clicks on any of these images, a short description of that particular duck is provided. To complete this example, we need images of three types of ducks that have been saved in the *res/drawables* folder for the app project. In addition, we need to define a string-array in the *res/values/strings.xml* file. We will name the array "duckinfo" and initialize it as shown in Table 7.7 (all text information is taken from *Wikipedia*).

Next, build a screen layout with three *ImageButton* widgets and one *TextView* component. The *TextView* component has *id* "displayinfo". The id's assigned to the three image buttons are "divingducks", mallards", and "woodduck". All three of these image buttons are assigned the *onClick* property value "getinfo". So, when the user clicks on any one of the duck images, the Java method named "getinfo" will execute. The logic of this method is to identify which button was clicked, retrieve its name from the string array named "duckstypes", and then retrieve its description from the string array

TABLE 7.7

Two String Arrays Set Up as Parallel Arrays

`activity_main.xml`

```
<resources>
    <string name="app_name">ExampleDynamicContent</string>
    <string-array name="ducktypes">
        <item>Diving Ducks</item>
        <item>Mallards</item>
        <item>Wood Duck</item>
    </string-array>
    <string-array name="ducksinfo">
        <item>
            The diving ducks, commonly called pochards or scaups, are a category of
            duck which feed by diving beneath the surface of the water.
            These are gregarious ducks, mainly found on fresh water or on
            estuaries, though the greater scaup becomes marine during the northern
            winter. They are strong fliers; their broad, blunt-tipped wings require
            faster wing-beats than those of many ducks and they take off with some
            difficulty. Northern species tend to be migratory.
        </item>
        <item>
            The mallard is a medium-sized waterfowl species.
            The breeding male mallard is unmistakable, with a glossy bottle-green
            head and white collar which demarcates the head from the purple-tinged
            brown breast, grey brown wings, and a pale grey belly. The rear of the
            male is black, with the dark tail having white borders. The bill of the
            male is a yellowish orange tipped with black while that of the female
            is generally darker ranging from black to mottled orange. The female
            mallard is predominantly mottled with each individual feather showing
            sharp contrast from buff to very dark brown, and has buff cheeks,
            eyebrow, throat and neck with a darker crown and eye-stripe.
        </item>
        <item>
            The wood duck is a medium-sized perching duck.
            It is about three-quarters of the length of an adult mallard.
            The adult male has distinctive multicolored iridescent plumage and red
            eyes,with a distinctive white flare down the neck. The female, less
            colorful, has a white eye-ring and a whitish throat. Both adults have
            crested heads. They usually nest in cavities in trees close to water,
            although they will take advantage of nesting boxes in wetland locations
            if available. Females line their nests with feathers and other soft
            materials, and the elevation provides some protection from predators.
            Unlike most other ducks, the wood duck has sharp claws for perching in
            trees.
        </item>
    </string-array>
</resources>
```

named "duckinfo". Java statements placed in *MainActivity.java* that affect this are shown in Table 7.8.

Run the app. Selecting the third image button of the diving ducks yields the output displayed in Figure 7.19.

Note that the order of the strings in the respective arrays is very important. They are an example of "parallel" arrays, which means that the first elements in each array are related, and the second elements in each array are related, and so on.

TABLE 7.8

One *onClick* Method for Three *ImageButton* Widgets

MainActivity.java - partial listing

```
public void getinfo(View v) {
    int arraySubscript;
    int id = v.getId(); // get the id of the button that was clicked
    if (id == R.id.divingducks) arraySubscript = 0;
    else if (id == R.id.mallards) arraySubscript = 1;
    else arraySubscript = 2;
    // now index into the two string arrays in strings.xml resources
    String[] duckGenres =
            getResources().getStringArray(R.array.ducktypes);
    String [] duckDescrips =
            getResources().getStringArray(R.array.ducksinfo);
    // set up the output display
    String displayThis = duckGenres[arraySubscript] + "\n\n" +
            duckDescrips[arraySubscript] ;
    TextView displayText = (TextView) findViewById(R.id.displayinfo);
    displayText.setText(displayThis);
}
```

FIGURE 7.19

Display from click on second *ImageButton* shared *onClick* method.

Generating Selection Input Options Dynamically

In this chapter, the selection inputs consisting of the spinner widget, radio buttons, and checkboxes were discussed with statically determined values at development time. But sometimes it may be desirable to determine the radio button options, checkbox selections, or spinner choices at run time, dynamically. For example, an app may display a list of options from a database, such as a client contacts list. This topic will therefore be revisited later in the chapter that discusses databases, and a full detailed example illustrating the loading of a spinner's options from a database will be provided. This can easily then be extended to dynamically create radio buttons and checkboxes.

Design Considerations

Multiple studies of user interface experiences have concluded that it is better in mobile apps to provide the user with the ability to specify input values using quick selection input whenever possible rather than keyboard typed input. The selection inputs discussed in this chapter consisted of the spinner control, which is Android's version of the web prevalent drop-down list, radio buttons, and checkboxes. Most people who have experienced a mobile device keyboard would wholeheartedly agree with this observation. It is still, however, important to be mindful of the spatial arrangement of selection inputs that require touch or tap in order to accommodate the size of the touch input source, such as a person's finger. As an app developer, you want to make sure that the spatial distance between touchable components is far enough to avoid accidental selection.

One experience with the display of checkboxes that can be somewhat frustrating occurs when the text color of the checkbox component is set. The color of the text associated with the checkbox will update, but the square box will remain the former color, thus not reflecting the text color change. To remedy this, set the "buttonTint" property of the checkbox to the same color as the text. The same is true for radio buttons.

As an Android developer, you may find the visual display of spinner text quite disappointing. The default font size for this text is very small. For example, when the "Annual Recertification" sample app is run, the spinner month displayed is very small as shown here. Currently, there is no text size property for the spinner control. In fact, to change the text size for the spinner displayed text, you need to specify a code sequence in the *values/styles.xml* file. This file will be discussed in more detail later in a later chapter where the topic of app themes is covered. In the meantime, if this discrepancy in spinner text size in relation to the rest of the text size on the screen proves as disturbing to you as it has to some of us, then you can use the code in Table 7.9 with some minor modifications in order to resolve this circumstance.

TABLE 7.9

Modifying the Text Style for a Spinner Widget

`res/values/styles.xml`

```
<resources>
    <style name="myspinnerItemStyle"
          parent="@android:style/Widget.Holo.DropDownItem.Spinner">
        <item name="android:textSize">24sp</item>
        <item name="android:textColor">#000000</item>
    </style>

    <style name="myspinnerDropDownItemStyle"
          parent="@android:style/Widget.Holo.DropDownItem.Spinner">
        <item name="android:textSize">30sp</item>
        <item name="android:textColor">#000000</item>
    </style>
    <!-- Base application theme. -->
    <style name="AppTheme" parent="Theme.AppCompat.Light.DarkActionBar">
        <!-- Customize your theme here. -->
        <item name="colorPrimary">@color/colorPrimary</item>
        <item name="colorPrimaryDark">@color/colorPrimaryDark</item>
        <item name="colorAccent">@color/colorAccent</item>
        <!-- For the resting Spinner style -->
        <item name="android:spinnerItemStyle">
            @style/myspinnerItemStyle
        </item>

        <!-- For each individual Spinner list item once clicked on -->
        <item name="spinnerDropDownItemStyle">
            @style/myspinnerDropDownItemStyle
        </item>

    </style>
</resources>
```

Exercises

The exercises below build the main screen for an eventual full functioning app that will be completed in later chapters. Samples images required by the app are provided for downloading. In some exercises, extensive text may be required for string arrays and have also been provided for download. You may wish to experiment with some of the different layout managers covered in Chapter 6. For this reason, the images that are available for download are meant to be screen-density-driven resources, so multiple versions of the same image have been made available where appropriate and are named descriptively. When multiple versions of the same image are made available, you will need to rename them and save them as the same named resource in the different drawable folders, as was discussed in Chapter 6. Feel free to substitute your own images in place of those provided. Be sure to specify "hints" for all input fields and content descriptions for all images.

E7.1 Begin the development of an Android app named *AttendeeLunchOrders* for a conference facility. The functionality for this app will be completed in Chapter 8. The purpose of the app is to manage lunch orders for conference participants. At the time of registration, the conference attendee is directed to use the app to order lunch from the conference facility. The conference facility staff will then utilize the app order information in order to fill the orders at lunch time with the food preparer staff at the facility.

Lunch consists of a choice of menu items and optional side dishes. The price of lunch for participants is included in the conference fee, except for the side dishes. The participant must pay for any side dish(es) selected. The extra charge for each side dish is $5.00.

The app is to consist of three screens. The first screen, or opening screen, is the most complex and will be developed in this exercise. The other two screens will be developed in Chapter 8. A logo image to be used as the background for each screen, and a sample has been provided in the online resources for this book. Since the conference facility logo color is evergreen, it should also be used as the color of the text. Make certain that the app renders attractively on both mobile phone platforms and tablets. It is left to you to decide which techniques of Chapter 6 to employ to accomplish this task.

If you are struggling with the layout for the components, note that a sample screenshot is provided online. The screen presents the user with the lunch meal options using a spinner widget to enable the user to select one of the following: Hot Dog, Pizza Slice, Hamburger, or Taco. These four choices for the spinner control are to be stored in a string-array within the *strings.xml* file. The condiments are clearly labeled checkboxes, which allows the user to select zero or more of them for no additional charge. Zero or more of the "Side dishes" can be selected for an extra charge. The side dishes are therefore presented as checkbox items. Selected side dishes are $5.00 each. A button labeled "Take My Order" will eventually (next chapter) take the user to a second screen. For now, the button will simply display the user's selections from this screen using a temporary *TextView* element added specifically for this purpose.

E7.2 Code the initial screen for a tablet app named *TicTacToeImplants* that allows a user to choose the icons used to play the game Tic Tac Toe. The functionality for this app will be completed in Chapter 8. There will be two screens eventually. The second screen will implement the game in a later assignment. The initial screen to be coded in this assignment asks the user to select the pair of icons that will be used as game markers, traditionally X's and O's. Before selecting, however, users are provided with on-demand fun factoid explanations of the selectable markers, most of which are implants. The initial screen to be coded in this assignment is meant to render on a tablet, but you should make certain that it is also functional on a mobile phone device. An idea for the layout of the initial screen components is provided online in the supplementary resources for this book. The string array of marker explanations is also available for download. When the user selects a game marker from the drop-down list and clicks an "Explain These" button, an explanation of the marker selected by the chosen radio button is to be provided. An example of such an explanation is shown in a screenshot that is provided online. The "Finalize My Choice" button will eventually (next chapter) take the user to a second screen. For now, the button will simply display the user's selections from this screen using a temporary *TextView* element added specifically for this purpose.

E7.3 Begin the development of an Android app named *TimeTravelInc*. The functionality for this app will be completed in Chapter 8. The desire to search for the legacy of our predecessors has fueled the human imagination for centuries. Vestiges of today's art, architecture, mathematics, astronomy, and even the gods we worship remain as laurels to their great triumph. And now it is your assignment to build an Android app that helps today's explorers to discover our origins. Your app will enable them to discover the great mysteries of the past by visiting their greatest sanctuaries, notably, Seven Wonders of the World. In essence, the user of this app is looking to experience time travel backward in time, and Time Travel, Inc. works to make the user travel experience so magical and awe-inspiring that he or she feels it is so. The app should render attractively on both smartphone and tablet devices. When completely coded after built upon in later chapters, this app will consist of three screens and one very simple introductory screen. The purpose of this exercise is to build the screen on which the user will select their travel preferences. The other screens will be coded in later exercises.

A sample screenshot is provided online in the supplementary resources for this book. A spinner element is to be loaded with entries from a string-array representing the "time travel" seven wonders destinations. The actual values contained in the string array can be downloaded for use and consist of seven strings: "Great Wall of China", "Colosseum in Rome", "Machu Picchu in Peru", "Chechen Itza in Mexico", "Taj Mahal in India", "Christ the Redeemer in Brazil", and "Pyramids of Giza".

There are two modes of travel represented as checkboxes labeled "Air" and "Air and Water". The checkboxes should be assigned a color consistent with the color scheme employed in the layout.

A radio button group is used to determine the duration of the trip, and the options are "4 days", "1 week", "2 weeks", or "1 month". The clickable radio buttons should be assigned the same color as that used for the color of the checkboxes.

A second radio button group is used to determine the type of travel package and will have implications for determining the cost of the trip in a future assignment. The three travel package options are "Standard", "Deluxe", or "First Class".

There are two clickable/pressable buttons. The first is labeled "MORE DETAILS" and is to appear adjacent to the spinner. The button will acquire functionality in a later assignment. The second button is an image button with text "BOOK MY TRIP!" and is to appear centered in the screen below the other UI elements. Its app operation will be determined in a later assignment, but for now when the user presses this button, the app should display the user inputs in a *TextView* that has been added temporarily for this purpose.

The background image and two sizes of *drawables* for the image button have been provided for download along with the string array of values to feed the spinner component and a sample screenshot.

E7.4 Begin the development of an Android app named *GolfScoreTracking* that can be used by a golfer to track his or her scores. The functionality of this app will be completed in Chapter 8. When completely coded after built upon in later chapters, this app will consist of three screens. The purpose of this exercise in this chapter is to build the first and most user interface (UI)-intensive screen as shown below. Make certain that the screen coded in this assignment renders attractively on both smartphone and tablet devices, using the information presented in Chapter 6. Programmatically force the screen orientation to portrait mode in the Java activity using the information provided in Chapter 6. A sample screenshot of the initial screen components and layout is provided online in the supplementary resources for this book. A sample background image, golf ball images, and button images have also been provided for download.

The first user input is an *editText* component and is provided with the hint *"Enter course name"*. The second user input is a spinner selection for the tees from which the user begins each hole of play. The choices are "Black Tees" (shown here), "Mens Tees", "Ladies Tees", and "Jr Tees". These choices are to be specified in a string-array within the *strings.xml* file and then specified as the *entries* attribute for the spinner.

There is a radio group containing two radio buttons representing the number of holes being played today. One radio button is labeled "18 holes", and the other radio button is labeled "9 holes".

Once the user has specified these three inputs, an image button is available that in future assignments will lead to the next screen. In this assignment, clicking the image button labeled with text value "RECORD MY SCORE" should simply display the user input values in a temporary *TextView* that you create for this purpose.

8

Apps with Multiple Activities

Learning Outcomes:

- ✓ *Successful programmatic movement between activities.*
- ✓ *Successful passing of information from one activity to another.*
- ✓ *Successful retrieval of information passed from another activity.*
- ✓ *Basic understanding of the lifecycle of an activity.*
- ✓ *Understanding of the declaration of app activities within the manifest file.*

An appreciation for multiple screens and the necessity to move among them within an app was established in the previous chapter. In this chapter, the mechanics for doing so is covered in detail. In the most general terms, an Android screen is presented to a user by an activity. One activity is generally specified as the "main activity". This is reflected in the naming convention

DOI: 10.1201/9781003286325-8

of the default screen layout file as *"activity_main.xml"*, the building of which has been the primary focus of the chapters thus far. The main activity generates the first screen that appears when the app is launched. This chapter focuses on the implementation of multiple screens, and thus multiple activities, within an app.

The Android Activity and Creating Activities

An Android activity is the core unit of an app. As documented in the Android Developer site, the activity functions as the entry point for the interaction of the app with the user. It generates the window in which the user interface (UI) is constructed by the app.

As has been demonstrated many times in this book, when Android Studio constructs a new project, an activity is automatically created. For the sake of simplicity, we have specified an "Empty Views Activity" as the type of activity to be generated. Every new activity created results in the production of a pair of new file additions to the project. One of the pair of files is an eXtensible Markup Language (XML) layout file for the screen representation of the activity. The second is a Java code file to manage the activity's function and lifecycle.

To demonstrate, let's create a second activity in the employee annual certification app created in the previous chapter. To create a new activity, follow the steps identified here:

1. Right-click on the app folder in the Project pane and then select *New → Activity → Empty Views Activity* as shown in Figure 8.1.

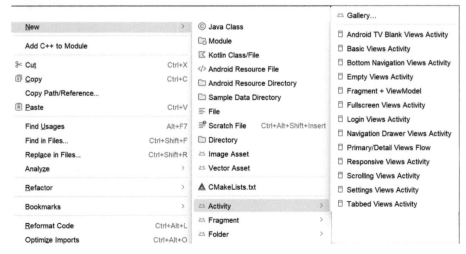

FIGURE 8.1
Adding a new activity to an app.

2. This opens the Configure Activity dialog window. By default, the second activity is named MainActivity2. This can be changed, of course, but for the sake of example, we will keep the default name. So just click the Finish button.

Looking at the app project view, it is apparent that two new files have appeared as shown in Figure 8.2. The names of the two files reflect the name indicated in the Configure Activity window that was displayed in the second step above. One of the files appears in the layout folder and is named *"activity_main2.xml"*. The other file appears in the Java folder and is named *"MainActivity2.java"*. Examining the *MainActivity2.java* file illustrates that other than the name of the activity class, "MainActivity2", the only other difference in this activity than in the original "MainActivity" is the argument in the "setContentView" method that references "activity_main2" as displayed in Figure 8.2.

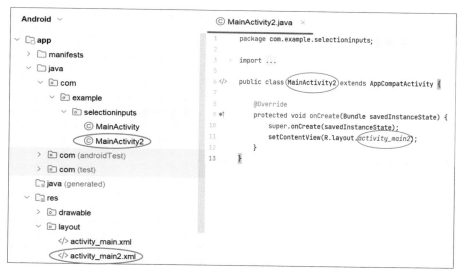

FIGURE 8.2
Second activity pair of files added to the app.

The process of creating a second activity that was described here can be used for creating a third activity, as well as any number of subsequent activities that are required by the functions and features of an app.

Run the app. Although it is the new activity file that is presently open, when the app executes, it is the original *activity_main.xml* layout that is rendered on the screen. This is because the app has a manifest file that controls what happens when the app is launched.

Activities and the Manifest File

In order for an app to use multiple activities, the activities must be declared within the app's manifest file. Within the app's folder is a folder named *manifests*. Expanding this folder in the Project view within Android Studio displays the folder contents shown in Figure 8.3. In addition, opening the *AndroidManifest.xml* file found in the *manifests* folder displays the contents shown in Figure 8.3.

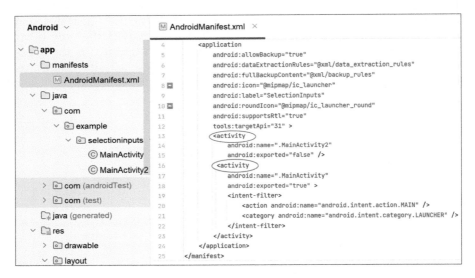

FIGURE 8.3
The *AndroidManifest.xml* file identifying all activities in the app.

We worked with this *AndroidManifest.xml* file briefly in Chapter 3 when specifying customized launcher icons for an app. The XML in this file identifies the occurrence of two *<activity>* tags. These tags distinguish two Android activities named "MainActivity" and "MainActivity2". It is important to note that these are the Java class names for the activities. Any activity not named in an activity tag within this XML file will remain unknown. Extracting the second of these activities, "MainActivity2" yields the code shown here.

```
<activity android:name=".MainActivity2">
  android:exported="false" />
```

This code identifies an activity named "MainActivity2" that can be referenced programmatically in Java code statements within the app and is referred to as an *explicit* intent.

Extracting the other of these activities, "MainActivity" yields the code shown here.

```
<activity android:name=".MainActivity">
      android:exported="true">
   <intent-filter>
      <action android:name="android.intent.action.MAIN" />
      <category android:name="android.intent.category.
      LAUNCHER" />
   </intent-filter>
</activity>
```

This code identifies an activity named "MainActivity" that can be referenced programmatically in Java code statements within the app but goes even further to associate an intent-filter with this activity. The intent filter specifies the type of implicit intents the activity accepts based on the intent's action, data, and category. The code listed above specifies an intent action and category. The action name "android.intent.action.MAIN" identifies this activity as the entry point of the app when it is launched. This specific action name is generally paired with the category named "android.intent.category. LAUNCHER",indicating that this is the activity that can be launched appearing in the app drawer of the device. The *exported* attribute specifies whether or not another app can launch the activity.

To change the launcher activity when the app is running, simply swap the activity named presently as the launch activity with the activity name that should be launched. So using our chapter example, if we wanted MainActivity2 to launch when the app is executed rather than MainActivity (*which we don't want but if we did just for example*), we would interchange the two activity names in the manifest file as shown in Table 8.1.

TABLE 8.1

Changing the Launch Activity

AndroidManifest.xml - partial code

```
   :
   :
   <activity android:name=".MainActivity">
       <intent-filter>
          <action android:name=
          "android.intent.action.MAIN" />

          <category android:name=
       "android.intent.category.LAUNCHER" />
          </intent-filter>
   </activity>
   <activity android:name=
            ".MainActivity2"></activity>
   .
   :
```

The Lifecycle of an Activity

When an activity is launched, its "onCreate" method is called. This method initializes the activity and so should be where the app developer places code required for an app's startup. The parameter specification of this method is a "Bundle", and if it is non-null, then it is used to provide values in the restoration of the activity. Such a Bundle is saved when a device orientation occurs, and the screen must be re-rendered, or at times when the app is placed in a background state. The "onCreate" method creates a window and fills it with the layout defined by the argument passed to the "setContentView" method. It is important to note that *findViewById* cannot reference the UI components in your layout until after the "setContentView" method operates on the layout. The "onCreate" method is always followed by the "onStart" method.

The "onStart" method is called when the activity is becoming visible to the user. Android uses this method to finalize the tasks required to bring the activity to the foreground to become interactive.

Android calls the "onResume" method just before the activity begins interaction with the user. Once an activity is in the foreground, it is considered to be in the "running" state. An app remains in the foreground until it loses focus, transitioning to a paused state. When this transition occurs, the Android system calls the "onPause" method.

The "onPause" method should be used by the app developer to save uncommitted program data, as discussed in a later chapter, and the system may use it for this purpose as well, especially target platforms running a version of the Android operating system prior to version 3.0, Honeycomb. Version 3.0 and later versions can safely do so in the "onStop" method. The UI of an activity in the paused state may continue to update, as the activity is still partially visible. The next method called when an activity has entered the paused state will be either the "onResume" method discussed above or the "onStop" method.

The "onStop" method is called by the system when the activity is no longer visible to the user. This method is followed by a call to the "onRestart" method if the user navigates back to the activity. Otherwise, if the system needs to destroy the activity or if the activity has been terminated, a call is made to the "onDestroy" method.

The "onRestart" method restores the state of the activity from the time at which it was stopped. Once the restoration occurs, a call is made to the "onStart" method discussed above.

The "onDestroy" method is the last method called within the activity. Its purpose is to release the resources of the activity before it is destroyed.

As an app developer, it is important to be familiar with the Android activity lifecycle. If it becomes relevant to add code to any of the methods described above, you will want to be sure to call the method's super class, as illustrated in the default "onCreate" method provided in every new activity.

Moving between Activities within an App

We can create several activities corresponding to several UI layouts, but by default only the main activity is ever called, consequently displaying only the main activity layout. For a second screen to be displayed, we will need to add appropriate Java code to the main activity. To illustrate, let's return to the annual recertification sample app created in Chapter 7, the main screen for which is displayed in Figure 8.4. At present, a main activity layout presents a screen for an employee user of the app to request recertification training in a chosen month, at a chosen time of day, with an option to specify preferred locations. The screen layout as rendered on a mobile phone device is displayed in Figure 8.4 for the purpose of review.

FIGURE 8.4
Revisiting the app begun in the previous chapter.

A second activity named *MainActivity2* was previously created earlier in this chapter. As previously noted, this resulted in the creation of two files. One file is named *MainActivity2.java*. There will be no changes to this file.

The second file is named *activity_main2.xml*. A UI layout will be created here for the sole purpose of thanking the employee for providing information, with an additional note that further seminar offering information will be forthcoming. So, add a *TextView* component and an *ImageView* component to the second activity screen named *activity_main2.xml*. The *TextView* component is to be assigned a string reflecting the message of thanks, and the *ImageView* component is to display the company logo. Thus, the only modification we will make for the second activity is to the layout in the *activity_main2.xml* file as displayed in Figure 8.5.

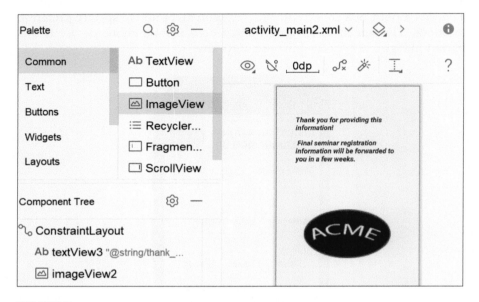

FIGURE 8.5
The layout for the second activity.

Now, in order for this screen to be displayed after the app user enters information on the first screen and then clicks the Submit button, we need to change the *onClick* action for the main activity "Submit" button so that it will transition the user to the second activity screen.

To do so, return to *MainActivity.java*, the <u>original</u> activity, and comment out the code that we added in the previous chapter to the *onClick* method named "processInput". We are commenting out the code because in the next section, we will use it in a different manner. After the commented-out code, add the two Java statements highlighted in Figure 8.6.

After typing "Intent nextActivity", the *Alt+Enter* prompt illustrated in Figure 8.6 will appear indicating the requirement to add the import statement for the *Intent* class, so just heed it.

Recall that the *MainActivity2* was declared in the manifest file as an activity that can be referenced programmatically in Java code statements within

```
public class MainActivity extends AppCompatActivity {
    @Override
    protected void onCreate(Bundle savedInstanceState) {
        super.onCreate(savedInstanceState);
        setContentView(R.layout.activity_main);
    }

    public void processInput(View v) {
/* COMMENTING OUT THE PREVIOUSLY CODED STATEMENTS -- TEMPORARILY
        Spinner monthChoice = (Spinner) findViewById(R.id.chosenmonth);
        String spinnerSelectedValue =
                            monthChoice.getSelectedItem().toString();
        .
        .
        .
    */
            // need to move onto the next activity screen:
? android.content.Intent? Alt+Enter

        Intent nextActivity = new Intent(this,MainActivity2.class);
        startActivity(nextActivity);
    }
}
```

FIGURE 8.6
Defining an *Intent* for transfer to another activity.

the app. Remember that this was referred to as an explicit *intent*. The first of the highlighted Java statements in Figure 8.6 is defining the explicit *Intent* and assigning it an identifier name of "nextActivity". The second highlighted Java statement is invoking the *startActivity* method and passing to it the "nextActivity" *Intent* object, which launches the *MainActivity2* in our app.

We need not code any additional statements within the *MainActivity2.java* file in this example. Relaunch the app. Upon clicking on the "Submit" button on the initial screen, the second activity should be started, and its UI layout should display.

So, moving from one activity to another activity, or from one screen to another screen, is relatively simple consisting of just two Java code statements. In general, these Java statements are as follows:

1. *Intent someIntent = new Intent(this, MoveToActivity.class);*
2. *startActivity(someIntent);*

Now that we know how to move between activities, let's discuss how we can pass information from one activity to the other as we move.

Passing Information between Two Activities within an App

There are a few ways of passing information from one activity to another, but the easiest technique is to use the *putExtra* method to add extended data to the *Intent* object created to make the transition. Then on the receiving side, the use of a version of the *getExtra* method is relatively straightforward. You can code as many *putExtra* method calls and *getExtra* type methods as is needed to pass and receive information.

Passing Scalar Information between Activities

On the sending side, the general syntax of the *putExtra* method is as follows:

```
intentObject.putExtra(key, value);
```

It is easiest if both key and value are of string type. On the receiving side, it is important to make certain that the retrieved *Intent* instance is non-null prior to retrieving the extended data. So, on the receiving side, it is relatively easy to use the *getStringExtra* method after making this check, the general syntax of which is provided in Table 8.2.

TABLE 8.2

Java Code for Retrieving String Data Passed to an Activity

```
Intent intentObject = getIntent();
if (intentObject!= null) {
// list all relevant getString Extra method calls here
String val1 = intentObject.getStringExtra("keyspec");
String val2 = intentObject.getStringExtra("key2spec");
...
}
```

For example, let's add a new activity to our sample annual recertification app. But let's name this new activity "VerifyInput". So right-click on the *app* folder in the Project pane and select *New → Activity → Empty View Activity*, then name it "VerifyInput". The purpose of this new activity is to serve as a check on the user input prior to the thank you message of the *MainActivity2* coded in the previous section. So, the original *MainActivity* will pass the user input to this new *VerifyInput* activity. It in turn will ask the user to verify the input and then give the user the choice of two buttons. One button will be labeled "REVISE INPUT" and will send the user back to the input screen. The other button labeled "INPUT CONFIRMED" will send the user to the thank you screen defined by *MainActivity2* as created in the previous section. Figure 8.7 provides a look at the layout for the *VerifyInput* activity.

Along with the two *TextView* components addressing the user input information that has been passed from the previous activity, *ImageView* and *TextView* highlighting the month input selection have been added to add a little interesting aspect to the screen. The *ImageView* will display an appropriate image to reflect the user's month selection from the previous screen. Image files have been supplied for the project and are *.png* files,

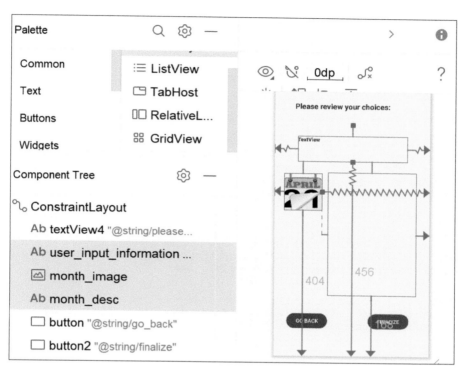

FIGURE 8.7
The layout for a third activity.

named after each of the possible months. Choose any of the *.png* files for the initial image.

The adjacent *TextView* component will display some fun factoids for the month selected. A *string-array* has been provided for the project, consisting of fun factoids for each of the possible month selections.

Two buttons are provided to the user for the purpose of moving back to the previous screen in order to change the input, or to move forward to the next screen, finalizing the input values.

In order to populate this activity screen layout with run-time content, it needs to be "called" by the first activity named *MainActivity* which along with the call forwards its data content.

So, before adding the necessary Java statements to the new activity *VerifyInput.java*, we need to add the statements to *MainActivity.java* that will pass the user information to the *VerifyInput* activity. The statements that we need to add to *MainActivity.java* include statements to create an *Intent*, statements to "putExtra" input items from the *activity_main.xml* layout, and then the statement required to call the *VerifyInput* activity. These necessary statements are highlighted in Table 8.3.

TABLE 8.3

Get User Input Data and Transfer the Data and Control to Another Activity

MainActivity.java

```java
package com.example.chapterexampleapp;

import androidx.appcompat.app.AppCompatActivity;

import android.content.Intent;
import android.os.Bundle;
import android.view.View;
import android.widget.CheckBox;
import android.widget.RadioGroup;
import android.widget.Spinner;
import android.widget.TextView;

public class MainActivity extends AppCompatActivity {

    @Override
    protected void onCreate(Bundle savedInstanceState) {
        super.onCreate(savedInstanceState);
        setContentView(R.layout.activity_main);
    }
public void processInput(View v) {
    Spinner monthChoice = (Spinner) findViewById(R.id.chosenmonth);
    String spinnerSelectedValue =
            monthChoice.getSelectedItem().toString();

    RadioGroup rg =
            (RadioGroup)findViewById(R.id.time_day);
    int checkedRadioButton = rg.getCheckedRadioButtonId();
    String whichRadioButton = "";
    if (checkedRadioButton == R.id.morning) {
        whichRadioButton = " Morning ";
        }
    else if (checkedRadioButton == R.id.afternoon) {
        whichRadioButton = " Afternoon ";
        }

    CheckBox locationNorth = (CheckBox) findViewById(R.id.north);
    CheckBox locationSouth = (CheckBox) findViewById(R.id.south);
    CheckBox locationWest = (CheckBox) findViewById(R.id.west);
    String possibleLocations = "";
    if (locationNorth.isChecked())
        possibleLocations += "Possible location is North";
    if (locationSouth.isChecked()) {
        if (possibleLocations.length() ==0)
            possibleLocations += "Possible location is South ";
        else
            possibleLocations += " or South";
    }
    if (locationWest.isChecked()) {
        if (possibleLocations.length() ==0)
            possibleLocations += "Possible location is West ";
        else
            possibleLocations += " or West";
    }
```

(Continued)

TABLE 8.3 (*Continued*)

Get User Input Data and Transfer the Data and Control to Another Activity

`MainActivity.java`

```
if (possibleLocations.length() == 0)
    possibleLocations = " No locations selected";

TextView output = (TextView) findViewById(R.id.result);
output.setVisibility(View.VISIBLE);
output.setText("You chose the month of " + spinnerSelectedValue
        + " in the " + whichRadioButton
        + "\nand " + possibleLocations
);

// So we now have the user input and need to
// pass it to the VerifyInput activity
// So first, create the Intent:
Intent nextActivity = new Intent(this,VerifyInput.class);
// Next add any data to be passed"
nextActivity.putExtra("monthname",spinnerSelectedValue);
nextActivity.putExtra("timeofday",whichRadioButton);
nextActivity.putExtra("locations",possibleLocations);
//move onto the VerifyInput activity:
startActivity(nextActivity);
    }
}
```

Now that the *MainActivity* is passing the user input to the *VerifyInput* activity, the statements to receive and decipher this input information can be added to the *VerifyInput.java* code. Basically, an *Intent* object must be created and after checking to ensure that nothing went wrong and it is not null, the data sent must be extracted, using in this example the "getStringExtra" method of the intent object. These statements are highlighted in the coded *VerifyInput.java* file listed in Table 8.4. The highlighted code is followed by code that utilizes the retrieved extended data to produce the desired output results.

A sample run of this code is presented in Figure 8.8.

And finally, we need to add functionality to the buttons in the *VerifyInput* layout. So, we code the method for the "GO BACK" button's *onClick* method which will be named "goback". And we code the method for the "FINALIZE" button whose *onClick* method will be named "finalize". The first button returns the user to the previously coded *MainActivity* input screen, and the second button moves the user onto the previously *MainActivity2* final screen. Neither of these transitions is to pass any extended data. Be sure to set the *onClick* property of each button to the appropriately named method.

TABLE 8.4

Retrieve the Data Passed from Another Activity

VerifyInput.java

```
package com.example.chapterexampleapp;

import androidx.appcompat.app.AppCompatActivity;
import android.content.Intent;
import android.os.Bundle;
import android.widget.ImageView;
import android.widget.TextView;

public class VerifyInput extends AppCompatActivity {
    @Override
    protected void onCreate(Bundle savedInstanceState) {
        super.onCreate(savedInstanceState);
        setContentView(R.layout.activity_verify_input);

        Intent intentObject = getIntent();
        if (intentObject != null) {
            // get the extended data elements passed from MainActivity
            String monthSelection = intentObject.getStringExtra("monthname");
            String timeofdaySelection = intentObject.getStringExtra("timeofday");
            String selectedLocations = intentObject.getStringExtra("locations");
            //now use this information in this activity to achieve its goals
            // We need to display this info and then display an image and text for
            //    the specific month selected
            String buildDisplayText = "You have selected the month of "
                    + monthSelection + " preferring the " + timeofdaySelection
                    + " time of day "
                    + selectedLocations;
            TextView displayText = (TextView)
                                    findViewById(R.id.user_input_information);
            displayText.setText(buildDisplayText);
            // Now just to make the screen content a little more interesting,
            // we need to use the user month selection to retrieve the image
            // file to display
            // and the fun factoids specific to the selected month as well
            // So to display an image file for the user selected month
            // we need to construct the filename for the drawable resource:
            String imagefilename = monthSelection.toLowerCase();
            ImageView myimage = (ImageView) findViewById(R.id.month_image);
            int xid = getResources().getIdentifier(getPackageName() + ":drawable/"
                    + imagefilename, null, null);
            myimage.setImageResource(xid);

            // And adjacent to the image we wish to display the fun factoid's about
            // the selected month that have been stored in a string-array.
            // We can use the displacement of the month
            // in the course_months array as a subscript into the string-array
            // The course_months array was used in MainActivity to load the spinner
            String [] monthsArray = getResources().getStringArray
                    (R.array.seminar_months);
            String [] monthFacts = getResources().getStringArray
                    (R.array.monthfacts);
            TextView funfactoids = (TextView) findViewById(R.id.month_desc);
            for (int i=0; i<monthsArray.length; i++) {
                if (monthsArray[i].equals(monthSelection)) {
                    funfactoids.setText(monthFacts[i]);
                }
            }}}}
```

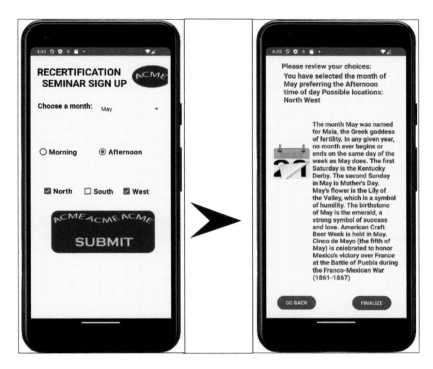

FIGURE 8.8
Sample run of the app showing the effects of data and control transfer.

The two Java *onClick* methods in the *VerifyInput.java* file consist of the code provided in Table 8.5.

Passing a Java Array of Information to an Activity

It is sometimes necessary to pass an array of information from one activity to another. For example, if our annual certification app example prompted the user for specific dates in a month rather simply the month, then it would be necessary to send the list of dates to the *VerifyInput* activity along with the other information that is presently transferred. An array of information is passed in an identical manner as was followed with the passing of simple scalar values. In fact, it is impossible to tell the difference in the *putExtra* method call. For example, the following passes an array to the *VerifyInput* activity, which is not obvious in this code, except for the named variable *selectedDatesArray*:

```
Intent nextAct = new Intent(this,VerifyInput.class);
nextAct.putExtra("selecteddates", selectedDatesArray);
```

On the receiving side, in the *VerifyInput* activity, however, the retrieval code is different from that of the scalar *getStringExtra* method previously used. To retrieve the values in the transferred array, assuming that the selected dates are integers and that *userDates* has been declared as a Java array, we retrieve the extras as a bundle and then extract the array from the bundle as shown here.

```
Bundle extras = getIntent().getExtras();
userDates = extras.getIntArray("selecteddates");
```

In addition to *getIntArray*, the *Bundle* class has methods for *getStringArray* and *getDoubleArray* as well.

Additional Considerations

Tangential to the activity topic of the chapter, we also saw how to dynamically construct an image file name from a string variable, and then to retrieve the image file for display purposes. As this was the first time doing so, it seems worthwhile to go over this code in some detail.

The drawable resources to be displayed for the user's month selection are *.png* files named after the month (*drawable/march.png, drawable/april.png*, etc.). The first of the statements that accomplish the task of displaying the month image converts the user's month selection retrieved from the spinner component to all lowercase. This is done because the spinner control lists the month choices as "March", "April", "May", "June", "October", and "November". But all resources in an Android *apk* must be specified in lowercase.

```
String imagefilename = monthSelection.toLowerCase();
```

The next statement retrieves the reference to the imageview that will eventually display the specific month drawing:

```
ImageView myimage = (ImageView) findViewById(R.id.monthimage);
```

Then, we retrieve the pointer to the actual file identified in the app's *drawable* folder within the *apk* that is named as dictated by the "imagefilename" string variable, and finally, assign this file resource to the *ImageView* using its resource *id*:

```
int xid = getResources().getIdentifier(getPackageName() +
        ":drawable/"
        + imagefilename, null, null);
myimage.setImageResource(xid);
```

Exercises

The exercises below build on the initial app screens developed in the exercises in Chapter 7. We are now adding additional screens to these apps to take a step further toward the implementation of attractive and completely functional apps. Later chapters build on these exercises to accommodate persistent data, databases, and web server information where appropriate. Be sure to specify "hints" for all input fields and content descriptions for all images.

E8.1 Continue the development of the Android app named *AttendeeLunchOrders* for which one activity was created in Exercise E7.1, toward an app that will eventually manage lunch orders for conference participants at a conference facility. The activity created in Chapter 7 presented the luncheon menu to the user that included some optional side dishes. It was previously mentioned but becomes more important now that the price of lunch for participants is included in the conference fee, except for the side dishes. The participant must pay for any side dish(es) selected. The extra charge for each side dish is $5.00. In this exercise, modify the button labeled "TAKE MY ORDER" so that when clicked, it now sends the user to a second activity that is created as part of this exercise.

The screen created by the new activity is to prompt the user for a conference registration code, explain the importance of this code, and summarize the user's order information together with any amount owed for the extra side dishes. In addition, two mutually exclusive radio buttons are to prompt the user for "cash" or "charge" ONLY IF there is an amount owed. A screenshot is provided online in the supplementary resources for this book to provide an example of what the second screen (MainActivity2) is to display, given the selected input on the first screen.

Two buttons are to be provided at the bottom of this new screen. One button is labeled "CHANGE MY ORDER", and when clicked, it sends the user back to the order screen. The other button is labeled "FINALIZE MY ORDER" and is to send the user to a third activity provided that the user has entered a registrant code. Prior to sending the user to the third activity named "FinalizeOrder", pass the registrant code, main dish selection, chosen condiments and extras, if any, and the computed extra charge due along with the display info through the intent (*this may seem excessive at this time, but this app could be expanded in later chapters to record this information in a database, and it will be easier to do so if the pieces are as itemized*).

If no registrant code has been entered and if the "FINALIZE MY ORDER" button is clicked, the user should remain with this screen, but a message should be displayed in red indicating that the registrant code must be entered.

The third activity should be named "FinalizeOrder" and from the information passed from the second activity will state "Thank you for your order", the details of the order, and if there is a charge for any extra side dishes, a message stating that "a cash (or charge depending on the user input specification) payment of $x is due upon delivery".

In addition, underneath this order summary are to be displayed an *ImageView* component and a *TextView* component. The *ImageView* is to display the image named for the selected main dish. A *"place-holder.png"* image has also been supplied for the initial setup of the layout. All image files are of size 250 px by 207 px. Download some royalty-free images to use for the different meal selections. The *TextView* component is to display a fun factoid of information regarding the specific main dish selection. A string-array has been provided for download that contains this fun factoid information.

A sample screen for the "FinalizeOrder" activity is provided online in the supplementary resources for this book. The two new screens (referenced as MainActivity2 and FinalizeMyOrder) added in this exercise are to use the same background, text colors, and text sizes as were used in Exercise 7.1 for the first screen. Note that a *ScrollView* may be necessary on a mobile smartphone, especially in the case of the finalize order screen layout.

E8.2 Continue the development of the Android app named *TicTacToeImplants* for which one activity was created in Exercise E7.2. The activity previously created allowed a user to choose a pair of icons to be used as markers in the game Tic Tac Toe. A screenshot is provided online to review that the pairs of markers are provided in a spinner control and explained prior to final selection as a game marker.

In this chapter's exercise, the second screen is to be implemented to support the play of the game. So, after the user chooses the pair of icons and then clicks the "FINALIZE MY CHOICE" button, the user is to be moved to a new screen that presents the 3 × 3 grid layout of a Tic Tac Toe board. In so doing, the first activity will pass the user chosen pair of icons to the new activity named "PlayGame". The new screen layout associated with the "PlayGame" activity is to force **landscape** orientation. The 3 × 3 layout is composed of *ImageButtons*. All image buttons are to specify the same *onClick* method. Initially all image buttons are sourced with the image *"blanksquarepc.png"*. An initial message signaling that the "human" player is to go first is displayed. A sample screenshot is provided online in the supplementary resources for this book to provide clarity on the layout components in this activity.

As the game is played, the blank square gets replaced with the player piece as determined by the user selected icons as explained above. Simply put, the user selected radio button on the initial screen is the user's game piece and the other icon in the pair is the computer's game piece. The icons used on the initial screen are too large to be game pieces, so another set of icons is available for download for this purpose. These icons are named the same except that there is a "pc" concatenated prior to the *.png* suffix. So, for example, the brain implant icon shown on the initial screen is named *"brainimplant.png"*, so if chosen in the pair as a marker on the *activity_play_game.xml* screen, the image named *"brainimplantpc.png"* should be used as the human player marker, and it is just a smaller version of the image displayed on the initial screen. The other image in the pair, in this case the "External device" in its smaller version, becomes the computer player marker.

The game of Tic Tac Toe is played with the human player clicking on one of the available squares and the computer alternately taking its turn until either one of the player wins, or the game results in a tie (which is called "cats"). Sample screenshots have been provided online in the supplementary resources for this book to illustrate a game that ends in "Cats" and a game that ends in a "Loss".

E8.3 Continue the development of the app named *TimeTravelInc* for which you began development in Exercise E7.3 in Chapter 7. In the exercise here, three screens and associated activities are to be added. To place these new activities and their sponsored screens in perspective, a reminder of the screen developed in Exercise 7.3 is provided online in the supplementary resources for this book. The app should render attractively on both smartphone and tablet devices, and it would be wise to utilize a *ScrollView* container in the layouts.

To review the first screen layout developed in Exercise E7.3, the spinner element is loaded with entries from a string-array representing the "time travel" seven wonders destinations. The actual values contained in the string array can be downloaded for use and consist of seven strings: "Great Wall of China", "Colosseum in Rome", "Machu Picchu in Peru", "Chechen Itza in Mexico", "Taj Mahal in India", "Christ the Redeemer in Brazil", and "Pyramids of Giza". There are two modes of travel represented as checkboxes labeled "Air" and "Air and Water". A radio button group is used to determine the duration of the trip, and a second radio button group is used to determine the type of travel package. There are two clickable/pressable buttons that are now to be given actions.

The first button labeled "MORE DETAILS", when clicked is to transfer the user to a new screen and corresponding activity. This new screen provides details and an image matching the spinner selected choice of destination. Sample images and the text details are available for download, as is a sample screenshot illustrating the layout requirements for this new screen. A button labeled "BACK" is present that returns the user back to the original screen.

The second button on the original screen is an image button with the text "BOOK MY TRIP". When clicked, it is to transfer the user to a third activity that summarizes the trip details selected by the user and provides a total cost for the booking of the trip. The cost is to be calculated according to the prices in Table 8.5. A screenshot of a sample run illustrating the content of this third activity is provided online in the supplementary resources for this book.

TABLE 8.5

Costs to Be Computed for Travel in Exercise 8.3

PACKAGES:	
Standard	$3000
Deluxe	$5000
First Class	$7000
MODE OF TRAVEL:	
Air	No extra charge and is assumed to be the default if the user does not select the Air or Air and Water checkboxes
Air and Water	Additional charge of $2500
DURATION:	
Four days	Default – no extra charge
More than 4 days	Extra charge of $400 a day after the first 4 days

* Assume that a month is 28 days for this purpose

The last new activity, the fourth activity in total, to be created in this exercise is the introductory screen, which consists of two text components and a button. The button is labeled "take off" and transfers the user to the original screen created in Exercise 7.3. Note that you will need to change the launch screen in the *AndroidManifest.xml* file to set this activity as the new launch activity. A screenshot illustrating an example for the screen layout of this activity is provided online.

E8.4 Continue the development of the Android app named *GolfScoreTracking* for which an initial screen was developed in Exercise 7.4 in Chapter 7, which can be used by a golfer to track his or her scores. An example to review the content of this initial screen is provided online in the supplementary resources for this book.

The temporary *TextView* previously created can now be deleted. Once the user has specified the three inputs, the image button labeled "RECORD MY SCORE" transfers the user to a new screen, identified by the new "ScoreEachHole" activity.

The new screen associated with the "ScoreEachHole" activity, defined in the file named *"activity_score_each_hole.xml"*, should display the course name and tee selection sent from the previous screen and is used to score each hole played. Note that this same screen records the scores for **every** hole played. The current hole number is displayed, and inputs are requested from the user for the total number of strokes scored for the hole and the number of putts that contributed to this score (golfers often keep track of putts in addition to total strokes). Two image buttons for moving the user between holes are to be made available on this screen layout, with one exception. A left arrow image is to indicate a "back" button, and a right arrow image is to indicate a next button. The next button is also to be labeled "RECORD MY SCORE". When displaying the prompts for the first hole obviously, there is no previous hole, and so this is an exception where there should be no back button. Sample screenshots illustrating the content for the first hole and that for subsequent holes are provided online in the supplementary resources for this book.

Your code must be able to recognize when the right arrow has been pressed on the last hole (18 or 9) in which case the user is transferred to the third activity. This third activity, "GameOver" with associated layout *activity_game_over.xml*, provides the user with a detail and summary of scores and putts as shown below. This activity is to force a landscape orientation. The "ScoreEachHole" activity will need to pass the information to be displayed via an intent as discussed in this chapter. A final screen for scores and putts recorded for each hole is displayed along with a total for each quantity as well. A sample screenshot to illustrate this content is provided online.

Note that there are only three activities in this app. The scoring for each hole is done in only one activity.

9

Saving App Data with Shared Preferences

Learning Outcomes:

- ✓ *Basic understanding of persistent storage.*
- ✓ *An understanding of Android shared preferences.*
- ✓ *Successful programmatic storage of shared preferences using the Editor class.*
- ✓ *Successful programmatic retrieval of shared preferences.*
- ✓ *Successful removal of shared preferences information.*
- ✓ *Understanding the device storage location of shared preferences information.*

The apps we have created this far execute without memory of past usage. For example, when indicating training preferences in the *recertification* sample app in the previous chapter, a user may have specified a "West" location in the morning as the preferred location and time of day. Why would an app require that a user specify this preference every subsequent time

 DOI: 10.1201/9781003286325-9

the app executes? Why not provide these preferences as default choices to improve the user experience?

In the apps developed in previous chapters, there is no history maintained before the app is closed. So, each time the app is executed, prior user choices are unavailable, as are all previous records that might be helpful to provide a consistent user experience.

In this chapter, we look at remedying the loss of information when an app closes. In order to save information associated with an app so that it is still available when the app terminates or when the device loses power, we make use of a feature called *persistent storage*.

What Is Persistent Storage?

Persistent storage refers to memory that retains its contents when an app closes or when a device loses its power. Persistent data persists even when the device is powered off. Disk storage is an example of persistent storage. There are several methods for implementing Android persistent storage, including device memory reserved for shared preferences, native databases, or simple files. This chapter focuses on the use of "shared preferences" for implementing persistent storage.

Android "shared preferences" refers to the device storage of an eXtensible Markup Language (XML) file where small amounts of primitive data are stored as *key-value* pairs. Primitive data refers to values identified as Java primitive types including *string, int, float*, and *Boolean*. Shared preference data is stored in the appropriate app's data folder on the mobile device.

In addition to shared preferences, persistent data can be stored in databases. Android native databases are SQLite databases. SQLite is a lightweight self-contained SQL database engine that is a component of Android OS and is "baked into" the Android runtime. SQLite is popular among mobile devices of many vendors as it has a very small footprint and yet supports SQL as a database standard. SQLite Android native databases are discussed in the next chapter.

Saving and Retrieving Android Shared Preferences

Shared preferences are values that have been associated with identifying "keys". The value representing a shared preference must be of a primitive type, which means that it must be either a string, or an integer, or a logical value or a decimal number. The key that is associated with the primitive value must be a string. So, for example, the string value "Joe Doe" could be associated with the key "name", and the integer value 1990 could be associated with the key "yearborn". Key-value pairs are saved and retrieved as shared preferences using the Android *SharedPreferences* API and *Editor* class.

Shared Preferences API and the Editor Class

A *SharedPreferences Editor* object is obtained by invoking the *getSharedPreferences edit* method. Once this object instance is created, its methods may be used to store the actual shared preferences data. Tracing these steps identifies the following tasks:

1. Define the shared preferences filename and location on the Android device:

   String spf = getPackageName() + "prefs";

2. Obtain a *SharedPreferences* object instance and associate it with a physical file on the device. In addition, specify the access rights to the data:

   SharedPreferences sp = getSharedPreferences(spf, MODE_PRIVATE);

3. Create an *Editor* instance in order to write shared preferences to the file:

   SharedPreferences.Editor myEditor = sp.edit();

Table 9.1 lists the "put" methods of the *Editor* instance that can be used to set up the key-value pairs in the file.

TABLE 9.1

The Various "put" Methods Available for Shared Preference Storage

`putString("key", "value")`	identifies a *String* value for later retrieval using key
`putInt("key",value)`	identifies an integer value for later retrieval using key
`putLong("key", value)`	identifies a long integer value for later retrieval using key
`putFloat ("key", value)`	identifies a value with a fractional portion for later retrieval using key
`putBoolean("key",value)`	identifies a *Boolean* value (true or false) for later retrieval using key

Table 9.2 lists some examples of key-value pairs that may be stored as shared preferences.

TABLE 9.2

Examples of "put" Methods for Storing a Variety of Types of Values

`myEditor.putString("firstname", "Joe")`	identifies "Joe" as the string value for the key "firstname"
`myEditor.putInt("favyear", 2018)`	identifies 2018 as the integer value for the key "favyear"
`myEditor.putLong("ID", 123456789)`	identifies 123456789 as the long integer value for the key "ID"
`myEditor.putFloat("amtdue",(float) 19.35)` **OR** `myEditor.putFloat("amtdue", 19.35f)`	identifies 19.35 as the float value for the key "amtdue"
`myEditor.putBoolean("member", true);`	identifies `true` as the logical value for the key "member"

Note in the previous explanation, the word "identifies" is used for the association of a value for a key. The word "identifies" is used rather than "save". This is because the methods "set up" key-value pair(s), but they are not saved until they are "committed". In order for the key-value pairs to actually be stored in the file, a "commit" type of method of the *Editor* must be used. For example:

myEditor.commit();

The *commit* method of the *Editor* class writes the data to the device storage immediately and returns a value of *true* to indicate success or *false* to indicate failure. There is an *apply()* method that commits the data to the in-memory *SharedPreferences* object immediately but starts an asynchronous commit to disk, meaning that the changes may not necessarily be written to the device storage immediately, so the return from the method is faster, and the UI is therefore more responsive.

The *remove* method is used to set up the deletion of a key-value pair from the *SharedPreferences* object. For example:

myEditor.remove("firstname");

To set up the removal of all key-value pairs, use the *clear()* method:

myEditor.clear();

And in all cases, do not forget to *commit*() or *apply*() the changes.

Retrieving Information from Shared Preferences

On the other side, to retrieve the information stored as a key-value pair, we need to use the *getSharedPreferences* function and then specify the appropriate key type using a get method. The *get-key-type* methods supply the key as the first method parameter and a default value of the appropriate type as the second parameter. The methods available to do this include those displayed in Table 9.3.

TABLE 9.3

Examples of "get" Methods for Retrieving Shared Preference Values

getString("key", default_value_spec)	"key" is actually a *String* value used in a corresponding "putString"
getInt("key", default_value_spec)	
getFloat("key", default_value_spec)	*default_value_spec* is a default value to be assigned if no shared preference is found
getBoolean("key", default_value_spec)	
getLong("key", default_value_spec)	

You can also determine if a shared preference exists, using the *contains* method. For example:

```
contains("key")
```

The *contains* method returns *true* if a key-value pair exists for this specified "key" parameter value. This method also belongs to the *SharedPreferences* class rather than the *Editor* class and is used in this way:

```
SharedPreferences sp = getSharedPreferences(spf,MODE_PRIVATE);
if (sp.contains("username") {
        String usern = sp.getString("username", "");  ...
```

Working with Stored Shared Preferences

As stated, "Shared Preferences" are key-value pairs stored in an XML file as a means of tracking primitive data belonging to one or more apps. Data that is meant to be global to an app or is meant to persist across sessions are examples of shared preferences. Specific examples of such data might be text size adjustments made within an app or selected color schemes, or in the case of some game apps, a best score to date, or a player's avatar selection.

Android stores shared preferences data in an XML file in a folder on the Android device under the *"data/data/{application package}"* directory. For example, considering an app named *SharedPrefsDemo* developed later in the chapter, the folder path is */data/data/com.example.sharedprefsdemo,* and the file is named *sharedprefsdemoprefs.xml*. Note that the filename must be unique and so should be named in accordance with the app package name.

Android Studio provides a *Device Explorer* tool that can be used to examine the files stored on an Android physical device or within a virtual Android emulator device. The only requirement is that the physical device be connected, or in the case of an Android emulator, the virtual Android emulator device be running when the file structure is examined.

To open the Android *Device Explorer* tool, click *View* → *Tool Windows* → *Device Explorer*. Then simply navigate to *data/data/{application package}* as illustrated in Figure 9.1 where the application has package named *com.example. sharedprefsdemo* and a file named *com.example.sharedprefsdemoprefs.xml* in the *shared_prefs* subfolder of the app.

Device Explorer				⋮ —
Pixel 3a API 34 Android 14.0 ("UpsideDownCake")				⌄
Files Processes				
▶️ ↓ ↥ 🗑 ↻				
Name		Permissio...	Date	Size
⌄ ▢ com.example.sharedprefsdemo		drwxrwx--x	2023-12-18 13:21	4 KB
› ▢ cache		drwxrws--x	2023-12-28 11:32	4 KB
› ▢ code_cache		drwxrws--x	2023-12-28 11:32	4 KB
⌄ ▢ shared_prefs		drwxrwx--x	2023-12-28 11:45	4 KB
	‹/› com.example.sharedprefsdemoprefs.xml	-rw-rw----	2023-12-28 11:45	273 B
› ▢ com.google.android.adservices.api		drwxrwx--x	2023-12-18 13:21	4 KB

FIGURE 9.1
File locations for the app including for the shared preferences values.

Saving Shared Preferences as String Values

Sometimes, it is preferable to store the data as type string even when the data is a numeric or Boolean value, and then convert it when it is required for an arithmetic or logical operation. This can be advantageous when the data is primarily or most frequently used for display purposes or record-keeping. The advantages include general app performance benefits and simplified coding since display of any data value requires conversion to text string assignment in a layout widget.

An additional advantage to storing and retrieving saved preferences as string data is associated with the exception handling of corrupted data or the input of data mistakenly of an incorrect type. In such cases, it is wise to make use of *try/catch* exception handling to surround the explicit conversion of the string value to that of a numeric or Boolean type.

Saving an Array of Values as Shared Preferences

In some cases, it may be desirable to store an array of values as a shared preference. To do so generally involves saving the array of values as a delimited string value. While you may choose to hard code the delimited values to build the string, an alternative means is to use the *Gson* library with a Java *ArrayList*.

Employing an *ArrayList* with Google *Gson* at this time requires that a dependency for *Gson* be added to the *build.gradle* file within the app. Specifically, the dependency highlighted below should be added to the dependencies section in the *build.gradle* file.

```
dependencies {
        implementation 'com.google.code.gson:gson:2.8.5'     }
```

Be sure to "Sync" the project after making any additions or changes to the *build.gradle* file.

Shared Preferences Code Example

The code in Tables 9.4 and 9.5 illustrates a sample use of shared preferences between two activities in an app. This sample app is just a test version of code that will be incorporated into a larger app. Currently, the app consists of two simplified activities. The first activity enables the user to store two shared preferences consisting of a single name as a string and a single year as an integer, the code for which is supplied in Table 9.4. The second activity simply displays the shared preference data that has been stored by the first activity, and the code for retrieving these values is included in Table 9.5.

TABLE 9.4

Sample Code for Storing a Username String and Birth Year Value as Shared Preferences

MainActivity.java

```java
// Simple example to share two shared preferences within this app
package com.example.sharedpreferencesdemo;
import androidx.appcompat.app.AppCompatActivity;
import android.content.Intent;
import android.content.SharedPreferences;
import android.os.Bundle;
import android.view.View;
import android.widget.EditText;

public class MainActivity extends AppCompatActivity {

    @Override
    protected void onCreate(Bundle savedInstanceState) {
        super.onCreate(savedInstanceState);
        setContentView(R.layout.activity_main);
    }
```

(Continued)

TABLE 9.4 *(Continued)*

Sample Code for Storing a Username String and Birth Year Value as Shared Preferences

MainActivity.java

```java
public void save_prefs(View v) {
    // data can come from anywhere hardcode for now
    String spfile = getPackageName() + "prefs";
    SharedPreferences sp = getSharedPreferences(spfile, MODE_PRIVATE);
    // create an Editor object to write info to this file
    SharedPreferences.Editor myEditor = sp.edit();

    // get the input
    EditText name_input = (EditText) findViewById(R.id.user_name);
    String users_name = name_input.getText().toString();
    EditText year = (EditText) findViewById(R.id.birth_year);
    String year_val = year.getText().toString();
    int year_born = Integer.parseInt(year_val);

    // Save the string name and the integer year as shared preferences
    myEditor.putString("name", users_name);
    myEditor.putInt("yearborn", year_born);
    myEditor.commit();
}
public void move_next(View v) {
    Intent secondAct = new Intent(this,MainActivity2.class);
    startActivity(secondAct);
}
}
```

TABLE 9.5

Sample Code for Retrieving a Username and Birth Year as Shared Preferences Data

MainActivity2.java

```java
// Simple example to retrieve two shared preferences within this app
package com.example.sharedpreferencesdemo;
import androidx.appcompat.app.AppCompatActivity;
import android.content.SharedPreferences;
import android.os.Bundle;
import android.widget.TextView;

public class MainActivity2 extends AppCompatActivity {

    @Override
    protected void onCreate(Bundle savedInstanceState) {
        super.onCreate(savedInstanceState);
        setContentView(R.layout.activity_main2);

        // retrieve shared preference data and display it
        TextView tv = (TextView) findViewById(R.id.display_data);
        String spf = getPackageName() + "prefs";
        SharedPreferences sp = getSharedPreferences(spf,MODE_PRIVATE);
        String usern = sp.getString("name", "");
        int year = sp.getInt("yearborn",0);
        tv.setText(usern + "   " + year);
    }
}
```

A sample run of this application is illustrated in Figure 9.2. In the first activity, the username and year of birth are solicited as input, and then each is stored as a shared preference. Then in the second activity, this data is retrieved and displayed. Once the shared preferences are saved, they can also be retrieved in later runs of the same app on the same device.

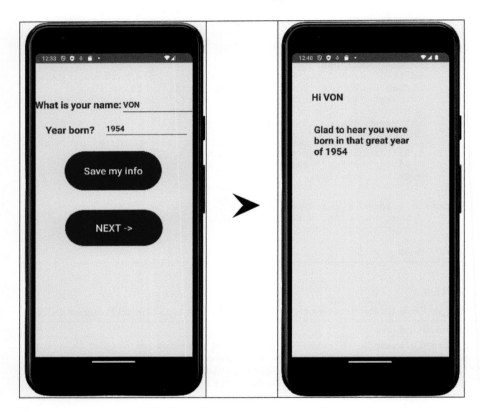

FIGURE 9.2
Sample run illustrating retrieval of shared preferences.

Design Considerations

Shared preferences can be a quick and simple way to store a small amount of data for use within an app or a set of apps. As a method of saving information, it yields better performance for storing and retrieving app data than does a database, when storing a limited number of items. These are situations where a database would be overkill. It is not, however, a particularly wise choice for the storage of a large amount of data.

When a large amount of data is to be stored for an app, a database is a much better solution. Another disadvantage of shared preferences is the requirement that the developer knows the exact key under which the value has been stored as well as its type.

The examples discussed in this chapter employ *MODE_PRIVATE*. There are two additional modes that can be specified as an alternative. The alternatives are *MODE_APPEND* and *MODE_PUBLIC*.

If the app referencing stored information requires any level of search facility or aggregate reporting, the database method of data storage and retrieval is the choice to be made over the option of shared preferences. Android database storage is the topic of the next chapter.

Exercises

The exercises below are scaled to accommodate a weekly schedule. Each can easily be expanded upon to achieve a lengthier exercise if needed or multiple assignments can be designated for more advanced skill sets. Sample images are available for download but can easily be substituted with any appropriate images. The assignments are also designed for adaptation to navigation views activities in later chapters. Be sure to specify "hints" for all input fields and content descriptions for all images.

E9.1 Add an avatar option to your previous homework, or a previous chapter exercise app. Add a new screen to the app that permits the user to select from one of four avatar images. Once selected, this avatar image is to appear in the top left corner or top right corner of every screen within the app. A change avatar button should also be provided within the app that takes the user back to the new screen for avatar selection. The selected avatar option is to be stored as a shared preference for the app. A set of avatar images is available for download, or you can create your own.

E9.2 Create a new app for a user who wishes to keep track of friends' birthdays. The initial activity for this app displays a welcome screen explaining the purpose of the app and its use. It includes two buttons. One button reads "DISPLAY FRIENDS", and the other button displays "ADD A FRIEND". An idea of this initial screen is provided online in the supplementary resources for this book.

The button that reads "DISPLAY FRIENDS" is to transfer the user to a second activity. This second activity displays a list of all friends stored as shared preferences for this app. This information is presented as a list of names and corresponding birthday dates. Of course, this list is empty until the user adds information. It is recommended that the count of the friends presently stored also be stored as a shared preference. It is recommended that a scroll feature be employed in the layout. At the end of this listing is a button labeled "BACK" that is to return the user to the initial screen. A sample screenshot for this content is provided online in the supplementary resources for this book.

A third activity is responsible for adding new friends as shared preference data. The user reaches this activity from the welcome screen when clicking the button labeled "DISPLAY FRIENDS". On the third screen are input fields for the name of a friend and the string representing a birthday month and day combination. When the user clicks the "Save information" button, this new friend information is stored. It is advised that a counter should be incremented as stored as a shared preference as well. There is a second button present that enables the user to return to the main activity's welcome screen. There is a sample screenshot indicating how this third screen layout may be organized provided online.

E9.3 (A little more advanced skills required) Create a new app for a grandmother who wishes to keep track of her grandchildren's favorite ice cream flavors. The initial activity for this app displays a welcome screen explaining the purpose of the app and its use. It includes three buttons. The first button reads "LIST ALL SWEETIES", the second button displays "ADD A SWEETIE", and the third button is labeled "CHANGE A SWEETIE". An idea of this initial screen is provided in a sample screenshot online in the supplementary resources for this book.

The button which reads "LIST ALL SWEETIES" is to transfer the user to a second activity. This second activity displays a list of the favorite flavors for each appropriate grandchild's name known to date. Of course, this list is empty until grandma adds the information. It is recommended that the number of grandchildren stored to date is also stored as a shared preference to facilitate the management of this list. It is also recommended that a scroll feature be employed in the layout as grandma might have many grandchildren to track. At the end of this listing is a button labeled "BACK" that is to return the user to the initial screen. An idea as to how to organize the content of this screen is provided in a sample screenshot online in the supplementary resources for this book.

A third activity is to add the information for a grandchild to those stored as shared preferences. The information stored in shared preferences consists of the name of the grandchild and their corresponding favorite flavor of ice cream. It is recommended that the count of grandchildren be updated and stored whenever a grandchild is added to the list. In addition to the input fields for the grandchild's name and favorite flavor, there is also a button labeled "BACK" so that the user can be returned to the main screen after adding the grandchild information. An idea as to how to organize the content of this screen is provided in a sample screenshot online.

The fourth activity enables the user to change the favorite flavor of one of the grandchildren's shared preference values. A spinner is provided to present a drop-down list of the stored grandchildren's names. Loading this spinner with information that has been stored as shared preferences will most likely necessitate the use of a Java "ArrayList" and "ArrayAdapter". A "BACK" button is also provided to return the user to the main screen when this task has been accomplished or aborted. Make certain to update the grandchild's favorite flavor as an update to the appropriate shared preference. An idea as to how to organize the content of this screen is provided in a sample screenshot online.

E9.4 Enhance exercise E8.2 in the previous chapter so that the pair of icons selected by the user for the game image buttons is stored in shared preferences. However, you must also modify the app so that if such a shared preference is stored, then the app automatically uses the shared preferences pair of icons but also provides a facility for the user to change the shared preferences.

In addition, keep track of the user's winning percentage (i.e. number of wins divided by total games played) as a shared preference that is displayed on the final screen for the game.

E9.5 Enhance exercise E8.4 in the previous chapter so that the user's minimum score for each hole played on a specific golf course is saved as a shared preference. Keep in mind that the specific golf course name is important in this preservation. Also maintain a minimum score for the entire golf game for the specific course as a shared preference as well. Add a "row" of information to the final screen that lists the minimum scores to date for each hole played on the course, as well as the minimum total score to date for the course.

10

Android Native Databases as Persistent Storage

Learning Outcomes:

- ✓ *Identification of import statements required for database use.*
- ✓ *Knowledge of an app's file and folder structure on a device or AVD.*
- ✓ *Successful creation of a database within an app.*
- ✓ *Successful use of SQL to create a table within a database.*
- ✓ *Successful addition of new records to a database table.*

DOI: 10.1201/9781003286325-10

✓ *Awareness of the advantages of using a try/catch structure with database operations.*
✓ *Successful creation of a record set from a database table.*
✓ *Successful traversal of a record set in Java.*

In our last chapter, we made use of persistent storage using a feature called "Shared Preferences". It was noted that the best use of shared preferences is for the saving of a handful of data elements or a homogeneous set of items. It becomes quite cumbersome and performance compromising, however, to store many different values as shared preferences information.

It is far more appropriate to store heterogeneous data elements in a database, especially when the data elements are logically related as records. Examples of records would include data values collectively describing a student, or an employee, or a sales transaction, or even an exercise activity. Databases facilitate not only record keeping but also record retrieval and reporting. Android provides support for native database usage within apps.

Android Native Databases

Android native databases are implemented as either SQLite databases or ORMLite data banks. We will work with SQLite databases in this chapter because they are more versatile and well-known even outside of Android, for example, in iOS and Windows.

SQLite is a server-less relational database management system that is incorporated into the Android operating environment and is embedded in the Android runtime environment. Server-less means that it doesn't need a different server process or system to operate. It has a very small footprint which makes it ideal for supporting mobile database applications. SQLite is an open-source library, cross-platform DBMS which, as was already mentioned, means that it can run on a wide variety of platforms. Database operations are SQL-based and are therefore compatible with the standard skills possessed by SQL users and database administrators.

ORMLite is based on a Lightweight Object Relational Mapper (ORM) package that serves as a wrapper around a database rather than serving as a database management system itself. While ORM can simplify programming with the use of function calls, it is limited in the types and sophistication of queries that can be typically used to retrieve desired kernels of information.

Overview of SQLite Databases in Android

An Android app can create a new database to support its operation or can utilize a previously created SQLite database. To reference an existing database, the database must be installed within the app as detailed below. In the discussion that follows, we will first look at the steps required to make an existing database accessible within an app before exploring apps that support the creation and maintenance of a database and its components. All such tasks make use of library packages that must be imported into an app and will include native methods and SQL operations.

There are many excellent books describing the design and intricacies of database design and development which should be consulted, since this topic of database design is beyond the scope of this book. Although not covered here, the author acknowledges that proper database design and analysis are essential to ensure the maximization of data integrity and the minimization of data redundancy. Such design and consideration require the use of substantiated practices, including modeling and normalization. Recognizing this import, the databases constructed and utilized in this text are overly simplified and consist of only a single table. In this chapter, we will focus on database support within an app and will use SQLite to create our databases and store and manage their information.

The java code required to work with a database within an Android app *activity* must include the following *import* statements:

➢ `import android.database.Cursor;`
➢ `import android.database.sqlite.SQLiteDatabase;`
➢ `import android.database.sqlite.SQLiteException;`

Installing a Database within an App

There are several reasons as to why an app may want or need to utilize a previously created database. Perhaps the database is an SQLite database that was created by a different Android app or maybe even an iOS app. Or it may be the case that the database was created by an SQLite user or program operating on a completely different platform, perhaps independent of an actual application.

In any case, it is possible to install an existing SQLite database within an app running on a physical Android device or a virtual Android emulator. It is necessary that the app be installed on the device prior to installing the database, so that the appropriate folder structure exists for the app. This folder and file structure can be confirmed using the Android Studio *Device Explorer* in a similar way to that which was previously explored in the implementation of shared preferences.

An SQLite database used within an Android app should be in the folder path given by *data/data/app_package_name/databases/*. The "databases" folder need not be named such; in fact, any valid name can be used successfully. But the convention is to use the name "databases" as it is most descriptive and well-recognized. A pre-existing database can be installed at this file location by using the *Device Explorer* in the Android Studio environment when a device is connected or when the emulator device is running. To open the Device *Explorer* tool, click *View* → *Tool Windows* → *Device Explorer*.

Then navigate to the folder location specified by the path *data/data/app_package_name/*. If there is no *databases* subfolder present, create it by right-clicking on the *app_package_name* subfolder and selecting "New" and then "Directory". Then enter "databases" in response to the dialog window prompt for a new folder name as shown in Figure 10.1.

FIGURE 10.1
Creating a subfolder for the database within the app file structure.

Creating a Database within an App

In simplest terms, a database consists of one or more tables. Most database-driven applications require the creation of a database within the app itself. Database data manipulation is done at the table level. A table consists of records. A record consists of fields that are also referred to as attributes. An attribute is a single data value. The records of the table are referred to as rows and the fields as columns. Table 10.1 provides an example of a very simple database table. The first row of the table identifies the name of each field. Each column is a distinct field.

TABLE 10.1

Example of a Simple Database Table

Table: Birthdays				
FirstName	**LastName**	**BirthMonth**	**BirthDay**	**FavoriteColor**
Elle	Vator	5	16	Fuchsia
Sean	Nee	8	11	Blue
Sara	Ross	9	9	Pink
Mike	Taylor	8	2	Black
Xavier	Wang	9	21	Blue

Prior to adding records to the database or retrieving records from the database, the database must be created if it does not exist, or simply opened if it does exist by specifying these statements:

```
1. SQLiteDatabase myDB = null;
2. myDB = openOrCreateDatabase("name.db",MODE _ PRIVATE, null);
```

where "name.db" is the name of the database file and can alternatively be qualified with the suffix *.sqlite* as in "name.sqlite", or with the suffix *.sql* as in "name.sql". The specification of *MODE_PRIVATE* is the default mode and is short for *Context.MODE_PRIVATE*. This indicates that the database can only be used by the current application, as was also the case with shared preferences in the previous chapter.

The third parameter specifies something called a "cursor factory" which is set to "null" for our purposes because we will use the standard *SQLiteCursor* object to manage data retrieval from databases within our apps. Loosely speaking, this cursor serves as a type of record set pointer, and we will refine this concept later.

Creating a New Table within an SQLite Database

After the database file is created, one or more tables of data must be created and added to the database. A table is conceptually defined as a series of rows of data for which specific field or attribute values are defined as the columns. This requires that we identify a name for the table as well as names for each of the data items that comprise the columns. Table 10.1 illustrated how a simple table might be organized. In Table 10.1, there are five fields of information. The names of the fields are important, but also of importance is the type of data each field can contain. This type must be strictly defined. Table 10.2 identifies the data type for each field initially identified in Table 10.1.

TABLE 10.2

Defining Table Fields

Table: Birthdays	
Field Name	**Field Type**
FirstName	VARCHAR
LastName	VARCHAR
BirthMonth	INT
BirthDay	INT
FavoriteColor	VARCHAR

To create a table in our database, we utilize the SQL "CREATE TABLE" operation. The general form of this statement is syntactically specified as:

```
CREATE TABLE IF NOT EXISTS tableName
(Field₁Name Field₁Type, Field₂Name Field₂Type,...);
```

To create the table displayed in Table 10.1, as an example, requires the coding of two Java statements. The first statement is the identification of the SQL operation required to create the table with the appropriate columns. The second statement is an SQLite statement to execute the SQL operation. To create the table displayed in Table 10.1 and further defined in Table 10.2 requires the Java statements:

```
1. String sql = "CREATE TABLE IF NOT EXISTS Birthdays (FirstName
   VARCHAR,
   Lastname VARCHAR, BirthMonth INT, BirthDay INT, FavoriteColor
   VARCHAR);" ;
2. myDB.execSQL(sql);
```

Once the database and table are created, data records can be added to the table.

Adding Records to an SQLite Database Table

Adding data to an SQLite database table requires the use of the SQL "INSERT INTO" statement. When using this SQL operation, the data should be added as a complete row of information. The order of the field data supplied does not matter when the field names are also supplied in this operation. However, it is very important to adhere to the defined datatype for the field when supplying a value. This necessitates the use of quotes for both text and character data, and the omission of quotes when specifying numeric values.

The general syntax for the SQL "INSERT INTO" statement is as follows.

```
INSERT INTO tableName (Field₁Name, Field₂Name, …)
VALUES (valueFor Field₁, valueFor Field₂, …);
```

So, to add a new record for a friend named Bea Sting born on May 8 to the table displayed in Table 10.1, we would specify two Java statements as a pair:

```
1. String sql2 = "INSERT INTO Birthdays   " +
   "(FirstName, LastName, BirthMonth, BirthDay, FavoriteColor)" +
   "VALUES ('Bea', 'Sting', 5, 8, 'Light Blue');"   ;
2. myDB.execSQL(sql2);
```

Note the importance of matching the values in the "VALUES" parenthesized expression with the order of fields enumerated in the first set of parenthesized field names. Also of importance is the use of the single quotes to enclose the text values.

The Advantages of a "try/catch" Structure and Remember to Close

So many different aspects of working with a database can be problematic that it is usually advantageous to enclose database operations with a Java "try/catch" structure. Just to consider a few errors that can occur, think about what happens if the database does not exist, or if a text value is not enclosed in quotes in an insert operation, or if the name of a table is misspelled. Given the extensive opportunity for errors to occur, there is a facility for capturing SQL exceptions. In general, the database operations are placed in a *try* block, and the *catch* block is set up to handle any exception that is triggered. Table 10.3 illustrates how a "try/catch" structure can be set up to gracefully handle any database operation exceptions that may occur.

TABLE 10.3

Sample Code Creating a Database and a Table Using a Try/Catch Structure

MainActivity.java

```java
import android.database.Cursor;
import android.database.sqlite.SQLiteDatabase;
import android.database.sqlite.SQLiteException;
import ...

public class MainActivity extends AppCompatActivity {
    @Override
    protected void onCreate(Bundle savedInstanceState) {
        super.onCreate(savedInstanceState);
        setContentView(R.layout.activity_main);
    }

  public void addbook(View v)
  {
    SQLiteDatabase myDB= null;
    String TableName = "booksimple";
    String insertSQL = "OOO";
    TextView r = (TextView) findViewById(R.id.result);
    /* Create the Database if it does not exist. */
    try {
        myDB =   openOrCreateDatabase("simplebooks1.
        db",MODE_PRIVATE,null);
        /* Create a Table in the Database. */
        myDB.execSQL("CREATE TABLE IF NOT EXISTS "
                    + TableName
                    + " (Title VARCHAR, "
                    + "Author VARCHAR, "
                    + "Year INT);" )

    /* add the new book to the database - not checking for duplicates */
            EditText titlein = (EditText) findViewById(R.id.booktitle);
            String bTitle = titlein.getText().toString();
            EditText authorin = (EditText) findViewById(R.
            id.bookauthor);
            String bAuthor = authorin.getText().toString();
            EditText yearInput =
                            (EditText) findViewById(R.
                            id.yearpublished);
            String userInput = yearInput.getText().toString();
            int bYear = Integer.parseInt(userInput);

            insertSQL = "INSERT INTO "
                    + TableName
                    + " (Title, Author,  Year)"
                    + " VALUES ('" + bTitle + "', '" + bAuthor +
                        "'," + bYear +  ");" ;
            myDB.execSQL(insertSQL);
            myDB.close();
        }
        catch (SQLiteException e)
            {r.setText(r.getText()+"Problem  adding to the database!"
                        +insertSQL);
        };
    }
}
```

Table 10.3 also includes a very important operation we did not yet discuss, namely the "close" operation. It is necessary to close the database so that future database operations can continue in the app, since create and insert operations tend to lock database access by code elsewhere in the app.

Accessing the Data in an SQLite Database

In order to retrieve data from a database, the import statements previously identified must be included in the appropriate activity *.java* file. Then the database must be opened for access, and an SQL statement to "SELECT" the desired information to load it into a record set must be executed. This is the first time in this chapter that we are using these operations so we will examine each of them closely. The use of a record set for handling the retrieved data is also examined.

Opening an Existing Database

When it is known that a database exists, the statements that should be used to access it involve the "openDatabase" SQL operation. The general syntax for the code to open a database for data retrieval is provided here:

```
SQLiteDatabase myDB = SQLiteDatabase.openDatabase("/data/data/" +
    getPackageName() + "/databases/name_of_database", null,
    SQLiteDatabase.OPEN_READONLY);
```

If the database does not exist, an exception is triggered. Therefore, it is wise to place the open operation in a *try* block with exception handling facilitated by the matching *catch* block.

Retrieving Data from a Database Table

Data is retrieved from an SQLite database using the SQL "SELECT" statement. It is possible to capture data for all of the fields for all of the records in a table, or a subset of fields for all of the records, or a subset of records. Which of the variety of options enacted is dependent upon the form of the SELECT statement. A full treatment of the SQL SELECT statement is beyond the scope of this book. But a brief examination of each of the most popular options is considered in the discussion that follows.

For the data to be retrieved by any SELECT statement in an app, the SELECT statement is passed to a method named "rawQuery" which returns the data in a "Cursor" object. The advantage of a "Cursor" object, also referred to as a "record set" or a "result set", is that the data is organized as a sequence of records with data access controlled one record at a time. In addition, the means of accessing the data in the individual fields of a single record is specified with a relative index, beginning with zero. This is further explained in the examples that follow. Conceptually, it may help to think of a record set as a "mini table".

The simplest form of the SQL SELECT statement retrieves the data found in all of the fields in all of the records. The data retrieved is placed in a record set that can then be processed record-by-record in a loop. For example, the following pair of statements will retrieve the data identified in Table 10.1.

```
1. String sql = "SELECT * FROM Birthdays";
2. Cursor record_set = myDB.rawQuery(sql, null);
```

The asterisk in the SELECT operation is a shorthand way to specify all fields without having to name each of them individually in a list. It is important to note that the data returned for each record will be in the order in which the fields in the table were specified when the table was first created. If a listing of the information returned in the record set is desired, the Java code displayed in Table 10.4 will prepare such a listing for output.

TABLE 10.4

Sample Code Retrieving the Database Table Matching Table 10.1

```
// display each record retrieved from the database
// by walking through the record set
if (crs.moveToFirst()) {
    // the database has at least one record
    do {
        dbInfo += crs.getString(0)  // since FirstName defined as VARCHAR
            + " " +                 // and was the first field defined so 0
            crs.getString(1)        // since LastName defined as VARCHAR
            + " " +                 // and was the second field defined so 1
            crs.getInt(2)           // since BirthMonth defined as INT
            + " " +                 // and was the third field defined so 2
            crs.getInt(3)           // since BirthDay defined as INT
            + " " +                 // and was the fourth field defined so 3
            crs.getString(4)        // FavoriteColor was defined as VARCHAR
            + "\n\n";               // and was the fifth field defined so 4
    } while (crs.moveToNext());
```

As a different example, let's say that we desire to simply list the first names and birthday months of the friends in the "Birthdays" table matching the table identified in Table 10.1. The pair of Java statements that retrieves only this information consists of the following:

```
1. String sql = "SELECT FirstName, BirthMonth FROM Birthdays";
2. Cursor record_set = myDB.rawQuery(sql, null);
```

The data record set that is obtained from these statements is presented in Table 10.5 and is prepared for an eventual output listing by the Java code provided in Table 10.6.

TABLE 10.5

Record Set Obtained from *"SELECT FirstName, BirthMonth FROM Birthdays"*;

Elle	5
Sean	8
Sara	9
Mike	8
Xavier	9
Bea	5

TABLE 10.6

Sample Code Retrieving the Data Presented in Table 10.5

```
// display each record retrieved from the database
// by walking through the record set
if (crs.moveToFirst()) {
    // the database has at least one record
    do {

        dbInfo += crs.getString(0) // since FirstName defined as VARCHAR
            + " " +                // and was the first field in the SELECT
            crs.getInt(1)          // since BirthMonth defined as INT
            + "\n\n";              // and was the second field in the SELECT

    } while (crs.moveToNext());
```

In our last example in this discussion, we will filter records and return from the "Birthdays" table the first names of those who were born in the month of September. The pair of Java statements that retrieves only these individuals consists of the following:

1. `String sql = "SELECT FirstName FROM Birthdays WHERE BirthMonth = 9";`
2. `Cursor record _ set = myDB.rawQuery(sql, null);`

The record set data that is obtained from these statements is presented in Table 10.7 and is prepared for an eventual output listing by the Java code provided in Table 10.8.

TABLE 10.7

Record Set Matching the First Names of People Born in September

Sara

Xavier

There are numerous other examples of filtered data that can be obtained from a table. The precise data retrieved from a database table is defined by the SQL SELECT statement as has been demonstrated by the examples. It is noteworthy to keep in mind that the "get" method used to retrieve a particular field within a record from the record set must match the field type, and the

TABLE 10.8

Sample Code Retrieving the Data Presented in Table 10.7

```
// display each record retrieved from the database
// by walking through the record set
if (crs.moveToFirst()) {
    // the database has at least one record
    do {
        dbInfo += crs.getString(0)  // since FirstName defined as VARCHAR
               + "\n\n";            // and the only field in the SELECT

    } while (crs.moveToNext());
```

specified index parameter supplied in the "get" must correspond to the order specified in the actual SELECT statement, with the count beginning at zero.

Again, it is wise to specify the code covered in this section within a "try/catch" block. Table 10.9 provides a comprehensive listing of a simple app that provides a single screen layout with database operations for the "Birthdays" table schema we have used in this chapter. The screen layout includes three buttons as illustrated in Figure 10.2. One button adds a new friend to the

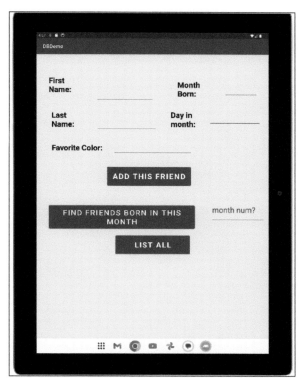

FIGURE 10.2
Putting it all together in a single activity.

TABLE 10.9

Code to Create a Database and a Table, Add Records to a Table, and List Records

MainActivity.java

```java
package com.example.dbdemo;

import androidx.appcompat.app.AppCompatActivity;
import android.database.Cursor;
import android.database.sqlite.SQLiteDatabase;
import android.database.sqlite.SQLiteException;
import android.os.Bundle;
import android.view.View;
import android.widget.EditText;
import android.widget.TextView;

public class MainActivity extends AppCompatActivity {
    @Override
    protected void onCreate(Bundle savedInstanceState) {
        super.onCreate(savedInstanceState);
        setContentView(R.layout.activity_main);
    }

    public void addfriend(View v)
    {
        SQLiteDatabase myDB= null;
        String TableName = "Birthdays";
        String insertSQL = "";
        TextView r = (TextView) findViewById(R.id.result);
        /* Create the Database if it does not exist. */
        try {
            myDB = openOrCreateDatabase
                ("FriendsAndBirthdays.db",MODE_PRIVATE,null);
            /* Create a Table in the Database. */
            myDB.execSQL("CREATE TABLE IF NOT EXISTS "
                + TableName
                + " (FirstName VARCHAR, " +
                "Lastname VARCHAR, " +
                "BirthMonth INT, " +
                "BirthDay INT, " +
                "FavoriteColor VARCHAR);" );
            /* add new friend to the db - not checking for duplicates */
            EditText fnamein = (EditText) findViewById(R.id.firstname);
            String fname = fnamein.getText().toString();
            EditText lnamein = (EditText) findViewById(R.id.lastname);
            String lname = lnamein.getText().toString();
            EditText monthInput = (EditText) findViewById(R.id.monthborn);
            String userInput = monthInput.getText().toString();
            int bMonth = Integer.parseInt(userInput);
            EditText dayInput = (EditText) findViewById(R.id.dayborn);
            String dInput = dayInput.getText().toString();
            int bDay = Integer.parseInt(dInput);
            EditText favcin = (EditText) findViewById(R.id.favcolor);
            String favcolor = favcin.getText().toString();
            r.setText("got here 3");
```

(Continued)

TABLE 10.9 *(Continued)*

Code to Create a Database and a Table, Add Records to a Table, and List Records

MainActivity.java

```
        insertSQL = "INSERT INTO " + TableName
            + " (FirstName,LastName,BirthMonth,BirthDay,FavoriteColor)"
                + " VALUES ('" + fname + "', '" + lname + "',"
                + bMonth + "," + bDay + ",'" + favcolor + "');" ;
        myDB.execSQL(insertSQL);
        myDB.close();
    }
    catch (SQLiteException e) {
        r.setText("Problem  adding to the database!");
    };
}

    public void displayall(View v) {
        String dbInfo="";  // using to concatenate the db records
        TextView list = (TextView) findViewById(R.id.result);

        try {
            SQLiteDatabase myDB = SQLiteDatabase.openDatabase(
                    "/data/data/" + getPackageName() +
                    "/databases/FriendsAndBirthdays.db",
                    null,
                    SQLiteDatabase.OPEN_READONLY);

            String q = "SELECT * FROM Birthdays;";
            Cursor crs = myDB.rawQuery(q, null);

            if (crs.moveToFirst()) {
                // ok the database has at least one record

                do {
                    dbInfo += crs.getString(0) + "  " +
                            crs.getString(1) + " " +
                            crs.getInt(2) +  " " +
                            crs.getInt(3) +  " " +
                            crs.getString(4) +  "\n\n ";
                } while (crs.moveToNext());
                myDB.close();
            }

        } catch (SQLiteException e) {
            dbInfo += "database does NOT exist yet."; }

        list.setText(dbInfo);
    }
    public void findfriend(View v) {
        EditText monthinput = (EditText) findViewById(R.id.whichmonth);
        String bmonth = monthinput.getText().toString();

        String sql =
"Select FirstName, LastName, BirthDay From Birthdays Where BirthMonth = "
        + bmonth + ";";
```

(Continued)

TABLE 10.9 *(Continued)*

Code to Create a Database and a Table, Add Records to a Table, and List Records

MainActivity.java

```java
        String dbInfo="No Friends born this month";  // Assume no
        matching
        TextView list = (TextView) findViewById(R.id.result);
        try
        {
            SQLiteDatabase myDB = SQLiteDatabase.openDatabase(
                    "/data/data/" + getPackageName() +
                    "/databases/FriendsAndBirthdays.db",
                    null,
                    SQLiteDatabase.OPEN_READONLY);

            Cursor crs = myDB.rawQuery(sql, null);

            if (crs.moveToFirst()) {
                // ok the database has at least one record
                dbInfo = "Friends born in this month:";
                do {
                    dbInfo += crs.getString(0) + " " +
                            crs.getString(1) + " " +
                            crs.getInt(2) +  "\n\n ";
                } while (crs.moveToNext());
                myDB.close();
            }

        } catch (SQLiteException e) {
            dbInfo += "Something went wrong here :("; }

    list.setText(dbInfo);
    }
}
```

database table using the input fields provided. A second button lists all friend information presently stored in the database table. And a third button displays the names of the friends born in a certain month and lists the day in the month on which they were born.

Note that we would not normally place all of this functionality with inputs on one screen layout. We would also make the screen much more attractive. We are providing only "bare bones" here in an effort to present the code as one comprehensive listing.

Removing Records from an SQLite Database

To delete records from an SQLite database, use the SQL DELETE operation. This operation will delete all records or a subset of records. Consult an SQL source for more information as this can be a dangerous operation if all records are accidentally deleted.

Loading a Spinner Widget with Database Information

Database information is often used to present choices to users. For example, if a user app maintains contact information and one of the features of the app is an ability to change the addressing information for a contact, it is much more efficient and secure to present a drop-down list of contact names from which the user can select. As detailed in previous chapters, the spinner widget provides such a drop-down list of options. Would it not be most efficient to load the spinner entries with the information that already exists in a database table maintained by the app?

For example, a database table contains a list of lunch menu items, from which a user may select. The name of the database is "lunch.sql". The name of the table within the database is "entrees", and one of the fields is named "maindish". A spinner widget has been defined in a layout and assigned the id "spinner_entree". Table 10.10 lists the Java code required to load the

TABLE 10.10

Code to Fill a Spinner with Data from a Database Table

```
try {
    SQLiteDatabase myDB = SQLiteDatabase.openDatabase(
            "/data/data/" + getPackageName() + "/databases/
            lunch.db",
            null,
            SQLiteDatabase.OPEN_READONLY);
    String q = "SELECT * FROM entrees;";
    Cursor crs = myDB.rawQuery(q, null);
    Spinner spinner = findViewById(R.id.spinner_entree);
    ArrayList<String> arrayList = new ArrayList<>();
    String dbdish = "";
    if (crs.moveToFirst()) {
        // ok the database has at least one record

        do {
            dbdish = crs.getString(0);
            arrayList.add(dbdish);
        } while (crs.moveToNext());
        myDB.close();
    }
    ArrayAdapter<String> arrayAdapter = new
    ArrayAdapter<String>(this,
            android.R.layout.simple_spinner_item, arrayList);
    arrayAdapter.setDropDownViewResource
            (android.R.layout.simple_spinner_dropdown_item);
    spinner.setAdapter(arrayAdapter);
} catch (SQLiteException e) {
    e.printStackTrace();
}
```

spinner with the values of the "maindish" field within the database table. The code listed uses a Java *ArrayList* and an *ArrayAdapter*. Since the values placed into the spinner exactly match the database information, it is preferable to provide them for user selection than to ask the user to input their preference in a text field. Doing so also significantly reduces the chances of SQL injection malice.

Design Considerations

Normally a database consists of several related tables. This chapter has purposely limited a database to one table. This has been done out of respect for the importance of database design principles. It should be noted that an app can support multiple databases as well. Databases can be very beneficial in Android apps, and the reader is encouraged to research their design and implementation in more detail. The goal of this chapter was to illustrate how SQLite databases can be used within an app to provide insight as to why they are important, and to demonstrate that a developer knowledgeable in SQL can directly take advantage of this skill when implementing Android apps and their database support.

Exercises

The following exercises are meant to provide practice with incorporating databases into apps. They are multiple activity apps. Each is a scaled down version of a full-featured functional app so that it can be scoped appropriately as a week assignment. Each can easily be expanded upon to achieve a lengthier exercise if needed or multiple assignments can be designated for more advanced skill sets. Sample images are available for download but can easily be substituted with any appropriate images. Sample databases are also available for download where indicated. The assignments are also designed for adaptation to navigation views activities in later chapters. Be sure to specify "hints" for all input fields and content descriptions for all images.

E10.1 At their recent meeting, your book club was discussing how nice it would be to have a mobile app for tracking exercise and workout activity. One of the members stated that a friend had downloaded such an app for a non-Android mobile device, but it supported only a few activities. Another friend stated that she had investigated such app ability but found that they were all either too expensive to purchase or too cumbersome to use. All agreed that it would be nice to have just a simple app that allowed you to keep track of exercise activity and time spent, but for a variety of different activities. Having previously bragged that you are developing apps, they asked you if you could code such an app. In addition, one of the members actually owns a workout facility named *Power Zone* and said that she would help you market your app in the future. But she stated that it would be most attractive to her clientele if it could also provide information on calories burned. She went on to explain that calories burned while performing an activity are significantly influenced by a person's body weight. She added that most people, especially the women to whom she would be marketing your app, are very reluctant to confess their actual weight but would be more inclined to report their weight in a category range.

You were thinking about this app and have decided to make such an app a reality. At this time, the app will require three* activity layouts and is to be designed for a mobile phone. The first of the activities is basically a welcome screen that describes the purpose of the app and provides button links to subsequent features. A background image with a fitness theme is to be utilized on every screen within this app. A sample layout for this welcome screen is provided online in the supplementary materials for this book.

The button labeled "Record an Activity" on the launch screen is to transfer the user to a second activity. A spinner containing the list of exercise activities that can be recorded is to be present on this screen layout. A database will load this information. A database is available for download*. There is a group of radio buttons for selecting a weight category. And there is a numeric input field for the specification of the number of minutes that were spent performing the activity. A button to record the activity will then calculate the calories burned based on this information. Specifically, if the input is valid, notably if the number of minutes is a positive number, then determine the burn rate information for the activity and weight estimate from the table named *activities* in the database named *exercises.sqlite*. Note that the database contains the value for the typical calories burned for this activity for each of the five possible weight values for ten minutes of activity. Therefore, the app must compute the total calories burned by factoring in the user-supplied time in minutes value. So, for example, if the user selects *aerobics high intensity* as the activity and selects 250 lbs as the approximate weight value and specifies 20 as the number of minutes the activity was performed, then your app will compute the total calories burned as 162 (returned from the database for the weight input) × 2 (for 20 minutes) which computes to 324 calories burned. This value for calories burned is then to be stored along with the exercise activity performed in a second database. A button labeled "Back" is to return the user to the main activity. A sample layout for this screen is provided online in the supplementary materials for this book.

The button labeled "Display all Activities" on the initial screen is to transfer the user to a third activity. The information stored in the second database of recorded activities performed is to be displayed on this screen. An idea for the organization of this screen is provided online. If no activities have yet been recorded, an appropriate message should indicate so. A "Back" button to return the user to the main activity must also be present.

* *If the database of exercise activities does not yet exist, then a fourth activity will be required to add exercises to a database of activities and calories. A database named "exercises.sqlite" containing a table named "activities" with this information is available for download, which eliminates the need for this fourth activity. The "activities" table has fields named and typed as "ID (int)", "exerciseactivity (VARCHAR)", along with fields for each of the weight categories defined with names and types "lbs124 (int)", "lbs150 (int)", "lbs175 (int)", "lbs200 (int)", and "lbs250 (int)".*

E10.2 Create an app that maintains an inventory of yoga ambient tunes. This assignment can be enhanced in later chapters with the playing of the tunes and the identification of appropriate web content. In the meantime, the app will consist of three activities. The main activity presents a welcome screen. Included in this screen layout are two buttons. One button is labeled "ADD MUSIC" and is to transfer the user to a second activity. The other button is labeled "LIST MUSIC" and is to transfer the user to a third activity. A background image with a musical theme is to be utilized on every screen in this app. A sample layout for this welcome screen is provided online in the supplementary materials for this book.

The button labled "ADD MUSIC" transfers the user to a second activity. This next activity presents a screen that solicits input from the user describing an appropriate tune. The solicited input is to consist of a tune title, the tune artist, and a length in minutes. The input for duration in minutes must be validated to be a number. There is a button present in the screen layout labeled "ADD TUNE INFO" that stores the input data in the database table with the other music tune records. The screen also includes a "BACK" button to return the user to the main activity welcome screen. A sample layout for this screen is provided online in the supplementary materials for this book.

The button labeled "LIST MUSIC" transfers the user to a third activity that lists the tunes that have been stored in the database table. An appropriate message is displayed if there are no tunes stored yet. An SQL statement to retrieve this data is "SELECT * FROM tableName;". There is also a "BACK" button to return the user to the main activity welcome screen. A sample layout for this screen is provided online.

E10.3 Create an app that supports a neighborhood sports coach (soccer, football, and baseball) in keeping contact information for players on a team. The information is to be stored in a single table in a database and consists of some basic data fields. The data fields tracked include the player's first name (VARCHAR), last name (VARCHAR), phone number (VARCHAR), team position (VARCHAR), and emergency contact's name (VARCHAR). Three activities are required for this app. The first activity is a "welcome" screen that explains the purpose of the app and contains two buttons on this screen, each of which transfers the user to a different activity. The buttons are labeled "List Team" and "Add a member". A sample layout for this welcome screen is provided online in the supplementary materials for this book.

When the user clicks the button labeled "List Team", the user is transferred to a second activity. This activity displays the data from the database table. The screen must also include a "BACK" button to return the user to the first screen. If there are no team members in the database table, display an appropriate message. An SQL statement to retrieve this data is "SELECT * FROM tableName;". A sample layout for this screen is provided online in the supplementary materials for this book.

When the user clicks the button labeled "Add a member", the user is transferred to a third activity. The screen layout associated with this activity prompts the user to input a new player's first name, last name, phone number, team position, and emergency contact's name. Two buttons are included on this screen. One button is labeled "Add Player" and when clicked inserts a new record with the screen input information into the database table. The other button is labeled "Back" and returns the user to the first screen. A message should be displayed when a record is successfully added to the database table. The record should be added using the SQL INSERT INTO statement. A sample layout for this screen is provided online in the supplementary materials for this book.

Follow-up Questions:

> *What additional information do you think should be collected to track player information?*

> *What additional activities/screen layouts do you think should be added to increase the functionality and use of this app?*

E10.4 Create an app that will help your grandfather to know which pills and medicine he should be taking in the morning and which pills and medicine he should be taking at night. The app will consist of three activities. The app gets right to its purpose without a welcome screen since grandpa does not feel all that comfortable with apps. So, the first activity opens to the most important feature. The screen layout for this first activity includes two radio buttons so that the user can select "AM" for morning or "PM" for evening. Neither of these buttons should be selected as a default as that would be considered potentially harmful. So, you are to provide a warning message and halt further action if the user clicks the image button labeled "Which pills?" without specifying a time of day. Once a radio button is selected, the app lists the records from the database table that have an "AM" or "PM" value matching the radio button in the time-of-day field. Two additional buttons labeled "List meds" and "Add meds", respectively, are provided to transfer the user to a different activity as discussed below. A sample layout for this initial screen is provided online in the supplementary materials for this book.

When the user clicks the button labeled "List meds", the user is transferred to a second activity. A list of all medications stored in the database table is listed on the screen, and a button labeled "BACK" is provided to return the user to the main screen. A sample layout for this screen is provided online.

The button labeled "Add meds" provided on the main screen when clicked transfers the user to a third activity. The layout for this third activity provides input fields to capture the information for one medication. The information captured includes the name of the medication, the "mg" or "oz" units, the number of pills, and a spinner containing selections "AM" and "PM" for the time-of-day. An "ADD" button validates the input data and then adds it as a record to the database table. The user is transferred back to the main activity when activating a second button that is labeled "BACK". A sample layout for this screen is provided online.

11

Navigation Drawers and Implementing Fragments

Learning Outcomes:

- ✓ *Ability to create navigation drawer activities.*
- ✓ *Knowledge of the anatomy of a navigation drawer activity.*
- ✓ *Ability to customize the navigation header.*
- ✓ *Ability to customize the navigation menu.*

DOI: 10.1201/9781003286325-11

✓ *Understanding of fragments.*
✓ *Ability to create a menu icon using the Image Asset Studio.*
✓ *Appreciation for how the main activity manipulates fragments.*
✓ *Ability to customize a fragment.*
✓ *Ability to add drawer menu items and new fragments.*
✓ *Understanding of the floating action button.*

Thus far, we have developed apps with one or more screen layouts, and movements between and among these different screens have been controlled programmatically based primarily on user button interaction. But no doubt you have experienced apps on your personal device whereby different screen layouts are presented in response to tabs you select at the bottom or top of the screen, or selections you choose from a "slide-in" navigation menu. Interaction of the former type involving tabs within an app layout is covered in the next chapter. In this chapter, we will code apps of the latter type, which are referred to as "navigation drawer" apps.

The Android Developers site describes a navigation drawer as a user interface panel that displays the app's main navigation menu. Such a navigation drawer slides in from the left in response to a right directional swipe action on the part of the user, or because of a user clicks on the hamburger menu icon displayed in the top left of the screen. The hamburger menu icon is also referred to as a "drawer" icon. A navigation drawer activity uses "fragments" to load versatile screen content within the navigation view content area as detailed below.

Introduction to Navigation Drawer Activities

A navigation drawer activity has a very different user interface than does an "empty views" project template such as those we have created in previous chapters. We will also note a different project folder organization than that experienced in our previous apps. In addition, when working with navigation drawer activities, we will make significant use of "fragments". And it will become apparent that a fragment is not equivalent to an activity, which will lead to differences in how screen components are referenced. All of these details are covered in this chapter.

To create a navigation drawer project, we select the "Navigation Drawer Views Activity" as the project template as illustrated in Figure 11.1.

After clicking "Next", assign the project name and location as we have done in the case of previous projects. The file structure is different for this type of project as is the interaction with the app. To appreciate this, run this app that has just been created. Upon launching the app, the "Home Fragment" is displayed by default as illustrated in Figure 11.2.

Click on the hamburger menu icon indicated in Figure 11.2 or swipe across the screen from left to right. Interact with the app by clicking each of the link

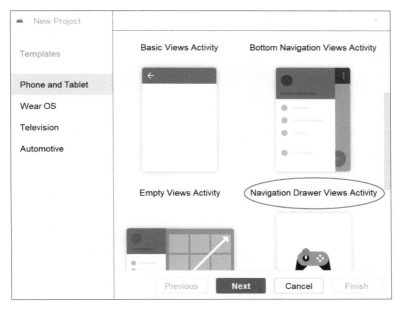

FIGURE 11.1
Create a "Navigation Drawer Views" activity.

FIGURE 11.2
Launching a Navigation Drawer app.

items labeled *Home*, *Gallery*, and *Slideshow* made available from the navigation menu shown in Figure 11.3.

FIGURE 11.3
Default navigation links.

As you test each of the navigation links, notice how each content message displayed identifies the display as a "fragment". By default, three fragments are provided with the creation of a "Navigation Drawer Activity". Much more will be said later regarding this concept of "fragment". First, however, let's look at the folder and files organization of a "Navigation Drawer Activity" project since it differs markedly from that of the projects with which we have been working in previous chapters.

Anatomy of a Navigation Drawer App

Expanding on the *app* folder displays the same subfolders we have seen in previous projects. But if we further expand the *res* folder, we see additional subfolders never encountered in the projects we have previously created. There is a new subfolder named *menu* and a subfolder named *navigation* as illustrated in Figure 11.4.

FIGURE 11.4
Folder structure associated with Navigation Drawer Activities.

Furthermore, if we expand the *layout* subfolder, we once again find the *activity_main.xml* file previously encountered, but now there are also several additional layout files present in this folder as shown in Figure 11.5, which we did not see in our previous apps.

Upon closer examination, we note that there are three eXtensible Markup Language (XML) files that contain a prefix of "fragment" in their file name. In fact, these files seemingly correspond to the link items encountered while exploring the user interface when this app was executed. In addition to the three "fragment" files, the other files listed in the *layout* subfolder consist of the files named *app_bar_main.xml*, *content_main.xml*, and *nav_header_main.xml*.

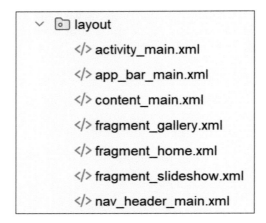

FIGURE 11.5
Additional files defined in the *layout* subfolder.

Before exploring these new XML files, let's take a closer look at the *activity_main.xml* file created for this project. While the name is familiar, a closer examination of the file contents reveals that the code is quite different from that of our previous projects. The first observations to note are the new widget members found in the Component Tree as shown in Figure 11.6. Of particular mention is the default layout of the *activity_main.xml* file which is no longer a constraint layout but is now instead a *drawer_layout*.

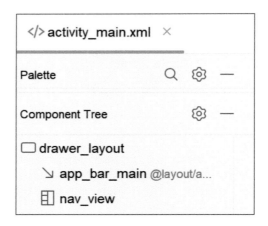

FIGURE 11.6
A different layout organizes the *activity_main.xml*.

The *drawer_layout* includes a layout resource named *app_bar_main* and a "NavigationView" widget. This *app_bar_main* references the same name xml file listed in the layout subfolder expansion shown in Figure 11.5.

Consideration of the code in the *app_bar_main.xml* file highlights organization by yet another type of layout, namely a "Coordinator Layout". Figure 11.7 illustrates the components within the *app_bar_main* layout with indications as to which portion of the screen each component is responsible for populating.

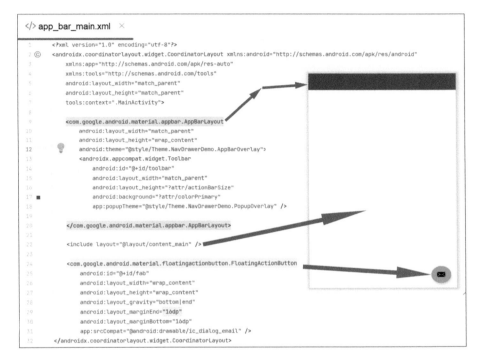

FIGURE 11.7
The area components defined by *app_bar_main*.

The "CoordinatorLayout" enables views within its layout to interact with each other. The "Floating Action Button" (FAB) that hovers over the screen content necessitates this layout. In the default code listed in Figure 11.7, there is an "AppBarLayout" present that contains a toolbar. Also included is a "content_main" layout which holds the content of individual drawer items as each is brought into user view when selected. Generally, developers do not find a reason to modify this file except for customization of the FAB.

What makes a navigation drawer app so different from the apps of previous chapters is the different way that the main activity functions and the role that it plays. Its layout represents a container for a fragment. So instead of unloading one activity to load another to present a different screen within the app, as we did with multiple activities, we now have an alternative and more efficient means of switching between different content views.

It is the *NavigationView* widget within *activity_main.xml* that represents a standard navigation menu for the app by identifying *app:headerLayout* and *app:menu* specifications. The header layout by default references the *nav_ header_main* XML file which until customized presents the top portion of the navigation view identified by the arrow in Figure 11.8.

FIGURE 11.8
The file content of *nav_header_main.xml*.

By default, this header layout as defined by the *nav_header_main.xml* content consists of an image view and two text view widgets. Most developers will want to customize this content. We will do so soon.

The *app:menu* specification in the *activity_main.xml* file is responsible for the menu items listed below the header layout, identified by the default values "Home", "Gallery", and "Slideshow" as shown in Figure 11.8. These menu items originate from a different layout file named *activity_main_drawer.xml* as a menu resource found in the *menu* subfolder of the *res* subfolder. The customization of these entries as well as the header layout is detailed in the next section.

After customizing the navigation user interface, we will look in detail at the very different main activity code that exists for navigation drawer activities to manipulate fragments.

Customizing the Navigation View

The *NavigationView* widget which is found in the "Containers" category in the editor palette and found within *activity_main.xml* was previously identified and said to represent a standard navigation menu for the app. Again, it includes *app:headerLayout* and *app:menu* specifications. We will now look at customizing these components.

Customizing the Header Layout of the Navigation View

As previously noted in Figure 11.8, the header layout as specified in the *nav_header_main.xml* file by default consists of an image view and two text view widgets. This is the content that developers generally wish to customize. The default code provided in Table 11.1 identifies the layout as a linear layout with

TABLE 11.1

Modifying the Navigation Header Image

nav_header_main.xml

```
<?xml version="1.0" encoding="utf-8"?>
<LinearLayout xmlns:android="http://schemas.android.com/apk/res/android"
    xmlns:app="http://schemas.android.com/apk/res-auto"
    android:layout_width="match_parent"
    android:layout_height="@dimen/nav_header_height"
    android:background="@drawable/side_nav_bar"
    android:gravity="bottom"
    android:orientation="vertical"
    android:paddingLeft="@dimen/activity_horizontal_margin"
    android:paddingTop="@dimen/activity_vertical_margin"
    android:paddingRight="@dimen/activity_horizontal_margin"
    android:paddingBottom="@dimen/activity_vertical_margin"
    android:theme="@style/ThemeOverlay.AppCompat.Dark">

    <ImageView
        android:id="@+id/imageView"
        android:layout_width="wrap_content"
        android:layout_height="wrap_content"
        android:contentDescription="@string/nav_header_desc"
        android:paddingTop="@dimen/nav_header_vertical_spacing"
        app:srcCompat="@drawable/oldbooks" />

    <TextView
        android:layout_width="match_parent"
        android:layout_height="wrap_content"
        android:paddingTop="@dimen/nav_header_vertical_spacing"
        android:text="@string/nav_header_title"
        android:textAppearance="@style/TextAppearance.AppCompat.Body1" />

    <TextView
        android:id="@+id/textView"
        android:layout_width="wrap_content"
        android:layout_height="wrap_content"
        android:text="@string/nav_header_subtitle" />
</LinearLayout>
```

a vertical orientation. All or part of the content can be removed or modified. For example, if we store an image in a file named *oldbooks.png*, we can modify the *app:srcCompat* property of the *ImageView* widget to reference this image as demonstrated in Table 11.1. Note that it is possible to modify this property in the Code view or in the Design view, the latter with which most developers find easier to navigate.

Likewise, we can modify either or both *TextView* widgets to reflect our choice of text value(s). Alternatively, we can choose to delete one or both default *TextView* widgets. To modify the text values of these *TextView* widgets, it is acceptable to modify the text string assignment in the *strings.xml* file to retain the descriptive string identifier such as *nav_header_title*. Sample effects of modifying the string values are illustrated in Figure 11.9.

FIGURE 11.9
Modification results of *nav_header_main.xml*.

Customizing the Menu Specification of the Navigation View

In the *menu* subfolder of the project, there is a file named *activity_main_drawer.xml*, which contains the components that appear in the lower part of the navigation view underneath the header layout. The default navigation menu items are displayed in Figure 11.10. The customization of these items requires the modification of the *NavigationView* widget *app:menu* specification, which again is found in the *activity_main_drawer.xml* file located in the *menu* subfolder of the app.

FIGURE 11.10
Contents of *activity_main_drawer.xml*.

Notice the "group" as an invisible container for the item elements. In this case, the group items are trios of "id", "icon", and "title" as shown in the code view of *activity_main_drawer.xml* in Figure 11.11. For reasons that should become clear shortly, in our initial navigation drawer apps, we will modify the "icon" and "title" properties but not the "id" property.

```
</> activity_main_drawer.xml  ×

1    <?xml version="1.0" encoding="utf-8"?>
2    <menu xmlns:android="http://schemas.android.com/apk/res/android"
3        xmlns:tools="http://schemas.android.com/tools"
4        tools:showIn="navigation_view">
5
6        <group android:checkableBehavior="single">
7            <item
8                android:id="@+id/nav_home"
9                android:icon="@drawable/ic_menu_camera"
10               android:title="@string/menu_home" />
11           <item
12               android:id="@+id/nav_gallery"
13               android:icon="@drawable/ic_menu_gallery"
14               android:title="@string/menu_gallery" />
15           <item
16               android:id="@+id/nav_slideshow"
17               android:icon="@drawable/ic_menu_slideshow"
18               android:title="@string/menu_slideshow" />
19       </group>
20   </menu>
```

FIGURE 11.11
Code view of the contents of *activity_main_drawer.xml*.

The "icon" property image is shown in the gray margin area adjacent to the line numbers as illustrated in Figure 11.11. To modify the "title" property for each menu item, we simply assign a new text string resource value to the "title" property. Customizing the icon property, however, requires a bit more work since an image asset of an icon type must be created for use. To demonstrate how to create such an image, let's create a book icon for a menu item intended to add a new book to our library.

Here are the steps required to create a "book icon" image asset:

1. In the project folder view of our app, right-click on the *res* subfolder and select *New* → *Image Asset* as shown in Figure 11.12.

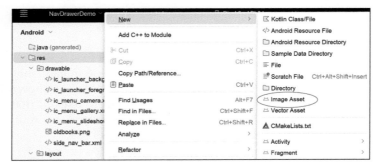

FIGURE 11.12
First step in creating a menu icon.

2. In the dialog box that opens, select Icon Type: "Action Bar and Tab Icons" and select the "Clip art" radio button as the Asset Type. Change the name to "ic_action_addbook" as shown in Figure 11.13 and then click on the Clip Art button to open the icon palette.

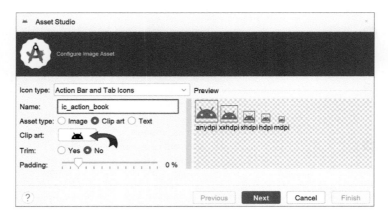

FIGURE 11.13
Configuring the icon as an Image Asset.

3. Scroll through the icons to locate the "Book" icon. Notice that a search facility is also available as observed in Figure 11.14.

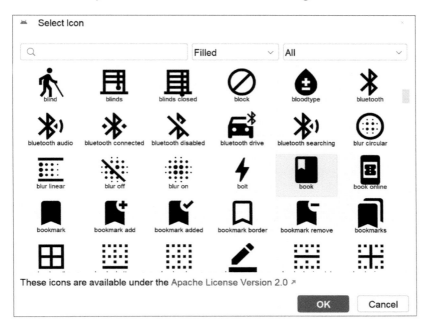

FIGURE 11.14
Scrolling to select the book icon.

4. Click OK and note that the button icon image has changed to the selected book icon as confirmed in Figure 11.15.

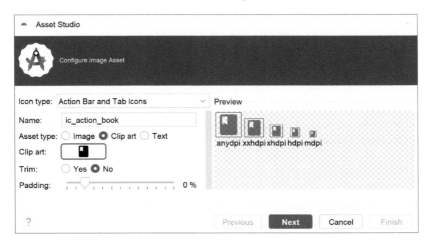

FIGURE 11.15
The book icon is now selected.

5. Click Next.

6. Click Finish.

Now that an icon image asset has been created, namely *ic_action_book*, we can assign it as the value for the icon property of the appropriate navigation item. We can also modify the text appropriately in the *activity_main_drawer.xml* file as shown in Figure 11.16.

FIGURE 11.16
Updated menu icon and title.

The first and third menu items may be modified in the same way. It is possible to specify additional menu items to augment the default three, and we will consider that task in a separate section later in the chapter. In the meantime, it is important to understand the core component of a navigation activity which is called a "fragment".

Introduction to Fragments and Their Relation to the MainActivity

According to the Android Developer website, a fragment is a modular component within an activity. A fragment is an independent component that runs in the context of an activity, has its own lifecycle, and controls access to its inputs.[1] Navigation controllers such as navigation drawer activities make extensive use of fragments. Developers desire to employ fragments in order to improve response time since it is faster to switch between fragments than it is to switch between activities. A fragment is similar to an activity in that it has its own layout (.xml file) and its own code (.java file), and some developers think of fragments as "sub-activities". This is evidenced by examining a relevant portion of our Navigation Drawer activity Project structure as shown in Figure 11.17. The java code and layout files have been highlighted for the "Home" fragment in Figure 11.17, but note that equivalent files exist for the "Gallery" fragment and "Slideshow" fragment as well.

FIGURE 11.17
Components defining the "Home" Fragment.

Examining the code view of each of the three default .*xml* fragment files does not reveal any surprises. In each, the layout container is a *ConstraintLayout*, and in each of the default layouts, one sees a *TextView* widget as the only child component.

The java code files for any of the default fragments however reveals content that is very different from the activity code files to which we have become accustomed to. First, note that there are two .*java* code files for each fragment. The two code files highlighted in Figure 11.17 for the default "Home" fragment identify *HomeFragment.java* and *HomeViewModel.java* which are in a subfolder named "home". Explore to confirm that there are two comparable files for the "Gallery" fragment situated in a subfolder named "gallery" and two similar files for the "Slideshow" fragment situated in a subfolder named "slideshow".

The "ViewModel" files associated with the fragments, for example, the *HomeViewModel*, are new with the infusion of the Model-View-ViewModel (MVVM) architecture. A thorough discussion of the MVVM and *LiveData* features is beyond the scope of this book, but a few notes are provided a little later in this book. In the meantime, we turn our attention back to the Java "fragment" files in the project.

Opening the *HomeFragment.java* file reveals the code displayed in Figure 11.18. An immediate indication that a fragment is not an activity is observed by the fact that the *onCreate* void method has been replaced with an *onCreateView* method that returns a *View* object. In addition to the *Bundle* parameter that we have seen in previous apps in the *onCreate* method of activities, the *onCreateView* method in fragments has two additional parameters. The *LayoutInflater* parameter is used to convert the fragment's XML layout file to a *View* object. The "container" parameter is the parent *ViewGroup* from the activity's layout in which our fragment layout will be inserted, and for all practical purposes, this will be *content_main.xml* found within the *activity_main.xml* file. Within the Java code is an assignment statement to a variable named *root* declared to be of type *View*. This statement is assigning to the variable *root* a pointer to the inflated layout (the fragment layout). It is this *View root* that is then returned from the *onCreateView* method. In addition, a new method named *onDestroyView* has been added to the fragment .java file. This permits developers to specify code that can be executed when the fragment loses focus.

A fragment has its own lifecycle and can handle user interaction with its components, but a fragment cannot stand on its own. Fragments must ultimately be hosted by an activity. Fragments lend versatility to apps for different screen sizes. For example, a landscape orientation or tablet might arrange fragments as adjacent elements, whereas a mobile phone might display the fragments in separate screens.

Understanding fragment manipulation, namely the swapping in and out of fragment layouts and execution of their associated code, requires an analysis of the *MainActivity.java* code, which is also very different from

```
 ⓒ HomeFragment.java  ✕                                                        ⋮

 1      package com.example.navdrawerdemo.ui.home;
 2
 3    > import ...
 14
 15     public class HomeFragment extends Fragment {
 16
            4 usages
 17         private FragmentHomeBinding binding;
 18
 19 •↑     public View onCreateView(@NonNull LayoutInflater inflater,
 20                                   ViewGroup container, Bundle savedInstanceState) {
 21            HomeViewModel homeViewModel =
 22                new ViewModelProvider( owner: this).get(HomeViewModel.class);
 23
 24            binding = FragmentHomeBinding.inflate(inflater, container,  attachToParent: false);
 25            View root = binding.getRoot();
 26
 27            final TextView textView = binding.textHome;
 28            homeViewModel.getText().observe(getViewLifecycleOwner(), textView::setText);
 29            return root;
 30        }
 31
 32        @Override
 33 •↑     public void onDestroyView() {
 34            super.onDestroyView();
 35            binding = null;
 36        }
 37     }
```

FIGURE 11.18
Default code in the "HomeFragment" Java file.

the activity-based similarly named file in the Android projects created in Chapters 1 through 10. To review this, Table 11.2 lists the code contained in a default *MainActivity.java* file when a project is first created in these earlier chapters.

TABLE 11.2

Default Code for the Main Activities in Non-Navigation Apps

MainActivity.java

```
public class MainActivity extends AppCompatActivity {

    @Override
    protected void onCreate(Bundle savedInstanceState) {
        super.onCreate(savedInstanceState);
        setContentView(R.layout.activity_main);
    }
}
```

Now in examining the default code created in the *MainActivity.java* file for a *NavigationDrawer* activity, we observe that there are three methods consisting in a total of over 60 lines of code. These statements cooperatively support the manipulation of the fragments hosted by this main activity. The three methods that comprise the main activity code are identified in Figure 11.19.

```
ⓒ MainActivity.java  ✕

1        package com.example.navdrawerdemo;
2
3   >    import ...
18
19 </>  public class MainActivity extends AppCompatActivity {
20
         3 usages
21           private AppBarConfiguration mAppBarConfiguration;
         6 usages
22           private ActivityMainBinding binding;
23
24           @Override
25 ●↑ >     protected void onCreate(Bundle savedInstanceState) {...}
51
52           @Override
53 ●↑ >     public boolean onCreateOptionsMenu(Menu menu) {...}
58
         5 usages
59           @Override
60 ●↑ >     public boolean onSupportNavigateUp() {...}
65       }
```

FIGURE 11.19
Three methods now present in *MainActivity.java*.

In addition to the *onCreate* method, there is now also an *onCreateOptionsMenu* method and an *onSupportNavigateUp* method that support navigation operations established by the *onCreate* method. The default code for the *onCreate* method in a *Navigation Drawer* activity is provided in Figure 11.20. It obviously consists of many more code statements than that which is present in the method of the same name in the apps developed in previous chapters. An examination of the most relevant statements in Figure 11.20 follows.

```
ⓒ MainActivity.java  ✕
25 ●↑      protected void onCreate(Bundle savedInstanceState) {
26             super.onCreate(savedInstanceState);
27
28             binding = ActivityMainBinding.inflate(getLayoutInflater());
29             setContentView(binding.getRoot());
30
31             setSupportActionBar(binding.appBarMain.toolbar);
32             binding.appBarMain.fab.setOnClickListener(new View.OnClickListener() {
33                 @Override
34 ●↑              public void onClick(View view) {
35                     Snackbar.make(view,  text: "Replace with your own action", Snackbar.LENGTH_LONG)
36                         .setAction( text: "Action",  listener: null).show();
37                 }
38             });
39             DrawerLayout drawer = binding.drawerLayout;
40             NavigationView navigationView = binding.navView;
41             // Passing each menu ID as a set of Ids because each
42             // menu should be considered as top level destinations.
43             mAppBarConfiguration = new AppBarConfiguration.Builder(
44                     R.id.nav_home, R.id.nav_gallery, R.id.nav_slideshow)
45                     .setOpenableLayout(drawer)
46                     .build();
47             NavController navController = Navigation.findNavController( activity: this, R.id.nav_host_fragment_content_main);
48             NavigationUI.setupActionBarWithNavController( activity: this, navController, mAppBarConfiguration);
49             NavigationUI.setupWithNavController(navigationView, navController);
50         }
```

FIGURE 11.20
Default code now found in the *onCreate* method.

Line 26 is the first statement in the *onCreate* method and is the only statement that is an exact duplicate of a statement in the default code for the
activities of which we are accustomed to in previous chapters. All statements that follow line 26 are new to navigation activities. In line 28, a binding class is now generated for the *activity_main* layout file, and a binding
object, named *binding*, is instantiated after inflating the layout. The *inflate*
method of the binding class creates a hierarchy of the view objects that
comprise the layout and binds the object to it. Line 29 references the root
view of this hierarchy and fills the current window with its UI content,
thereby effectively displaying the layout. Since much of the explanation
that follows refers to components found in the *activity_main.xml* layout, you
may want to review the contents of Figures 11.6 through 11.11 with the discussion that follows.

Line 31 is retrieving the toolbar widget from the *activity_main.xml* layout
file where it has been assigned the *id appBarMain* and is establishing it as the
activity's action toolbar. Lines 32–38 are collectively setting up the implementation for the "floating action button" identified as *fab* in the *appBarMain*
layout and setting up an event listener to respond to its use.

Line 39 retrieves the *Drawer* layout identified by *id* "drawerLayout" in
activity_main.xml for use as the hamburger menu container later in line 45.
Line 40 instantiates a *NavigationView* instance from the *activity_main.xml* layout's component widget named "nav_view". Both of these elements are used
a few lines later in the code to complete the navigation user interface.

As identified in the comments in lines 41–42, lines 43–46 build the sliding drawer navigation items that are added to the navigation user interface and organized into the *drawer* object previously created. Recall that we examined these menu items in a previous discussion of the menu items defined in the *activity_main_drawer.xml* file.

Next, in line 47, a *NavController* is created by the *findNavController* method of the *Navigation* API. It becomes responsible for coordinating the contents of the *View* identified by *nav_host_fragment_content_main*, which is the *id* of the fragment found in *content_main.xml*. and is where fragment layouts for "home", "gallery", and "slideshow" are displayed. The *content_main.xml* file was mentioned previously when the folder and subfolder hierarchy of the project was explored, but it is only now that its role takes on added significance. This *content_main.xml* initially contains an empty fragment placeholder and is included in the *app_bar_main.xml* layout which is in turn included in the *activity_main.xml* layout. Recall that this fragment is an empty container where destination fragments are swapped in and out as a user navigates through the app.

Simply stated but representative of a significant workload for the entire navigation architecture, the *navController* then manages all user navigation. It is strongly associated with the navigation graph, which is defined in the file named *mobile_navigation.xml*. More is said about this file shortly.

Finally, line 48 associates the *AppBarConfiguration* built in lines 43–46 with the navigation controller and the drawer icon to render the navigation user interface visible and usable. Line 49 links the menu items with the actual destinations. Without line 49, clicking the menu items would produce no response.

The Navigation User Interface

In addition to rendering the fragment content in response to user interaction, the "Navigation User Interface" (*NavigationUI*) must also update the app bar to reflect the appropriate content. So, notice that when you select "Gallery" for example from the slide-in menu, the app bar at the top of the screen displays the drawer icon, "Gallery", and the vertical ellipsis symbol to display "Settings".

The NavigationUI is very dependent upon the navigation graph as defined in the *mobile_navigation.xml* file displayed in Figure 11.21. The label properties highlighted in Figure 11.21 have been modified to reflect appropriate destination names for the fragments within our "My Library" sample app being developed in this chapter. Notice that the *label* attribute is the only attribute whose value has been changed. The other attributes have not been changed. They still read according to the original fragment names associated with "home", "gallery", and slideshow. This is because making a change to any one of these components necessitates a ripple of modifications that must occur to maintain a functioning app. Later discussion on adding a fourth navigation item will clarify the modifications that become necessary.

```
    </> mobile_navigation.xml  ✕

1    <?xml version="1.0" encoding="utf-8"?>
2    <navigation xmlns:android="http://schemas.android.com/apk/res/android"
3         xmlns:app="http://schemas.android.com/apk/res-auto"
4         xmlns:tools="http://schemas.android.com/tools"
5         android:id="@+id/mobile_navigation"
6         app:startDestination="@+id/nav_home">
7
8         <fragment
9             android:id="@+id/nav_home"
10            android:name="com.example.navdrawerdemo.ui.home.HomeFragment"
11            android:label="Home"
12            tools:layout="@layout/fragment_home" />
13
14        <fragment
15            android:id="@+id/nav_gallery"
16            android:name="com.example.navdrawerdemo.ui.gallery.GalleryFragment"
17            android:label="Add a Book"
18            tools:layout="@layout/fragment_gallery" />
19
20        <fragment
21            android:id="@+id/nav_slideshow"
22            android:name="com.example.navdrawerdemo.ui.slideshow.SlideshowFragment"
23            android:label="List Books"
24            tools:layout="@layout/fragment_slideshow" />
25    </navigation>
```

FIGURE 11.21
Destination names for the various fragments.

As developers, we need only to ensure that the fragment content and their named labels are coded appropriately, unless we add menu items, an effort that is discussed later in the chapter. Before considering the addition of menu items, however, we will next customize the content of the three default navigation fragments that are provided when the project is created.

Customizing the Content of the Fragments

Since the main activity in a Navigation Drawer app swaps fragments in and out of a placeholder "host" fragment, it is the individual fragments initially created in the files named *fragment_home.xml*, *fragment_gallery.xml*, and *fragment_slideshow.xml* that should be modified to achieve the "easiest" customization. In this, our first example, as previously mentioned, we will leave the fragments as named by default. Therefore, we will choose only to modify their content.

Modifying the "Home" Fragment to Serve as a "Welcome" in Our Sample App

In this example, let's modify the "Home" fragment content in the file named *fragment_home.xml* so that it will display an image and an explanation of the app. We will continue working with the project that we started earlier in this chapter that implements an inventory of a personal library of books. So, to keep the application relatively simple, let's modify the "Home" fragment so that it renders as shown in Figure 11.22.

FIGURE 11.22
Illustrating changes to the content of the "Home" fragment layout.

To achieve this rendering, we must modify the content within the *fragment_home.xml* file by supplying and valuing widgets as has been done in previous chapters. As detailed in Table 11.3, an *Image* widget has been added with content from a *drawable* resource and the default *TextView* widget has been modified with a new appropriately valued resource string.

TABLE 11.3

Customized Code for "Home" Fragment in Sample App

fragment_home.xml

```xml
<?xml version="1.0" encoding="utf-8"?>
<androidx.constraintlayout.widget.ConstraintLayout
    xmlns:android="http://schemas.android.com/apk/res/android"
    xmlns:app="http://schemas.android.com/apk/res-auto"
    xmlns:tools="http://schemas.android.com/tools"
    android:layout_width="match_parent"
    android:layout_height="match_parent"
    tools:context=".ui.home.HomeFragment">

    <ImageView
        android:id="@+id/imageView2"
        android:layout_width="211dp"
        android:layout_height="358dp"
        android:src="@drawable/bookcase"
        app:layout_constraintBottom_toBottomOf="parent"
        app:layout_constraintEnd_toEndOf="parent"
        app:layout_constraintHorizontal_bias="0.44"
        app:layout_constraintStart_toStartOf="parent"
        app:layout_constraintTop_toTopOf="parent"
        app:layout_constraintVertical_bias="0.042" />

    <TextView
        android:id="@+id/textHome"
        android:layout_width="384dp"
        android:layout_height="222dp"
        android:layout_marginStart="8dp"
        android:layout_marginEnd="8dp"
        android:fontFamily="sans-serif-medium"
        android:text="@string/text_home_mod"
        android:textColor="@color/black"
        android:textSize="20sp"
        app:layout_constraintBottom_toBottomOf="parent"
        app:layout_constraintEnd_toEndOf="parent"
        app:layout_constraintHorizontal_bias="0.0"
        app:layout_constraintStart_toStartOf="parent"
        app:layout_constraintTop_toBottomOf="@+id/imageView2"
        app:layout_constraintVertical_bias="0.133" />

</androidx.constraintlayout.widget.ConstraintLayout>
```

WARNING: If you were to run the app, a runtime error would occur. This is due to the fact that we have modified the fragment content and removed an item that the *HomeViewModel.java* code required. The purpose of a *ViewModel* is to facilitate the sharing of data between fragments or between a fragment and its "host" activity. In the apps we are developing in this book, we are not engaged in such sharing of data. Therefore, it is critical that the two highlighted statements in Figure 11.23 be commented out in the *HomeFragment.java* file and every other fragment's modified primary *.java* file as well.

```
© HomeFragment.java    ×

 2   >   import ...
13
14       public class HomeFragment extends Fragment {
             3 usages
15           private FragmentHomeBinding binding;
16
17 ●↑      public View onCreateView(@NonNull LayoutInflater inflater,
18                                    ViewGroup container, Bundle savedInstanceState) {
19             HomeViewModel homeViewModel =
20                     new ViewModelProvider( owner: this).get(HomeViewModel.class);
21
22             binding = FragmentHomeBinding.inflate(inflater, container, attachToParent: false);
23             View root = binding.getRoot();
24
25             //   final TextView textView = binding.textHome;
26             //   homeViewModel.getText().observe(getViewLifecycleOwner(), textView::setText);
27             return root;
28         }
29
30         @Override
31 ●↑      public void onDestroyView() {
32             super.onDestroyView();
33             binding = null;
34         }
35     }
```

FIGURE 11.23
Necessary code commenting in *HomeFragment.java*.

If you are a seasoned developer and understand the MVVM pattern, then by all means employ it within your app. The intended audience of this book is not generally yet familiar with MVVM, and so it is not utilized throughout this book. Those unfamiliar with MVVM, however, are encouraged to study it further in their future educational endeavors. It is a very important technique for separating code and logic from the user interface that supports applications and is a topic in and of itself.

The personal library inventory that we are implementing in this chapter's sample app is significantly based on the code developed in the previous chapter. Therefore, the label for the "Gallery" fragment as previously noted has been changed to read "Add a Book", and the label for the "Slideshow" fragment has been modified to the string value "List Books". The "Gallery" fragment will be used in our app to add a book to a native database maintained to track the books in the personal library and so will require modification as follows.

Modifying the "Gallery" Fragment to "Add a Book" in Our Sample App

Both the layout and the code file for this second fragment need to be modified to support our sample application. Specifically, the layout defined in the *fragment_gallery.xml* file needs to be modified to present the fields required for the addition of a new book record to the database. These required fields are the same as were identified in our sample app in Chapter 10. This modified layout is displayed in Figure 11.24.

FIGURE 11.24
Updated "Gallery" fragment layout for new book fields.

The Java code file for this fragment will contain much the same code as was used in Chapter 10 when a new book was added to the personal library database. There are however two very important differences. These differences are due to the fact that the code lives within a fragment rather than an activity. One primary difference is that we now need to import a reference for "R" to reference the app's resources. We can no longer simply use *".findViewById(R."* to do so. An *import* statement is now required to reference app resources directly. The *import* statement is specifically:

```
import com.example.yourprojectname.R;
```

This *import* statement can be obtained with the "Quick-Fix" applied numerous times in previous apps by making the selection illustrated in Figure 11.25.

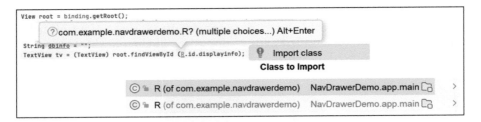

```
View root = binding.getRoot();
        ⑦com.example.navdrawerdemo.R? (multiple choices...) Alt+Enter
String dbinfo = "";
TextView tv = (TextView) root.findViewById (R.id.displayinfo);    💡  Import class
                                                                        Class to Import

                             © ⬍ R (of com.example.navdrawerdemo)    NavDrawerDemo.app.main ⬚   >
                             © ⬍ R (of com.example.navdrawerdemo)    NavDrawerDemo.app.main ⬚   >
```

FIGURE 11.25
"Quick-Fix" to remedy the resource references in fragments.

Another significant difference between activities and fragments is in the handling of *onClick* events. In the case of activities, the developer has a choice. The developer can do as we have in the last several chapters and assign a method name to the *onClick* attribute of a button and then code a method of that name in the activity .java file. Or the developer can code an event handler to "listen" for a click of the button. In the case of fragments, the developer does not have the same choice. In a fragment, a button *onClick* event listener must be employed. Such an event handler for a button component in Java is referred to as an *onClickListener* method. Therefore, such an *onClickListener* event handler is required for the "Add a Book" image button displayed in Figure 11.24. Using the *onClick* attribute to define a method by name will not work with fragments as it did with activities. So, Figure 11.26 illustrates in highlighted lines 33–36 a means of addressing the requirement to set a listener for the user click of the button, which must override the default *onClick* method.

Modifying the "Slideshow" Fragment to List Books in the Database in Our App

The "Slideshow" fragment must be modified to list the books presently in the database table. The code used within the layouts and .java code files for these fragments also borrow heavily from the code developed in Chapter 10. In fact, the .java code to list the books within this fragment is provided in Table 11.4. The code is similar to that in Chapter 10 that accomplished this task. This very important exception regarding how a layout View widget is accessed must be addressed in this fragment as it was addressed in the previous fragment. Again, this exception is due to the fact that our layouts are now fragments rather than activities. And this requires that the references made to the fragment .*xml* layout components be altered to access the app's resources using an app name qualified reference. This is again accomplished with the *import* statement identified in

```
ⓒ GalleryFragment.java   ✕

33        ImageButton book = (ImageButton) root.findViewById(R.id.btn_addabook)  ;
34        book.setOnClickListener(new View.OnClickListener(){
35            @Override
36            public void onClick(View v) {
37                // Get user data and store in the database as a new record
38                // assuming the database already exists so don't need CREATE TABLE
39                try {
40                    SQLiteDatabase myDB = SQLiteDatabase.openDatabase(
41                        "/data/data/" + getActivity().getPackageName() +
42                            "/databases/simplebooks1.db",
43                        null,
44                        SQLiteDatabase.OPEN_READWRITE);
45                    String insertSQL = "000";
46                    EditText bt = (EditText) root.findViewById(R.id.btitle);
47                    EditText ba = (EditText) root.findViewById(R.id.bauthor);
48                    EditText by = (EditText) root.findViewById(R.id.byear);
49                    String btitle = bt.getText().toString();
50                    String bauthor = ba.getText().toString();
51                    String year = by.getText().toString();
52                    int byear = Integer.parseInt(year);
53                    insertSQL = "INSERT INTO booksimple (TITLE, AUTHOR, YEAR) " +
54                        "VALUES('" + btitle + "', '" + bauthor + "'," + byear + ");";
55                    myDB.execSQL(insertSQL);
56                    myDB.close() ;
57                } catch (SQLiteException e) {
58                    tv.setText("OOPS");
59                }
60            }
61        });
62        //   final TextView textView = binding.textGallery;
63        //   galleryViewModel.getText().observe(getViewLifecycleOwner(), textView::setText);
64        return root;
65    }
```

FIGURE 11.26
A button in a fragment requires an *OnClick* listener.

line 12 of Table 11.4, which facilitates the root qualified call to the *find-ViewById* method found later in line 25 referencing the *TextView* widget used to display the information.

The app coded thus far now performs the same functions as did the app featured in the previous chapter. It accomplished this using the three tabs provided when the project was created. It is quite possible that a navigation drawer app will require more than three drawer items to accomplish its purpose. This requires the addition of one or more menu items. The tasks required to add an additional menu item and its associated fragment are detailed in the next section.

TABLE 11.4

Modifying the Fragment to Display Table Records

SlideshowFragment.java

```java
1   package com.example.navdrawerdemo.ui.slideshow;
2   import android.database.Cursor;
3   import android.database.sqlite.SQLiteDatabase;
4   import android.os.Bundle;
5   import android.view.LayoutInflater;
6   import android.view.View;
7   import android.view.ViewGroup;
8   import android.widget.TextView;
9   import androidx.annotation.NonNull;
10  import androidx.fragment.app.Fragment;
11  import androidx.lifecycle.ViewModelProvider;
12  import com.example.navdrawerdemo.R;
13  import com.example.navdrawerdemo.databinding.FragmentSlideshowBinding;
14  public class SlideshowFragment extends Fragment {
15      private FragmentSlideshowBinding binding;
16      public View onCreateView(@NonNull LayoutInflater inflater,
17                              ViewGroup container, Bundle savedInstanceState) {
18          SlideshowViewModel slideshowViewModel =
19                  new ViewModelProvider(this).get(SlideshowViewModel.class);
20
21          binding = FragmentSlideshowBinding.inflate(inflater, container, false);
22          View root = binding.getRoot();
23          // Get the database records and display them
24          String dbinfo = "Books in my library:\n\n";
25          TextView tv = (TextView) root.findViewById (R.id.displayinfo);
26          try {
27              SQLiteDatabase myDB = SQLiteDatabase.openDatabase(
28                      "/data/data/" + getActivity().getPackageName() +
29                              "/databases/simplebooks1.db",
30                      null,
31                      SQLiteDatabase.OPEN_READONLY);
32              // now get data to display
33              String sql = "SELECT * FROM booksimple;";
34              Cursor crs = myDB.rawQuery(sql, null);
35              if (crs.moveToFirst()) {
36                  // ok database has records
37                  do {
38                      dbinfo += crs.getString(0) + "   " +
39                              crs.getString(1) + "   " +
40                              crs.getInt(2) + "\n\n";
41                  } while (crs.moveToNext());
42              }
43              tv.setText(dbinfo);
44              myDB.close();
45          }   catch (Exception e) {
46              tv.setText("OOPs something is wrong");
47          }
48  //      final TextView textView = binding.textSlideshow;
49  //      slideshowViewModel.getText().observe(getViewLifecycleOwner(),
50  //              textView::setText);
51          return root;
52      }
53      @Override
54      public void onDestroyView() {
55          super.onDestroyView();
56          binding = null;
57      }
58  }
```

Adding Drawer Menu Items and Corresponding Fragments

Most navigation drawer apps require more than three menu items. In fact, when there are only three or four menu items, it may be easier to implement a "tabbed" app, which is the subject of the next chapter. The point here is that the requirement for additional drawer menu items and corresponding fragments is very real. Therefore, the process for adding an additional drawer menu item and its corresponding fragment is outlined in a stepwise procedure that follows.

1. Right-click on the *ui* subfolder folder in the Project view and select *New → Fragment → Fragment* with *ViewModel* as illustrated in Figure 11.27.

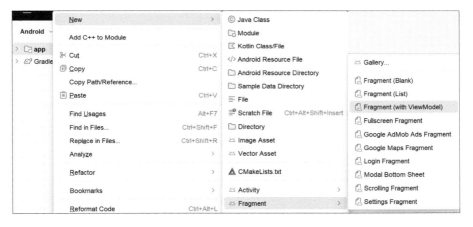

FIGURE 11.27
Adding a new fragment to the app.

2. Assign a name to the new fragment. For the sake of example in this chapter app, the new fragment has been named "DeleteAnAuthorsBooks".

3. Open the *activity_main_drawer.xml* layout file in the *menu* subfolder to add this fragment as a fourth navigation menu item. To do so, open the Code view and then just copy the third item and modify the *id* in the copy as appropriate along with the icon and title values. An example is provided in Figure 11.28.

4. Open *MainActivity.java* and add "R.id.new_items_id" to the list of menu items for the navigation drawer as illustrated in Figure 11.29.

5. Finalize the navigation for this new fragment by adding it to the navigation graph. To do so, open the *mobile_navigation.xml* file found in the *navigation* folder in the Code view. Copy the last fragment

```
</> activity_main_drawer.xml  ×

1      <?xml version="1.0" encoding="utf-8"?>
2      <menu xmlns:android="http://schemas.android.com/apk/res/android"
3          xmlns:tools="http://schemas.android.com/tools"
4          tools:showIn="navigation_view">
5
6          <group android:checkableBehavior="single">
7              <item
8                  android:id="@+id/nav_home"
9                  android:icon="@drawable/ic_action_myhome"
10                 android:title="Home" />
11             <item
12                 android:id="@+id/nav_slideshow"
13                 android:icon="@drawable/ic_action_name"
14                 android:title="Add a Book" />
15             <item
16                 android:id="@+id/nav_gallery"
17                 android:icon="@drawable/ic_action_listbooks"
18                 android:title="@string/menu_gallery" />
19             <item
20                 android:id="@+id/nav_deleteauthor"
21                 android:icon="@drawable/ic_action_delete"
22                 android:title="Delete An Author" />
23         </group>
24     </menu>
```

FIGURE 11.28
A new item corresponding to the new fragment is added to the *activity_main_drawer.xml* file.

```
// Passing each menu ID as a set of Ids because each
// menu should be considered as top level destinations.
mAppBarConfiguration = new AppBarConfiguration.Builder(
        R.id.nav_home, R.id.nav_gallery, R.id.nav_slideshow,
        R.id.nav_deleteauthor)
        .setOpenableLayout(drawer)
        .build();
```

FIGURE 11.29
A reference to the new fragment must be added to the *AppBar* in the main activity.

and modify it to reflect the information appropriate for the new fourth fragment. This requires modifying all of the attributes. An example appropriate to the sample app in this chapter is provided in Table 11.5.

TABLE 11.5

Modifying the Navigation Graph

navigation/mobile_navigation.xml

```
<?xml version="1.0" encoding="utf-8"?>
<navigation xmlns:android="http://schemas.android.com/apk/res/android"
    xmlns:app="http://schemas.android.com/apk/res-auto"
    xmlns:tools="http://schemas.android.com/tools"
    android:id="@+id/mobile_navigation"
    app:startDestination="@+id/nav_home">

    <fragment
        android:id="@+id/nav_home"
        android:name="com.example.navdrawerdemo2.ui.home.HomeFragment"
        android:label="@string/menu_home"
        tools:layout="@layout/fragment_home" />

    <fragment
        android:id="@+id/nav_gallery"
        android:name="com.example.navdrawerdemo2.ui.gallery.GalleryFragment"
        android:label="@string/menu_gallery"
        tools:layout="@layout/fragment_gallery" />

    <fragment
        android:id="@+id/nav_slideshow"
        android:name="com.example.navdrawerdemo2.ui.slideshow.SlideshowFragment"
        android:label="@string/menu_slideshow"
        tools:layout="@layout/fragment_slideshow" />

    <fragment
        android:id="@+id/nav_deleteauthor"
        android:name="com.example.navdrawerdemo2.ui.DeleteAnAuthorsBooks"
        android:label="Delete an Author's Books"
        tools:layout="@layout/fragment_delete_an_authors_books" />

</navigation>
```

6. Modify the fragment layout and corresponding Java code files to enact the behavior desired for the fourth fragment you are adding to the app.

The Floating Action Button

The default floating action button (fab) in the Navigation Drawer activity is a placeholder that presents an email icon as its image. To make this email action operational, replace the default code in the MainActivity.java file that is associated with the fab event listener. This code is in Figure 11.20 in lines 32 through 38.

Other popular possibilities for a floating action button include a "share" feature, a camera access, a search facility, an alarm element, a "play/pause" control, and a shopping cart button access. The "play/pause" feature is explored in Chapter 14.

To remove the floating action button entirely from a Navigation Drawer activity, delete all codes related to the fab in the *app_bar_main.xml* file and in the *MainActivity.java* file.

Design Issues

Navigation Drawer activities are not as common as tabbed activities. But the implementation of Navigation Drawer activities is strongly preferred when the number of tabs exceeds four or five. The Navigation Drawer activity also makes it easy to create groups and subgroups of navigation items that can be hierarchically arranged for presentation on the slide-in menu.

Exercises

Choose an exercise in either Chapter 9 (shared preferences) or Chapter 10 (databases) and code the application as a navigation drawer activity. Be sure to remove any buttons that are used to transfer the user to a different activity since they are no longer needed (including the "Back" button). Be sure to specify "hints" for all input fields and content descriptions for all images.

Note

1. https://developer.android.com/guide/fragments/create (last accessed on November 20, 2023).

12

Tabbed Apps, Styles, and Themes

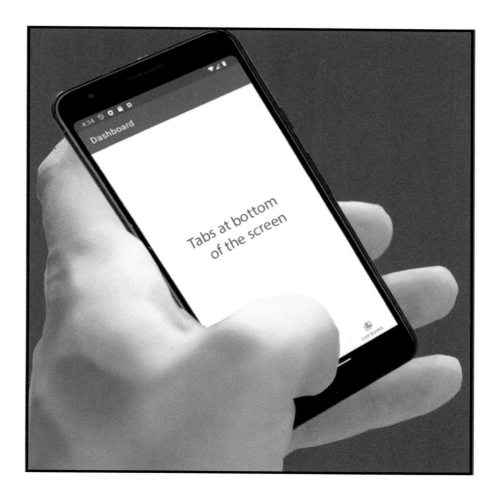

DOI: 10.1201/9781003286325-12

Learning Outcomes:

  ✓ *Ability to create bottom navigation activities.*
  ✓ *Understanding of the differences and similarities between navigation drawer activities and bottom navigation activities.*
  ✓ *Ability to customize the tabs in the app.*
  ✓ *Ability to customize the fragments in the app.*
  ✓ *Ability to add new tab items.*
  ✓ *Understanding of the difference between styles and themes in an app.*
  ✓ *Ability to specify a style.*
  ✓ *Ability to specify a theme.*
  ✓ *Ability to apply a theme across all relevant widgets within an app.*

In the previous chapter, we explored navigation drawer activities where the navigation items were presented in an itemized slide-in menu. This type of app was created by selecting the "Navigation Drawer Views Activity" when creating a new Android project. There is another type of Android navigation activity that is commonly referred to as a "tabbed app" that can be created by selecting the "Bottom Navigation Views Activity" project type. As the project type suggests, the navigation tabs in such an app are located at the bottom of the screen layout rather than as items in a slide-in menu. Many years ago, the tabs were actually incorporated into an action bar located at the top of the screen layout. But as apps and mobile phone technology evolved, it became clear that due to the way that users hold the mobile phone device, tabs at the bottom of the screen are easier to thumb access.

Tabs or bottom navigation is considered best when the maximum number of tabs is four or five, with the exact number being dependent on the width required to identify the tab. Tabs provide faster access between different views or features of an app. They tend to provide a clearer overview of the features and functionality of the app as well. The disadvantage of a tabbed app is the limitation on the number of tabs that can be clearly displayed horizontally across the width of a screen, especially on a mobile phone device.

While different in their presentation, navigation drawer-based activities and bottom navigation activities do possess similarities. One basic similarity is that they both manipulate fragments. Another similarity is their respective Java code. For the discussion that follows, it is assumed that the reader has read through Chapter 11 and is comfortable with the topics. Therefore, the similar code and mechanics between navigation drawer activities covered in Chapter 11 and bottom navigation activities will not be addressed in detail in this chapter. The Java code associated with the main activity and the individual fragments in a bottom navigation activity is so similar to that found in navigation drawer activities that it will not be covered in the same extensive detail in which it was covered in Chapter 11, and the reader is advised to carefully review the code discussion in Chapter 11 if they have not already done so.

Introduction to Bottom Navigation Activities

To create a bottom navigation project to implement a tabbed app, we select the "Bottom Navigation Views Activity" for the project template as illustrated in Figure 12.1.

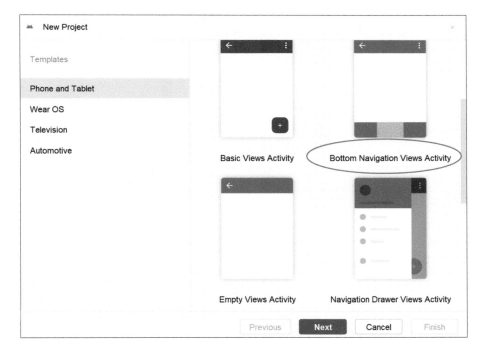

FIGURE 12.1
Create a "Bottom Navigation Views" activity.

After clicking "Next", assign the project name, folder location, and the Java language as we have done in all previous projects. Once created, the file structure is different for this type of project as is the interaction with the app. To appreciate this, run this app that has just been created. Upon launching the app, the "Home Fragment" is again displayed by default as illustrated in Figure 12.2.

FIGURE 12.2
Launching a Navigation Drawer app.

There is no menu. Click on the bottom tabs to interact with the app by click-ing each of the link items made available that are labeled *Home, Dashboard,* and *Notifications* as displayed in Figure 12.2. As you test each of the naviga-tion links, notice how each content message displayed identifies the display as a "fragment". By default, three fragments are provided with the creation of a "Bottom Navigation Views Activity". The fragments themselves are vir-tually the same as in the case of the navigation drawer type activity. Before considering the frames, however, let's look at the folder and file organization of a "Bottom Navigation Drawer Activity" project.

Anatomy of a Bottom Navigation App

Expanding on the *app* folder displays the same subfolders we have seen in previous projects. But if we further expand the *res* folder, we see once again that subfolders have been created named *menu* and *navigation*. In addition, if we expand the *layout* subfolder, we find once again that there are one *activity_main.xml* file and three fragment layout files as well. While some filenames are different, the folder and subfolder structure appear to be analogous to that encountered with the navigation drawer activities. In fact, the names of the fragment files and the menu file, namely *bottom_nav_menu.xml*, are different, but the overall organization is the same.

Upon a closer examination of the *activity_main.xml* file this project created, it appears that the component tree for this layout as shown in Figure 12.3 is actually quite different from that of the file with the same name in a navigation drawer activity. Figure 12.3 illustrates the components within a bottom navigation project's *activity_main.xml* layout with indications as to which portion of the screen is populated by each component.

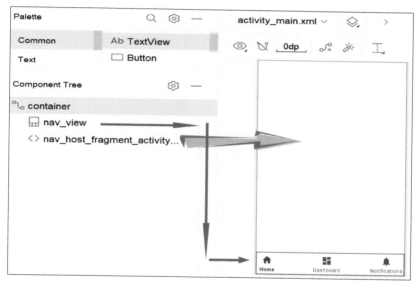

FIGURE 12.3
A different layout organizes the *activity_main.xml*.

The code view of this layout, as displayed in Table 12.1, reveals a constraint layout container and its children consisting of a "BottomNavigationView" widget and a fragment. The navigation view widget includes a menu file named *bottom_nav_menu.xml*. The fragment is assigned the *id* "nav_host_fragment_activity_main" indicating that it is a host fragment placeholder, similar to that encountered in the previous chapter. Furthermore, this fragment identifies a navigation graph located in the file named *mobile_navigation.xml* in the *navigation* subfolder.

In Chapter 11, it was the *activity_main_drawer.xml* file that defined the top-level navigation menu items. Here in bottom navigation activities, it is the

TABLE 12.1

Code behind *activity_main.xml* in a Bottom Navigation Activity

activity_main.xml

```xml
<?xml version="1.0" encoding="utf-8"?>
<androidx.constraintlayout.widget.ConstraintLayout
xmlns:android="http://schemas.android.com/apk/res/android"
    xmlns:app="http://schemas.android.com/apk/res-auto"
    xmlns:tools="http://schemas.android.com/tools"
    android:id="@+id/container"
    android:layout_width="match_parent"
    android:layout_height="match_parent"
    android:paddingTop="?attr/actionBarSize">

    <com.google.android.material.bottomnavigation.BottomNavigationView
        android:id="@+id/nav_view"
        android:layout_width="0dp"
        android:layout_height="wrap_content"
        android:layout_marginStart="0dp"
        android:layout_marginEnd="0dp"
        android:background="?android:attr/windowBackground"
        app:layout_constraintBottom_toBottomOf="parent"
        app:layout_constraintLeft_toLeftOf="parent"
        app:layout_constraintRight_toRightOf="parent"
        app:menu="@menu/bottom_nav_menu" />

    <fragment
        android:id="@+id/nav_host_fragment_activity_main"
        android:name="androidx.navigation.fragment.NavHostFragment"
        android:layout_width="match_parent"
        android:layout_height="match_parent"
        app:defaultNavHost="true"
        app:layout_constraintBottom_toTopOf="@id/nav_view"
        app:layout_constraintLeft_toLeftOf="parent"
        app:layout_constraintRight_toRightOf="parent"
        app:layout_constraintTop_toTopOf="parent"
        app:navGraph="@navigation/mobile_navigation"
        tools:ignore="FragmentTagUsage" />

</androidx.constraintlayout.widget.ConstraintLayout>
```

bottom_nav_menu.xml file that contains the navigation menu items. Examining the code view in Figure 12.4 of this file reveals a familiarity involving menu items and their attributes for id values, titles, and icons.

It is once again desirable to customize the titles and icons for the navigation menu items. Relevant icons can once again be created using the Image Asset Studio, and the titles can simply be assigned new string values. Just to review, the Image Asset Studio is obtained by right-clicking on the app folder in the project view and selecting *New → Image Asset*. The remaining instructions for obtaining a new icon can be found in Chapter 11. Let's customize the sample app to achieve the same functionality as did the sample app in Chapter 11. Figure 12.5 illustrates how the bottom navigation menu can be modified to accommodate this sample app. Recall that the purpose of the app is to maintain an inventory for a personal library of books.

```
</> bottom_nav_menu.xml  ✕

1      <?xml version="1.0" encoding="utf-8"?>
2      <menu xmlns:android="http://schemas.android.com/apk/res/android">
3
4          <item
5              android:id="@+id/navigation_home"
6 🏠          android:icon="@drawable/ic_home_black_24dp"
7              android:title="Home" />
8
9          <item
10             android:id="@+id/navigation_dashboard"
11 ▦         android:icon="@drawable/ic_dashboard_black_24dp"
12             android:title="Dashboard" />
13
14         <item
15             android:id="@+id/navigation_notifications"
16 🔔         android:icon="@drawable/ic_notifications_black_24dp"
17             android:title="Notifications" />
18
19     </menu>
```

FIGURE 12.4
Default *bottom_nav_menu.xml*.

```
</> bottom_nav_menu.xml  ✕

1      <?xml version="1.0" encoding="utf-8"?>
2      <menu xmlns:android="http://schemas.android.com/apk/res/android">
3
4          <item
5              android:id="@+id/navigation_home"
6 🏠          android:icon="@drawable/ic_home_black_24dp"
7              android:title="Home" />
8
9          <item
10             android:id="@+id/navigation_dashboard"
11 ▪         android:icon="@drawable/ic_action_addbook"
12             android:title="Add a Book" />
13
14         <item
15             android:id="@+id/navigation_notifications"
16 ▫         android:icon="@drawable/ic_action_listbooks"
17             android:title="List books" />
18
19     </menu>
```

FIGURE 12.5
Customized *bottom_nav_menu.xml*.

Run the app. Figure 12.6 shows the changes that have been made to this point.

FIGURE 12.6
Running the app to examine the changes made thus far.

Customizing the Fragments and Checking Their Management

Fragments were extensively covered in Chapter 11, and so the reader is advised to go back to review that material if they have not already done so. Fragments are the same in bottom navigation activities as they are in navigation drawer activities. The only difference is the file names. To prove the point, Figure 12.7 illustrates the duplication of fragment code in the two types of navigation activities. The code on the left in Figure 12.7 is the default Java code from *HomeFragment. java* in the navigation drawer activity covered extensively in Chapter 11. The code on the right is the default Java code from the *HomeFragment.java* file for the topic of this chapter, the bottom navigation activity.

In addition, once again there are two java code files for each of the default fragments. The two code files for the default "Home" fragment identify *HomeFragment.java* and *HomeViewModel.java* which are in a subfolder named "home". This is also what was observed in Chapter 11. Explore to confirm that there are two comparable files for the "Dashboard" fragment situated in

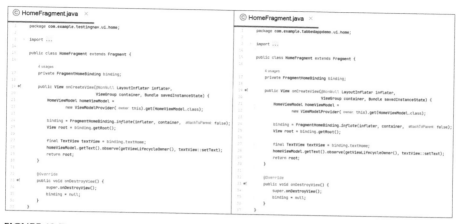

FIGURE 12.7
The Java code for fragment is exactly the same in both types of *nav* activities.

a subfolder named "dashboard" and two similar files for the "Notifications" fragment situated in a subfolder named "notifications".

So far, except for the navigation components, the organization and contents of the files are the same in the navigation drawer and bottom navigation activities. The exception could be the contents of the *MainActivity.java* file in each, as we have not yet compared them. Figure 12.8 displays the *MainActivity.java* code for the bottom navigation activity. It is different in that there are fewer statements. The missing statements are those that deal with

```java
package com.example.tabbedappdemo;

import ...

public class MainActivity extends AppCompatActivity {
    3 usages
    private ActivityMainBinding binding;

    protected void onCreate(Bundle savedInstanceState) {
        super.onCreate(savedInstanceState);

        binding = ActivityMainBinding.inflate(getLayoutInflater());
        setContentView(binding.getRoot());

        BottomNavigationView navView = findViewById(R.id.nav_view);
        // Passing each menu ID as a set of Ids because each
        // menu should be considered as top level destinations.
        AppBarConfiguration appBarConfiguration = new AppBarConfiguration.Builder(
                R.id.navigation_home, R.id.navigation_dashboard, R.id.navigation_notifications)
                .build();
        NavController navController = Navigation.findNavController( activity: this, R.id.nav_host_fragment_activity_main);
        NavigationUI.setupActionBarWithNavController( activity: this, navController, appBarConfiguration);
        NavigationUI.setupWithNavController(binding.navView, navController);
    }
}
```

FIGURE 12.8
Contents of *MainActivity.java* in a bottom navigation activity.

the slide-in menu. Other than these missing statements, the only difference is in line 24 of Figure 12.8 which creates a *BottomNavigationView* object instead of a *NavigationView* object. And the file names used in the two main activity code files are different. Other than these few differences, the code is the same.

The *NavController* created in line 30 by the *findNavController* method of the *Navigation* API will again manage all user navigations. It is still also strongly associated with the navigation graph, which is defined in the file named *mobile_navigation.xml*.

The Navigation User Interface

In addition to rendering the fragment content in response to user interaction, the "Navigation User Interface" (*NavigationUI*) must also update the app bar to reflect the appropriate content. So, run the app and take notice that when you select the "Add a Book" tab as shown in Figure 12.9, the app bar at the top of the screen displays "Dashboard". Similarly, if you tap the "List books" tab, the app bar displays "Notifications".

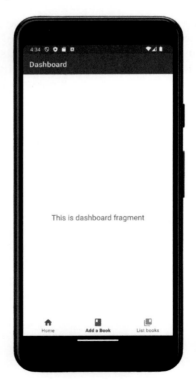

FIGURE 12.9
AppBar displays content specified in *mobile_navigation.xml*.

To remedy this, we must once again modify the content of *mobile_navigation. xml*. The necessary changes are highlighted in Figure 12.10. The label properties highlighted in Figure 12.10 have been modified to reflect appropriate destination names for the fragments within the sample app being developed in this chapter. Notice that the *label* attribute is the only attribute whose value has been changed. The other attributes have not been changed. They still read according to the original fragment names associated with "home", "dashboard", and "notifications". These fragments have simply been repurposed rather than deleted, since deletion would necessitate the creation of new fragments in their place with other significant ramifications.

```xml
</> mobile_navigation.xml   ×

1    <?xml version="1.0" encoding="utf-8"?>
2    <navigation xmlns:android="http://schemas.android.com/apk/res/android"
3        xmlns:app="http://schemas.android.com/apk/res-auto"
4        xmlns:tools="http://schemas.android.com/tools"
5        android:id="@+id/mobile_navigation"
6        app:startDestination="@+id/navigation_home">
7
8        <fragment
9            android:id="@+id/navigation_home"
10           android:name="com.example.tabbedappdemo.ui.home.HomeFragment"
11           android:label="Home"
12           tools:layout="@layout/fragment_home" />
13
14       <fragment
15           android:id="@+id/navigation_dashboard"
16           android:name="com.example.tabbedappdemo.ui.dashboard.DashboardFragment"
17           android:label="Add a Book"
18           tools:layout="@layout/fragment_dashboard" />
19
20       <fragment
21           android:id="@+id/navigation_notifications"
22           android:name="com.example.tabbedappdemo.ui.notifications.NotificationsFragment"
23           android:label="List books"
24           tools:layout="@layout/fragment_notifications" />
25   </navigation>
```

FIGURE 12.10
Customization of *mobile_navigation.xml*.

These modifications to *mobile_navigation.xml* will update the app bar at the top of the screen as the user clicks the tabs of an app in execution. But the content of the fragments must, of course, be updated as well.

Customizing the Content of the Fragments

Since the main activity in a Navigation Drawer app swaps fragments in and out of a placeholder "host" fragment, it is the individual fragments initially created in the files named *fragment_home.xml*, *fragment_dashboard.xml*, and *fragment_notifications.xml* that should be modified to achieve the "easiest" customization. As previously mentioned, we will leave the fragments as named by default. Therefore, we will choose only to modify their content.

In this example, let's modify the "Home" fragment content in the file named *fragment_home.xml* so that it will display an image and an explanation of the app. We will continue working with the project that we started earlier in this chapter that implements an inventory of a personal library of books. So, to keep the application relatively simple, let's modify the "Home" fragment so that it renders as shown in Figure 12.11.

FIGURE 12.11
The updated "Home" fragment for the sample app.

Figure 12.11 should look familiar. It is the same content as that displayed in Figure 11.22 in the "Home" fragment back in Chapter 11. In fact, the code in the file named *fragment_home.xml* is the same as the code that produced the home fragment content in Chapter 11. Note that again the *HomeFragment.java* file needs to be modified to comment out the reference to the text view referencing the *HomeViewModel* to avoid a runtime error. This modification is documented in Table 12.2.

```
ⓒ HomeFragment.java  ✕
─────────────────────────────
 1      package com.example.tabbedappdemo.ui.home;
 2
 3  ›   import ...
14
15      public class HomeFragment extends Fragment {
16
           3 usages
17         private FragmentHomeBinding binding;
18
19 •↑     public View onCreateView(@NonNull LayoutInflater inflater,
20                                  ViewGroup container, Bundle savedInstanceState) {
21             HomeViewModel homeViewModel =
22                 new ViewModelProvider( owner: this).get(HomeViewModel.class);
23
24             binding = FragmentHomeBinding.inflate(inflater, container, attachToParent: false);
25             View root = binding.getRoot();
26
27             //    final TextView textView = binding.textHome;
28             //    homeViewModel.getText().observe(getViewLifecycleOwner(), textView::setText);
29             return root;
30         }
31
32         @Override
33 •↑     public void onDestroyView() {
34             super.onDestroyView();
35             binding = null;
36         }
37     }
```

FIGURE 12.12
Reminder to modify the *HomeViewModel.java* file content.

This is necessary for the same reason that it was so in Chapter 11. The modified fragment content removed an item that the *HomeViewModel.java* code required. Recall that the purpose of a *ViewModel* is to facilitate the sharing of data between fragments or between a fragment and its "host" activity. In the apps we are developing in this text, we are not engaged in such sharing of data. Therefore, it is critical that the two highlighted statements in Figure 12.12 be commented out in the *HomeFragment.java* file and every other fragment's modified primary *.java* file as well.

It may be surprising to discover that the other fragments can utilize the very same code developed for the fragments in the sample app developed in Chapter 11. Specifically, the "Dashboard" fragment here can utilize the very same code from the "Slideshow" fragment previously coded in Chapter 11. Likewise, the "Notifications" fragment can utilize the very same code from the "Gallery" fragment.

To clarify, Table 12.2 lists the Java code for the "Dashboard" fragment, which should duplicate the code shown in Figure 11.26 for the "Gallery" fragment in Chapter 11, and Table 12.3 lists the code for the "Notifications" fragment.

TABLE 12.2

Code behind the "Dashboard" Fragment

DashboardFragment.java

```java
package com.example.tabbedappdemo.ui.dashboard;

import android.database.Cursor;
import android.database.sqlite.SQLiteDatabase;
import android.database.sqlite.SQLiteException;
import android.os.Bundle;
import android.view.LayoutInflater;
import android.view.View;
import android.view.ViewGroup;
import android.widget.EditText;
import android.widget.ImageButton;
import android.widget.TextView;
import androidx.annotation.NonNull;
import androidx.fragment.app.Fragment;
import androidx.lifecycle.ViewModelProvider;
import com.example.tabbedappdemo.R;
import com.example.tabbedappdemo.databinding.FragmentDashboardBinding;

public class DashboardFragment extends Fragment {

    private FragmentDashboardBinding binding;

    public View onCreateView(@NonNull LayoutInflater inflater,
                             ViewGroup container, Bundle savedInstanceState)
{
        DashboardViewModel dashboardViewModel =
                new ViewModelProvider(this).get(DashboardViewModel.class);

        binding = FragmentDashboardBinding.inflate
                                        (inflater, container, false);
        View root = binding.getRoot();
        ImageButton book = (ImageButton)
                        root.findViewById(R.id.btn_addabook);
        book.setOnClickListener(new View.OnClickListener(){
            @Override
            public void onClick(View v) {
    // Get user data and store in the database as a new record
    // assuming the database already exists so don't need CREATE TABLE
    try {
        SQLiteDatabase myDB = SQLiteDatabase.openDatabase(
                "/data/data/" + getActivity().getPackageName() +
                        "/databases/simplebooks1.db",
                null,
                SQLiteDatabase.OPEN_READWRITE);
        String insertSQL = "000";
        EditText bt = (EditText) root.findViewById(R.id.btitle);
        EditText ba = (EditText) root.findViewById(R.id.bauthor);
        EditText by = (EditText) root.findViewById(R.id.byear);
        // year as an integer
        String btitle = bt.getText().toString();
        String bauthor = ba.getText().toString();
        String year = by.getText().toString();
        int byear = Integer.parseInt(year);

        insertSQL = "INSERT INTO booksimple (TITLE, AUTHOR, YEAR) " +
                "VALUES('" + btitle + "', '" + bauthor + "'," + byear +
");" ;
```

(Continued)

TABLE 12.2   (*Continued*)

Code behind the "Dashboard" Fragment

DashboardFragment.java

```
                myDB.execSQL(insertSQL);
                myDB.close();

            } catch (SQLiteException e) {
              e.printStackTrace();
            }
        }
    });
    //    final TextView textView = binding.textDashboard;
    //    dashboardViewModel.getText().observe
    //                      (getViewLifecycleOwner(), textView::setText);
        return root;
    }

    @Override
    public void onDestroyView() {
        super.onDestroyView();
        binding = null;
    }
}
```

TABLE 12.3

Code behind the "Notifications" Fragment

NotificationsFragment.java

```
package com.example.tabbedappdemo.ui.notifications;

import android.database.Cursor;
import android.database.sqlite.SQLiteDatabase;
import android.os.Bundle;
import android.view.LayoutInflater;
import android.view.View;
import android.view.ViewGroup;
import android.widget.TextView;

import androidx.annotation.NonNull;
import androidx.fragment.app.Fragment;
import androidx.lifecycle.ViewModelProvider;

import com.example.tabbedappdemo.R;
import com.example.tabbedappdemo.databinding.FragmentNotificationsBinding;

public class NotificationsFragment extends Fragment {

    private FragmentNotificationsBinding binding;

    public View onCreateView(@NonNull LayoutInflater inflater,
                ViewGroup container, Bundle savedInstanceState) {
        NotificationsViewModel notificationsViewModel =    new
            ViewModelProvider(this).get(NotificationsViewModel.class);

        binding = FragmentNotificationsBinding.inflate
                                (inflater, container, false);
        View root = binding.getRoot();
        //copied and pasted this code
```

(*Continued*)

TABLE 12.3   *(Continued)*

Code behind the "Notifications" Fragment

NotificationsFragment.java

```java
        String dbinfo = "";
        TextView tv = (TextView) root.findViewById(R.id.displayinfo);
        try {
            SQLiteDatabase myDB = SQLiteDatabase.openDatabase(
                    "/data/data/" + getActivity().getPackageName() +
                        "/databases/simplebooks1.db",
                null,
                SQLiteDatabase.OPEN_READONLY);
            // now get data to display
            String sql = "SELECT * FROM booksimple;";
            Cursor crs = myDB.rawQuery(sql, null);

            if (crs.moveToFirst()) {
                // ok database has records
                do {
                    dbinfo += crs.getString(0) + "   " +
                                crs.getString(1) + "   " +
                                crs.getInt(2) + "\n\n";
                } while (crs.moveToNext());
            }
            tv.setText(dbinfo);
            myDB.close();
        }   catch (Exception e) {
            tv.setText("OOPs something is wrong");

        }
        // final TextView textView = binding.textNotifications;
        // notificationsViewModel.getText().observe
        //                      (getViewLifecycleOwner(), textView::setText);
        return root;
    }

    @Override
    public void onDestroyView() {
        super.onDestroyView();
        binding = null;
    }
}
```

Again, since the code is situated in a fragment rather than an activity, we again needed to import a reference for "R" to reference the app's resources. As was the case with the fragments in Chapter 11, we cannot simply use *".findViewById(R."* to do so. An *import* statement is again required to reference app resources directly. The *import* statement is specifically:

import com.example.yourprojectname.R;

To reiterate that which was discussed in Chapter 11, another significant difference between activities and fragments is in the handling of *onClick* events. In the case of fragments, the developer does not have a choice. In a fragment, a button *onClick* event listener must be employed. Such an event handler for a button component in Java is referred to as an *onClickListener* method. Therefore, such an *onClickListener* event handler is required for the "Add a Book" image button as reflected in the Java code in Table 12.2.

Adding Tab Menu Items and Corresponding Fragments

It is not uncommon for a tabbed app to require more than three tabs. Therefore, the process for adding an additional tab menu item and its corresponding fragment is outlined in a stepwise procedure that follows.

1. Right-click on the *ui* subfolder folder in the Project view and select *New → Fragment → Fragment* with *ViewModel* as illustrated in Figure 12.13.

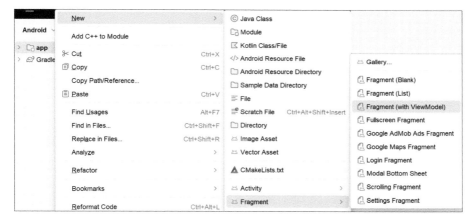

FIGURE 12.13
Adding another tab fragment to the project.

2. Assign a name to the new fragment. For the sake of example in this chapter app, the new fragment has been named "DeleteAnAuthorsBooks".

3. Open the *bottom_nav_menu.xml* layout file in the *menu* subfolder to add this fragment as a fourth navigation menu item. To do so, open the code view for the file in Android Studio and then just copy the third item and modify the *id* in the copy as appropriate along with the icon and title values. An example is provided in Figure 12.14. The Image Asset Studio was used as was the case earlier in this chapter to create an appropriate icon.

4. Open *MainActivity.java* and add "R.id.new_items_id" to the list of menu items for the navigation drawer as illustrated in line 24 in Figure 12.15.

5. Finalize the navigation for this new fragment by adding it to the navigation graph. To do so, open the code view for the *mobile_navigation. xml* file found in the *navigation* subfolder. Copy the last fragment and modify it to reflect the information appropriate for the new

```
</> bottom_nav_menu.xml ✕

1      <?xml version="1.0" encoding="utf-8"?>
2      <menu xmlns:android="http://schemas.android.com/apk/res/android">
3
4          <item
5              android:id="@+id/navigation_home"
6              android:icon="@drawable/ic_home_black_24dp"
7              android:title="Home" />
8
9          <item
10             android:id="@+id/navigation_dashboard"
11             android:icon="@drawable/ic_action_addbook"
12             android:title="Add a Book" />
13
14         <item
15             android:id="@+id/navigation_notifications"
16             android:icon="@drawable/ic_action_listbooks"
17             android:title="List books" />
18         <item
19             android:id="@+id/navigation_deleteauthor"
20             android:icon="@drawable/ic_action_deletebooks"
21             android:title="Delete Author" />
22
23     </menu>
```

FIGURE 12.14
Updating the navigation menu to accommodate another tab.

```
© MainActivity.java ✕

1      package com.example.tabbedappdemo;
2  >   import ...
13 </> public class MainActivity extends AppCompatActivity {
       3 usages
14     private ActivityMainBinding binding;
15 ⊙↑     protected void onCreate(Bundle savedInstanceState) {
16             super.onCreate(savedInstanceState);
17             binding = ActivityMainBinding.inflate(getLayoutInflater());
18             setContentView(binding.getRoot());
19             BottomNavigationView navView = findViewById(R.id.nav_view);
20             // Passing each menu ID as a set of Ids because each
21             // menu should be considered as top level destinations.
22             AppBarConfiguration appBarConfiguration = new AppBarConfiguration.Builder(
23                     R.id.navigation_home, R.id.navigation_dashboard,
24                     R.id.navigation_notifications, R.id.navigation_deleteauthor)
25                     .build();
26             NavController navController = Navigation.findNavController( activity: this,
27                     R.id.nav_host_fragment_activity_main);
28             NavigationUI.setupActionBarWithNavController( activity: this, navController,
29                     appBarConfiguration);
30             NavigationUI.setupWithNavController(binding.navView, navController);
31         }
32     }
```

FIGURE 12.15
Adding the new tab fragment to the *MainActivity.java* code.

fourth fragment. This requires modifying all of the attributes. An example appropriate to the sample app in this chapter is provided in Table 12.4.

TABLE 12.4

Update the Navigation Graph

mobile_navigation.xml

```xml
<?xml version="1.0" encoding="utf-8"?>
<navigation xmlns:android="http://schemas.android.com/apk/res/android"
    xmlns:app="http://schemas.android.com/apk/res-auto"
    xmlns:tools="http://schemas.android.com/tools"
    android:id="@+id/mobile_navigation"
    app:startDestination="@+id/navigation_home">
  <fragment
      android:id="@+id/navigation_home"
      android:name="com.example.tabbedappdemo.ui.home.HomeFragment"
      android:label="@string/title_home"
      tools:layout="@layout/fragment_home" />
  <fragment
      android:id="@+id/navigation_dashboard"
      android:name="com.example.tabbedappdemo.ui.dashboard.
DashboardFragment"
      android:label="@string/menu_title_add_a_book"
      tools:layout="@layout/fragment_dashboard" />
  <fragment
      android:id="@+id/navigation_notifications"
      android:name="com.example.tabbedappdemo.ui.notifications.
NotificationsFragment"
      android:label="@string/menu_title_list_books"
      tools:layout="@layout/fragment_notifications" />
  <fragment
      android:id="@+id/navigation_deleteauthor"
      android:name="com.example.tabbedappdemo.ui.DeleteAnAuthorsBook"
      android:label="@string/delete_author"
      tools:layout="@layout/fragment_delete_an_authors_book" />
</navigation>
```

6. Modify the fragment layout and corresponding Java code files to enact the behavior desired for the fourth fragment you are adding to the app.

Further Customization – Styles and Themes

Android styles and themes influence the visual appearances of the widgets in an app. A style defines a collection of attribute values that apply to a widget instance. For example, a style can be defined to apply to a *TextView* or a *Button*. Thus, the scope of a style is focused on an individual widget level.

For example, in the sample app developed in this chapter, there is a *TextView* widget defined in one of the layouts as shown in Table 12.5. A style could be defined for this widget as shown in Table 12.6 and then applied as illustrated in Table 12.7.

TABLE 12.5

A TextView Widget with Various Attributes

fragment_dashboard.xml - partial

```
<TextView
    android:id="@+id/textView4"
    android:layout_width="167dp"
    android:layout_height="55dp"
    android:text="@string/book_author"
    android:textColor="@color/black"
    android:textSize="@dimen/txtsize"
    app:layout_constraintBottom_toBottomOf="parent"
    app:layout_constraintEnd_toEndOf="parent"
    app:layout_constraintHorizontal_bias="0.139"
    app:layout_constraintStart_toStartOf="parent"
    app:layout_constraintTop_toBottomOf="@+id/textView3"
    app:layout_constraintVertical_bias="0.086" />
```

TABLE 12.6

Defining a Style

```
<style name="PromptTextStyle">
    <item name="android:textColor">#000000</item>
    <item name="android:textSize">24sp</item>
</style>
```

TABLE 12.7

Applying a Style

```
<TextView
    android:id="@+id/textView4"
    android:layout_width="167dp"
    android:layout_height="55dp"
    android:text="@string/book_author"
    style="@style/PromptTextStyle"
    app:layout_constraintBottom_toBottomOf="parent"
    app:layout_constraintEnd_toEndOf="parent"
    app:layout_constraintHorizontal_bias="0.139"
    app:layout_constraintStart_toStartOf="parent"
    app:layout_constraintTop_toBottomOf="@+id/
textView3"
    app:layout_constraintVertical_bias="0.086" />
```

Such a style can be stored in a file of styles usually named *styles.xml* located in the *values* subfolder of the project. Or a style can be specified in the *themes* subfolder of the *values* subfolder in the default file named *themes.xml*. This file is initialized at project creation time, and styles can be added as the app is developed.

The default *themes.xml* file content can vary with the various types of projects. Figure 12.16 shows the default content of the *themes.xml* file that was created for the sample app in this chapter.

```xml
</> themes.xml ✕

1     <resources xmlns:tools="http://schemas.android.com/tools">
2         <!-- Base application theme. -->
3         <style name="Theme.TabbedAppDemo" parent="Theme.MaterialComponents.DayNight.DarkActionBar">
4             <!-- Primary brand color. -->
5             <item name="colorPrimary">@color/purple_500</item>
6             <item name="colorPrimaryVariant">@color/purple_700</item>
7             <item name="colorOnPrimary">@color/white</item>
8             <!-- Secondary brand color. -->
9             <item name="colorSecondary">@color/teal_200</item>
10            <item name="colorSecondaryVariant">@color/teal_700</item>
11            <item name="colorOnSecondary">@color/black</item>
12            <!-- Status bar color. -->
13            <item name="android:statusBarColor">?attr/colorPrimaryVariant</item>
14            <!-- Customize your theme here. -->
15        </style>
16    </resources>
17
```

FIGURE 12.16
Contents of the default *themes.xml* file.

The style in this file is affecting the visual appearance of the app bar, status bar, and tab items. A theme generally applies one or more styles as a collection to an entire activity or application. The principle is to provide a consistent look and feel across the app.

Applying a Spinner Style

One of the concerns developers often have revolves around the spinner widget. Many times, the spinner entries convey a font size that seems too small or a color combination that does not match the visual style of the app. These attributes can be modified with appropriate styling. But the spinner is a special widget in that it already has an associated style. We are looking to modify the style of its entries rather than the spinner widget itself. Therefore, to modify its entries, we use the "theme" attribute.

For example, in the recertification app example in Chapter 8, there is a spinner that provides a drop-down list of month names as shown in Figure 12.17. This spinner can be styled so that the month names appear in larger font and in a text color more appropriate to the visual styling of the app. For example, Table 12.8 identifies a style named "SpinnerItemStyle" that changes the text size of the spinner entries to 24 sp and changes the text color of the entries to a maroon color.

FIGURE 12.17
Default style for spinner entries.

TABLE 12.8

Defining a Style for a Spinner's Entries

```
<style name="SpinnerItemStyle">
    <item name="android:textSize">24sp</item>
    <item name="android:textColor">#800000
</item>
    <!-- You can include other styling attributes here if needed -->
</style>
```

Table 12.9 shows this style applied to the spinner. But notice that it is applied as a theme because the spinner widget already has a style attribute value. The goal is not to override it. A theme applies to the entire spinner widget including its entries. If this approach was not taken, the alternative would be to define a custom layout file and then use a custom adapter on the spinner widget that applies the custom layout. It is much simpler to just apply the custom style as a theme.

TABLE 12.9

Apply a Style to the Entries in a Spinner

```
<Spinner
    android:id="@+id/chosenmonth"
    android:layout_width="195dp"
    android:layout_height="48dp"
    android:entries="@array/seminar_months"
    style="@style/Widget.AppCompat.Spinner"
    android:theme="@style/SpinnerItemStyle"
    app:layout_constraintBottom_toBottomOf="parent"
    app:layout_constraintEnd_toEndOf="parent"
    app:layout_constraintHorizontal_bias="0.261"
    app:layout_constraintStart_toEndOf="@+id/textView2"
    app:layout_constraintTop_toBottomOf="@+id/textView"
    app:layout_constraintVertical_bias="0.054" />
```

Figure 12.18 displays the effect of the spinner item style when applied as a theme to the spinner entries. The text size is exaggerated for demonstration purposes.

FIGURE 12.18
Example of coded style applied to spinner entries.

The Application of a Theme

One advantage of themes over styles is the ability to apply a theme across an entire app. For example, it might be desirable to apply the same background color to all of the screen layouts in an app. Rather than setting a background attribute value in each layout file, a theme can be defined for the app which applies to all layouts across the app.

To apply a style across an entire app, the *AndroidManifest.xml* file contains a specification for an app theme. Figure 12.19 illustrates the location of this attribute. In this example, it is located at line 12 where there is a specification for "android:theme".

Ⓜ **AndroidManifest.xml** ✕

```
1    <?xml version="1.0" encoding="utf-8"?>
2    <manifest xmlns:android="http://schemas.android.com/apk/res/android"
3        xmlns:tools="http://schemas.android.com/tools">
4        <application
5            android:allowBackup="true"
6            android:dataExtractionRules="@xml/data_extraction_rules"
7            android:fullBackupContent="@xml/backup_rules"
8            android:icon="@mipmap/ic_launcher"
9            android:label="SelectionInputsChapter7"
10           android:roundIcon="@mipmap/ic_launcher_round"
11           android:supportsRtl="true"
12           android:theme="@style/Theme.SelectionInputsChapter7"
13           tools:targetApi="31">
14           <activity
15               android:name=".VerifyInput"
16               android:exported="false" />
17           <activity
18               android:name=".MainActivity2"
19               android:exported="false" />
20           <activity
21               android:name=".MainActivity"
22               android:exported="true">
23               <intent-filter>
24                   <action android:name="android.intent.action.MAIN" />
25                   <category android:name="android.intent.category.LAUNCHER" />
26               </intent-filter>
27           </activity>
28       </application>
29   </manifest>
```

FIGURE 12.19
Location of the app theme specification in the Android Manifest.

The definition of this theme can be modified to reflect default style(s) to be applied across the app. For example, to specify a text color to be used in every activity in the app unless overridden, articulate an item where the name is assigned the value "android:textColor". An example is provided in the *themes. xml* file listed in Table 12.10. Note the comment indicating where the styles should be placed along with an example. The text color to be applied in this example is highlighted in Table 12.10.

TABLE 12.10

Specifying a Style to be Applied across the Entire App

themes.xml

```
<resources xmlns:tools="http://schemas.android.com/tools">
    <!-- Base application theme. -->
    <style name="Base.Theme.SampleAppChapter12"
            parent="Theme.Material3.DayNight.NoActionBar">
     <!-- Customize your light theme here. -->
     <!-- <item name="colorPrimary">@color/my_light_primary</item> -->
     <item name="android:textColor">#800000</item>
    </style>

    <style name="Theme. SampleAppChapter12"
            parent="Base.Theme. SampleAppChapter12" />
</resources>
```

Note that the app background attribute of the primary layout container (e.g. the "ConstraintLayout" container) is specified using the item with name "android:windowBackground". This is the attribute to which a default background color for the layout area of the screen should be assigned. Using the "background" attribute instead will also color the app bar and the status bar and any other components that are present.

Design Issues

Tabbed applications are more common than navigation drawer activities. But the implementation of navigation drawer activities is strongly preferred when the number of tabs exceeds four or five. A navigation drawer activity also makes it easy to create groups and subgroups of navigation items that can be hierarchically arranged for presentation on the slide-in menu.

Styles are a means of collectively fashioning specific attributes for a widget. If a text color, for example, is part of an app's color scheme but is only applied to certain widgets, it should be defined as a style. On the other hand, themes are a means of collectively styling multiple views across the app. So, a theme is more appropriate if all text in the app is to be of the same color. Themes can also be adapted more easily to support light and dark modes based on device settings as well.

Exercises

Choose an exercise in either Chapter 9 or Chapter 10 and code the application described as a Tabbed app. Be sure to remove any buttons that are used to transfer the user to a different activity since they are no longer needed (including the "Back" button)! Be sure to specify "hints" for all input fields and content descriptions for all images.

Apply at least one style to the entire application and at least one style to an individual widget.

13

Hybrid Apps

DOI: 10.1201/9781003286325-13

Learning Outcomes:

- ✓ *Understanding of the benefits of incorporating a web view within an app.*
- ✓ *Ability to successfully include a web view within an app.*
- ✓ *Understanding when a google map benefits an app.*
- ✓ *Understanding of the various ways that a google map can enhance the purpose of an app.*
- ✓ *Understanding how to incorporate a Google map into an app.*
- ✓ *Understanding how to customize the basic visuals of a google map.*

In the previous chapter, we explored Android native apps. Native apps are self-contained and independent of any access outside of the device on which they execute. A hybrid app includes web content. This content is usually a web view component, but many developers consider the incorporation of a Google Maps activity a hybrid application as well since it requires access to information external to its host device. This chapter explores both web view content and Google Maps content in the discussion that follows.

Introduction to WebView

Google provides a *WebView* widget so that applications can display web content within an app, thereby keeping the user within the app rather than losing them in a sense to an external web browser. The *WebView* is a child of the parent *View* class and as such can be easily placed within a screen layout. The Java code used to manage a web view is also not complicated and provides features that enable a developer to control the user activity within the web view.

Before considering the "how to" for a web view, it may be helpful to consider relevant applications. The primary purpose of a web view is usually to display web content within an app. From a developer perspective, it enables web pages to be embedded within an otherwise native application without using a traditional web browser. It uses Chromium rather than Chrome, so it does not track browser data and offers more privacy than Chrome. It displays web page content without browser tabs.

The use of web views can be advantageous to developers whose content is meant for Android users and iOS users alike, since web view content consists of codes that can be shared among different platforms in a way that native app code cannot. Web views can also be very helpful in providing information that is updated often such as help facilities, reference guides, and user agreements. In addition, they provide a means of sharing third party content such as blog posts, real-time news updates, or social media feeds.

A disadvantage of web views is their reduced capability to manipulate a device's hardware components, such as the camera, sound, and files stored in a device's memory. They can also experience slow load times and become less responsive than native app code. There is also always a security risk involved with web content and a possible vulnerability to malicious code.

Embedding WebView Content within an App

Use the *WebView* widget to load a web page or share content from a web application within your Android app. As an extension of the *View* class, the *WebView* widget facilitates the display of online content within a layout. With some additional code, it is also possible to enable hyperlink navigation and JavaScript, neither of which may be enabled by default. Listed below are the steps and requirements for displaying web content within your Android app.

1. Drag a *WebView* widget from the Palette onto the layout. The *WebView* component is found in the *Widgets* category in the Palette. Assign it an id as it will be required for later access. Figure 13.1 displays the code view of a layout file that contains a *WebView*.

```
</> activity_main.xml  ×
```

```xml
1      <?xml version="1.0" encoding="utf-8"?>
2  ©   <androidx.constraintlayout.widget.ConstraintLayout
3          xmlns:android="http://schemas.android.com/apk/res/android"
4          xmlns:app="http://schemas.android.com/apk/res-auto"
5          xmlns:tools="http://schemas.android.com/tools"
6          android:layout_width="match_parent"
7          android:layout_height="match_parent"
8          tools:context=".MainActivity">
9
10         <WebView
11             android:id="@+id/my_webview"
12             android:layout_width="369dp"
13             android:layout_height="655dp"
14             app:layout_constraintBottom_toBottomOf="parent"
15             app:layout_constraintEnd_toEndOf="parent"
16             app:layout_constraintHorizontal_bias="0.38"
17             app:layout_constraintStart_toStartOf="parent"
18             app:layout_constraintTop_toTopOf="parent"
19             app:layout_constraintVertical_bias="0.671" />
20     </androidx.constraintlayout.widget.ConstraintLayout>
```

FIGURE 13.1
Code for a WebView widget.

2. Before the contents of a URL can be loaded into *WebView*, the application must have permission to access the Internet. To set up authorization for Internet access, request the "INTERNET" permission in the manifest file. So, add the content highlighted in Figure 13.2 before the *<application>* tag in the *AndroidManifest .xml* file.

```
Ⓜ AndroidManifest.xml    ✕

1       <?xml version="1.0" encoding="utf-8"?>
2       <manifest xmlns:android="http://schemas.android.com/apk/res/android"
3           xmlns:tools="http://schemas.android.com/tools">
4       <uses-permission android:name="android.permission.INTERNET" />
5           <!-- may need this permission as well:  -->
6       <uses-permission android:name="android.permission.ACCESS_NETWORK_STATE" />
7           <application
8               android:allowBackup="true"
9               android:dataExtractionRules="@xml/data_extraction_rules"
10              .
11              .
```

FIGURE 13.2
Add required permission.

3. If the app is running on the emulator or using wi-fi in a campus-like setting, network access permission may also be required. In this case, add an additional permission for ACCESS_NETWORK_STATE" as also displayed in Figure 13.2.

4. If the data to be loaded is not encrypted, then the application requires the flagged use of the *usesClearTextTraffic*, so in the *AndroidManifest. xml* file, add to the application the attribute and value:

```
<application
        android:usesCleartextTraffic="true"
```

5. After these preliminary specifications are complete, the content loading can proceed. So, as illustrated in Figure 13.3, in the relevant activity, create a *WebView* object to point to the *WebView* widget in the layout and then use this object to load the URL web content. If the web page that you plan to load in your *WebView* uses JavaScript, you may very well need to enable JavaScript, or the web page might not render in the web view. In most versions of Android, JavaScript is disabled by default. So, if the web view remains blank after the container layout appears, enable JavaScript. It can be enabled in the Java code through the web settings attached to the *WebView*. To do so, retrieve a web settings object and use one of its methods to enable JavaScript before the load operation as shown in Figure 13.3 lines 16–17.

© MainActivity.java ×

```
1          package com.example.chapter13demo;
2
3          import androidx.appcompat.app.AppCompatActivity;
4          import android.os.Bundle;
5          import android.webkit.WebSettings;
6          import android.webkit.WebView;
7
8 </>      public class MainActivity extends AppCompatActivity {
9
10             @Override
11 •↑         protected void onCreate(Bundle savedInstanceState) {
12                 super.onCreate(savedInstanceState);
13                 setContentView(R.layout.activity_main);
14
15                 WebView myWebView = (WebView) findViewById(R.id.my_webview);
16                 WebSettings webSettings = myWebView.getSettings();
17                 webSettings.setJavaScriptEnabled(true);
18                 myWebView.loadUrl("http://www.yahoo.com"); // or whatever URL
19
20             }
21         }
```

FIGURE 13.3
Loading web content into a layout.

Run the app. It should load the web page content. An access message may precede this load in the running emulator that asks if a Chrome account should be used or not. This choice is left to the user and does not affect the web content display.

Note that this code has run successfully on close to a hundred different computers. However, there have been a handful of instances on Windows OS computers where the emulator crashes just as the URL content is about to load. The remedy that has worked in such a situation requires that a Windows file named *advancedFeatures.ini* located in *C:/Users/%username%/.android/*be modified (created if it does not exist) to include the following specifications:

```
Vulkan = off
GLDirectMem = on
```

Once this file includes these specifications, exit Android Studio completely before re-starting Android Studio to run the app.

WebView Client to Control WebView Experience

Page navigation and loading events can be monitored or controlled in Java code by a developer using the *WebViewClient* class. There is a method named *shouldOverrideUrlLoading* that can be used to control page navigation by intercepting user clicks on a link or any other means taken to initiate a URL request. There are also *onPageStarted, onPageFinished,* and *onReceivedError* methods associated with the *WebViewClient* that can be used to react to page loading events. The first two of these methods identify the URL involved. Finally, there is also a *shouldInterceptRequest* method that enables a developer to intercept and even modify the resource requests made by a web page loaded in a web view. Such resource requests include those required for the loading of images and scripts.

A web view also maintains a history of web pages that have been visited. This history can be monitored and maintained in Java code as well.

Apps with Google Maps

A Google map can be included in an app by incorporating a "Google Maps Views Activity". Such a feature can be beneficial in an app that desires a geolocation presentation. For example, a Google map can be used to guide users to a physical site location such as a retail store or service center, possibly even mapping out a route. As another example, Amazon will often provide a map with the delivery truck's whereabouts when a customer is awaiting an immediate delivery. An app could make use of a Google map for a similar application or could provide a route for a customer to traverse a physical route to a destination.

A fitness app could make use of a Google map to track a user's distance covered over a period of time. A real estate app can use a map to display the locations of available properties matching a user's property requirements. These are just some of the examples where a Google map can enhance an app.

A disadvantage of Google maps from a developer's perspective is the requirement that a developer obtain an API key for the use of a Google map even for testing purpose. More is said on this in the discussion that follows.

A Google map should be the sole or primary occupant of an activity or fragment on a mobile screen. Several important steps are required to successfully incorporate a Google map within an app. These steps are as follows.

1. Right-click on the *app* folder within the Project view and then select *New → Google → GoogleMapsViewActivity* as illustrated in Figure 13.4.

2. Google requires that the developer obtain an API key in order to make a Google map functional. For this reason, the *AndroidManifest. xml* file contains instructions and a link for obtaining such a key. Details regarding the mechanics to obtain such a key are not covered

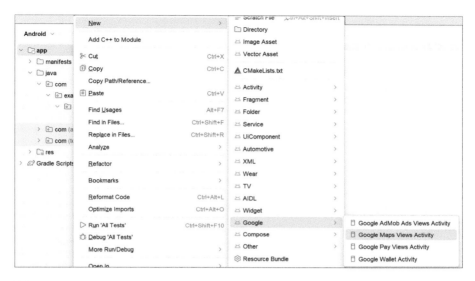

FIGURE 13.4
Adding a Google Maps feature.

    in this text since these instructions are very detailed by following the link provided in the manifest file, and these instructions may very well change over time. It is best to carefully follow the directions found in the manifest file.

3. The contents of the *build.gradle* module level file must contain a dependency, so add this to the file if it is not already present: *implementation 'com.google.android.gms:play-services-maps:18.2.0'*. The version may be different from that presented here in which case it is most likely a later version and should not be changed.

4. It is likely that permissions will be required for accessing the Internet and the location information for the device. Therefore, the permissions identified in Table 13.1 should be added to the Android manifest file prior to the *<application>* setup code.

TABLE 13.1

Permissions That Must Be Added to the Manifest File

AndroidManifest.xml - partial

`<uses-permission android:name="android.permission.INTERNET" />`
 `<uses-permission android:name="android.permission.ACCESS_FINE_LOCATION" />`
 `<uses-permission android:name="android.permission.ACCESS_COARSE_LOCATION" />`

5. As is the case with all activities added to an app, the Google maps activity is present in an eXtensible Markup Language (XML) file named *activity_maps.xml* and a companion Java file named

MapsActivity.java. The default contents of the *activity_maps.xml* layout file should resemble the code displayed in Figure 13.5.

```
</> activity_maps.xml  ✕                            ☰  ☰⃞  ⊠

1          <?xml version="1.0" encoding="utf-8"?>
2 ©        <fragment xmlns:android="http://schemas.android.com/apk/res/android"
3              xmlns:map="http://schemas.android.com/apk/res-auto"
4              xmlns:tools="http://schemas.android.com/tools"
5              android:id="@+id/map"
6              android:name="com.google.android.gms.maps.SupportMapFragment"
7              android:layout_width="match_parent"
8              android:layout_height="match_parent"
9              tools:context=".MapsActivity" />
```

FIGURE 13.5
Contents of the *Google Maps Activity* layout.

6. After an API maps key is obtained from the Google site and stored correctly within the app, run the app. If an error is encountered with the API key, after fixing the error be sure to "Clean" the project. The first time the app is run, permission must be granted for accessing the device's location. The choices from which to select are provided in Figure 13.6.

FIGURE 13.6
Granting permission to access device's location.

7. Once permission to access the device's location is granted, the screen layout for the maps activity should resemble that shown in Figure 13.7. The default location displayed within a map is Sydney, Australia.

FIGURE 13.7
Default Google map.

Customizing Map Properties

When examining the *MainActivity.java* file, it becomes apparent that the *onMapReady* method is responsible for setting the marker icon on the map and proving the text placed on the map adjacent to the location icon. These items can be modified within the *onMapReady* method using the *MarkerOptions* class by setting attribute values ".title" and ".icon", respectively. The statement that reads *"googleMap.addMarker(markerOptions);"* in the *onMapReady* method applies these customizations.

In addition, it is possible to set a position using a *Location* object. By default, the map activity obtains the current location's latitude and longitude values. This is the reason for the permissions in the manifest file and the follow-up requests in the companion Java code. To alter the location, use a *Location* object to supply appropriate values using the ".setLatitude" and ".setLongitude" methods.

It is also possible to use a ".snippet" method to display additional information over the marker in response to a user tap. In addition, there are several types of map presentations available from which to choose. These various types are specified using the built-in constants associated with the *GoogleMap* class. A sample of the named constants associated with map types include *MAP_TYPE_NORMAL*, *MAP_TYPE_SATELLITE*, and *MAP_TYPE_TERRAIN*.

Figure 13.8 illustrates a sample of customization options as specified in the Java code *onMapReady* method provided in Figure 13.9. As observed in Figure 13.9, the location has been modified, a snippet has been provided, and the default marker icon has been altered on the google map.

FIGURE 13.8
Google map resulting from options customized in Figure 13.9.

```
© MainActivity.java  ×
62              @Override
63 ◆≡ @         public void onMapReady(GoogleMap googleMap) {
64                  currentLocation.setLatitude(41.8948);
65                  currentLocation.setLongitude(-87.6242);
66                  googleMap.setMapType((GoogleMap.MAP_TYPE_NORMAL));
67                  LatLng latLng = new LatLng(currentLocation.getLatitude(), currentLocation.getLongitude());
68                  MarkerOptions markerOptions = new MarkerOptions().position(latLng).title( s: "I am here!");
69                  markerOptions.snippet( s: "The Magnificant Mile in Downtown Chicago, Illinois ");
70                  markerOptions.icon(BitmapDescriptorFactory.defaultMarker(BitmapDescriptorFactory.HUE_BLUE));
71                  googleMap.animateCamera(CameraUpdateFactory.newLatLng(latLng));
72                  googleMap.animateCamera(CameraUpdateFactory.newLatLngZoom(latLng,  v: 5));
73                  googleMap.addMarker(markerOptions);
74              }
75
```

FIGURE 13.9
Customizing options in a Google map.

Exercises

E13.1 Choose an earlier exercise in Chapter 11 or Chapter 12 and add a new fragment that incorporates a web view into the app. The URL for the web view content should be appropriate to the focus of the app and might be a web page that you find that includes information on the primary topic of the app, for example, soccer rules or an explanation of yoga ambient music.

E13.2 Choose an earlier exercise in Chapter 11 or Chapter 12 and add a new fragment that incorporates a google map. Customize some of the map options including a snippet, the marker icon, and the type of map displayed.

14

Media and Communication

Learning Outcomes:

- ✓ *Ability to incorporate audio in an app.*
- ✓ *Understanding of the benefits of appropriate audio applications.*
- ✓ *Understanding of the audio file types supported by native Android.*
- ✓ *Ability to include video content within an app.*
- ✓ *Understanding of video file types supported by native Android.*
- ✓ *Ability to supply user controls for video management.*
- ✓ *Ability to send text messages from within an app.*
- ✓ *Understanding of the permissions required for text messaging and phone call initiation.*
- ✓ *Ability to establish a telephone session within an app.*

                    DOI: 10.1201/9781003286325-14

This chapter explores the ways to incorporate music and sound files, as well as videos, within an app. In addition, the code required to send SMS messages and make telephone calls is revealed as well. Most of these features will be a component of a larger application. For example, a developer might choose to play a tune on a welcome screen as background music. As another example, an app might include a "Help" activity or fragment that invites the user to review an instructional video. Or an app might include a link to phone or text a message to a service center. Each of these features is covered individually in the discussion that follows.

Incorporating Audio within an App

Android supports three groups of audio file formats. These file formats are (a) uncompressed audio formats, (b) formats with lossless compression, and (c) formats with lossy compression. There are several audio file format types associated with each of these formats. A brief description of each format together with the identification of the more popular file types is provided below. Most of this information was obtained from Wikipedia.[1]

The uncompressed audio file format is also sometimes referred to as the raw audio format. The file type most popularly associated with the uncompressed audio file format is the .wav format, but Android supports .wav and .pcm files. The .pcm files may require an audio player app, depending on the version of Android running on the device.

The .mp3 format is the most popular lossy audio file format. A lossy format enables a greater reduction in file size but does so by eliminating some of the audio information. The claim is that the human ear will not miss the information that is gone when the sound file is later uncompressed. In addition to .mp3, Android also supports OggVorbis, .midi, .opus, and AMR file types, but depending on the actual Android device, an appropriate media player app may be necessary.

On the other hand, a lossless compression preserves all of the original audio information but still achieves a compressed format. FLAC is a popular lossless compression audio file format.

To play an audio file in an app, the file must be located in a resource directory. A popular name for this resource directory is "raw". So right-click on the *res* subfolder of the app project in Android Studio and select *New → Android Resource Directory* and then select the "Resource type:" "raw" as shown in Figure 14.1. Then move the audio file into this new subfolder named "raw".

Table 14.1 lists the Java code required to create an instance of a *MediaPlayer* object that is used to play, pause, or stop the audio file wherever appropriate within the app. Usually, the developer will supply buttons for the user to control these operations of the media player.

⚓ New Resource Directory	✕

D̲irectory name:	raw

R̲esource type:	raw ⌄

S̲ource set:	layout
A̲vailable qualifier	menu
🏳 Country Cod	mipmap
⟪ Network Cod	navigation
⊕ Locale	raw
⊟ Layout Direc	transition
⊞ Smallest Scr	values
⬚ Screen Width	xml

| | OK | Cancel |
| ? | | |

FIGURE 14.1
Creating the folder required for audio files.

TABLE 14.1

Use a Java MediaPlayer to Play, Pause, or Stop Audio

```
MediaPlayer audiotune = MediaPlayer.create(MainActivity.this,
                R.raw.audiofilename);

// These operations may be placed in methods invoked by the click of an
// appropriate button in the layout

audiotune.start();
audiotune.pause();
audiotune.stop();  // which also clears the MediaPlayer object
```

Remember that the volume controls for the emulator are located on the Android Virtual Device (AVD) control bar as displayed in Figure 14.2.

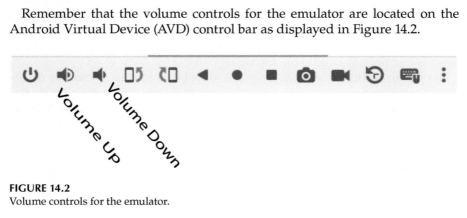

FIGURE 14.2
Volume controls for the emulator.

Providing Video Content within an App

An Android app can also play a video within a layout. Android supports several video file formats in its various versions, so consult the Android developers' site if you wish to use a video format other than .mp4.

Any video that is to be played within an app should be moved into a sub-folder created with the name *raw*. Figure 14.1 describes how to create this subfolder after right-clicking on the *res* subfolder with the Android project and then selecting *New → Android Resource Directory*.

Within the appropriate eXtensible Markup Language (XML) layout file to contain the video, drag a *VideoView* widget from the *Widgets* category in the Palette onto the layout file. Assign this widget an appropriate *id*. Figure 14.3 lists the Java code that should be placed in the appropriate Java source file. If for some reason you do not wish to provide media controls to the user, then omit lines 15–21. Supplying the media controls permits the user to pause and play the video as well as reverse or fast-forward. Figure 14.4 displays the rendering of the app screen layout associated with this code, illustrating the implementation of a *VideoView* with provided controls.

```java
package com.example.demovideo;
import ...
public class MainActivity extends AppCompatActivity {
    4 usages
    MediaController userControls; // global in case add activities that could return
    @Override
    protected void onCreate(Bundle savedInstanceState) {
        super.onCreate(savedInstanceState);
        setContentView(R.layout.activity_main);
        VideoView myVideo = (VideoView) findViewById(R.id.myvideo);
        if (userControls == null) {
            // create an object of media controller class
            userControls = new MediaController( context: MainActivity.this);
            userControls.setAnchorView(myVideo);
        }
        // set the media controller for video view
        myVideo.setMediaController(userControls);
        // set the uri for the video view
        myVideo.setVideoURI(Uri.parse( uriString: "android.resource://" +
                getPackageName() + "/" + R.raw.mygirl));
        // start a video
        myVideo.start();
    }
}
```

FIGURE 14.3
Java code to supply media controls for and initialize a video.

FIGURE 14.4
Sample app layout containing video.

Sending a Text Message from within an App

Sending a text message, also known as text messaging, is accomplished using a feature referred to as SMS. SMS is an acronym for "Short Message Service". The *SMSManager* API is utilized in this chapter to programmatically send a text message. This capability can be very beneficial within an app. Some examples of such benefits include the ability to confirm an appointment with a service technician, or the opportunity to reschedule a delivery, or the occasion for a user to easily share a phone number with a vendor.

Sending a text message within an app is relatively easy. The most complicated code has to do with the checking of permissions. Text messages require access to an external communications network, and such access may incur costs to the user. In addition, permission for text messaging is considered a security risk. Therefore, the code required for securing messaging permissions is covered in some detail before the code required to generate a text message.

One of the first permissions is acknowledged by including a *uses-permission* in the *AndroidManifest.xml* file as indicated in line 8 in Table 14.2. In addition, a *uses-feature* declarative is required as well as indicated in lines 5–7. The "SEND_SMS" and "RECEIVE"SMS" permissions require that this *uses-feature* for the telephony resource be specified. Adding the *required="false"* specification as done in Table 14.2 indicates that although permission is requested, the app can still handle situations where the user does not have the telephony feature.

TABLE 14.2

SMS-Related Permissions that Must Be Added to the Manifest File

AndroidManifest.xml

```
1   <?xml version="1.0" encoding="utf-8"?>
2   <manifest xmlns:android="http://schemas.android.com/apk/res/android"
3       xmlns:tools="http://schemas.android.com/tools">
4
5       <uses-feature
6           android:name="android.hardware.telephony"
7           android:required="false" />
8       <uses-permission android:name="android.permission.SEND_SMS" />
9       <application
10          android:allowBackup="true"
11          android:dataExtractionRules="@xml/data_extraction_rules"
12          android:fullBackupContent="@xml/backup_rules"
13          android:icon="@mipmap/ic_launcher"
14          android:label="@string/app_name"
15          android:roundIcon="@mipmap/ic_launcher_round"
16          android:supportsRtl="true"
17          android:theme="@style/Theme.SendingSMS"
18          tools:targetApi="31">
19          <activity
20              android:name=".MainActivity"
21              android:exported="true">
22              <intent-filter>
23                  <action android:name="android.intent.action.MAIN" />
24
25                  <category android:name=
26                          "android.intent.category.LAUNCHER" />
27              </intent-filter>
28          </activity>
29      </application>
30
31  </manifest>
```

Figure 14.5 illustrates how a message to be texted might be solicited from a user, and Figure 14.6 displays the message that will be represented to the user asking permission to send the SMS message. Two buttons are presented, one to allow and one to disallow text messaging.

FIGURE 14.5
Sample screen soliciting input for an SMS message.

FIGURE 14.6
Requesting permission to send the SMS.

Table 14.3 provides sample Java code for texting the user message to a help center. There are several aspects to this code. First, the manifest file must be imported into the .java code file as shown in line 2. Then in line 14, a global variable named "permission_denied" is set to false. Not because permission has been granted, but only because permission is not yet known. It will be set to *true* as described later if permission is denied by the user. When the user clicks the button to send their message, the *onClick* method declared in lines 26–38 is called. Line 28 retrieves the permission status for SMS. Line 30 tests if permission has been granted, and if so, line 31 calls a method to send the text message. If permission has not been granted, then line 33 checks to see if permission has been denied, and if so, it returns without sending any message. Otherwise, permission is still pending, and so permission is requested in lines 36–37, and a screen resembling Figure 14.6 is presented to the user unless the user settings on the device have already granted SMS permission.

TABLE 14.3

Requesting Permission and Then Sending the Text Message

```
1  package com.example.sendingsms;
2  import android.Manifest;
3  import androidx.appcompat.app.AppCompatActivity;
4  import androidx.core.app.ActivityCompat;
5  import androidx.core.content.ContextCompat;
6
7  import android.content.pm.PackageManager;
8  import android.os.Bundle;
9  import android.telephony.SmsManager;
10 import android.view.View;
11 import android.widget.TextView;
12
13 public class MainActivity extends AppCompatActivity {
14    boolean permission_denied = false;
15    @Override
16    protected void onCreate(Bundle savedInstanceState) {
17       super.onCreate(savedInstanceState);
18       setContentView(R.layout.activity_main);
19    }
20    public void ok2send() {
21       TextView usermsg = (TextView) findViewById(R.id.userText);
22       String msg = usermsg.getText().toString();
23       SmsManager smgr = SmsManager.getDefault();
24       smgr.sendTextMessage("+12625247877", null, msg, null, null);
25    }
26    public void sendtext(View v) {
27      // Setting up permission coordination
28      int smsPermission =
             ContextCompat.checkSelfPermission(this,Manifest.permission.
             SEND_SMS);
29      // check permission is given
30      if (smsPermission == PackageManager.PERMISSION_GRANTED)   {
31          ok2send();
32      }
```

(Continued)

TABLE 14.3 *(Continued)*

Requesting Permission and Then Sending the Text Message

```
33        else if (permission_denied) return; // user disallowed sms
34        else
35          // request permission
36            ActivityCompat.requestPermissions(this,new
37              String[]{Manifest.permission.SEND_SMS}, 0);
38    }
39
40    public void onRequestPermissionsResult(int requestCode,
41              String permissions[], int[] grantResults) {
42        super.onRequestPermissionsResult(requestCode, permissions,
43              grantResults);
44        if (requestCode == 0) { // this was the code sent in lines 37
45            if (grantResults.length > 0 &&
46                grantResults[0] == PackageManager.
                  PERMISSION_GRANTED) {
47                // permission was granted
48                ok2send();
49            } else permission_denied = true;
50        }
51    }
52 }
```

When the user responds to the choice given in Figure 14.6, the method named "onRequestPermissionsResults" is automatically called by the Android system. The implementation of this method is displayed in Table 14.3 in lines 40–51. Since an app may request more than one permission, line 44 checks for the result code matching that which was specified for SMS permission in line 37. Lines 45–46 then check to see if permission was granted or denied. If permission was granted, line 48 calls a method to send the text message. Otherwise, line 49 sets the "permission_denied" global flag to the value true.

The method named "ok2send" is called as referenced above when permission has been granted to send a text message, and the user has indicated the readiness to do so. Lines 21–22 retrieve the multi-line text input, and line 24 sends the text message to the destination after line 23 has created an *SmsManager* object. The assumption is that the text obtained from the user is non-null, and if uncomfortable with that assumption, be sure to double-check. Figure 14.7 displays the results obtained when the text messaging app is opened on the device to check messages that have been sent. The presence of the message entered as input in Figure 14.7 confirms that the code in Table 14.3 is working.

FIGURE 14.7
Checking the messaging app for the text sent.

Establishing a Telephone Session within an App

The process of making a telephone call with an app is very similar to that employed for sending a text message. As in the case of texting, an app intending to place a phone call must also arrange for appropriate permissions. A primary permission request is again specified in the manifest file. Table 14.4 lists the code required for phoning permission within an app. Again, the feature specifying a telephony resource is specified. In the case for making a call within the app, the permission is that of "CALL_PHONE" as displayed in Table 14.4.

TABLE 14.4

Permissions That Must Be Added to the Manifest File for Placing a Call

AndroidManifest.xml – partial code

```
<?xml version="1.0" encoding="utf-8"?>
<manifest xmlns:android="http://schemas.android.com/apk/res/android"
    xmlns:tools="http://schemas.android.com/tools">

    <uses-feature
        android:name="android.hardware.telephony"
        android:required="false" />
    <uses-permission android:name="android.permission.CALL_PHONE" />
    <application
        .
        :
    </application>

</manifest>
```

The Java code addressing permissions for making a call is very similar to that previously discussed for text messaging. Table 14.5 lists the code involved with asking permission as appropriate, recognizing when permission has been granted, and then actually making the phone call. The primary differences are in the "CALL_PHONE" constant utilized rather than the SMS constant, and the request code is assigned a different integer value to shed additional light on it use. The other difference is found in the method that makes the call. This method is defined in Table 14.5 in lines 21–25. As shown, an *Intent* object is defined for a call action. This intent is equipped with a string property value representing the call number, and then the intent is started, thereby placing the phone call. The method named "make_call" is the *onClick* method assigned to the button displayed in Figure 14.8 where the call is initiated by the user. Figure 14.9 shows the device asking the user for permission for the app to be able to make and manage phone calls. If permission is granted, the device displays a call event as illustrated in Figure 14.10.

TABLE 14.5

Requesting Permission and Then Making a Phone Call

```
1   package com.example.makingcall;
2   import androidx.appcompat.app.AppCompatActivity;
3   import androidx.core.app.ActivityCompat;
4   import androidx.core.content.ContextCompat;
5   import android.Manifest;
6   import android.content.Intent;
```

(Continued)

TABLE 14.5 (*Continued*)

Requesting Permission and Then Making a Phone Call

```
 7   import android.content.pm.PackageManager;
 8   import android.net.Uri;
 9   import android.os.Bundle;
10   import android.telephony.SmsManager;
11   import android.view.View;
12   import android.widget.TextView;
13
14   public class MainActivity extends AppCompatActivity {
15       boolean permission_denied = false;
16       @Override
17       protected void onCreate(Bundle savedInstanceState) {
18           super.onCreate(savedInstanceState);
19           setContentView(R.layout.activity_main);
20       }
21       public  void ok2call() {
22           Intent callIntent = new Intent(Intent.ACTION_CALL);
23           callIntent.setData(Uri.parse("tel:" + "18884444357"));
24           startActivity(callIntent);
25       }
26       public void make_call(View v) {
27           int callPermission = ContextCompat.checkSelfPermission(this,
28                   Manifest.permission.CALL_PHONE);
             // check permission is given
29           if (callPermission == PackageManager.PERMISSION_GRANTED) {
30               ok2call();
31           }
32           else if (permission_denied) return; // user disallowed sms
33           else
34               // request permission
35               ActivityCompat.requestPermissions(this,
36                   new String[]{Manifest.permission.CALL_PHONE}, 101);
37       }
38
39       public void onRequestPermissionsResult(int requestCode,
40                   String permissions[], int[] grantResults) {
41           super.onRequestPermissionsResult(requestCode, permissions,
42               grantResults);
43           if (requestCode == 101){ // this was the code set in line 36
44               if (grantResults.length > 0 &&
45                   grantResults[0] == PackageManager.PERMISSION_GRANTED) {
46                   // permission was granted
47                   ok2call();
48               } else permission_denied = true;
49           }
50       }
51   }
52
```

FIGURE 14.8
Sample screen offering to make a phone call.

FIGURE 14.9
Requesting permission for call management.

FIGURE 14.10
Call in process initiated within an app.

Exercises

E14.1 Choose an earlier exercise from any chapter and play an audio tune on the welcome screen of the app.

E14.2 Choose an earlier exercise in Chapter 11 or Chapter 12 and add a new fragment that adds an instructional video to an app.

E14.3 Choose an earlier exercise from any chapter and include a button that will take the content of an input text field and send it as a message to a phone number. Be sure to check the device's record of text messages to make sure that the message was sent.

E14.4 Choose an earlier exercise from any chapter and include a button that will call a "help" number. Be sure to check the device's record of calls to confirm that the call was made.

Note

1. https://en.wikipedia.org/wiki/Audio_file_format (last accessed on September 1, 2024).

Index

Note: Page numbers in **bold** and *italics* refer to tables and figures, respectively.